Poverty and Inequality in the UK
The Effects on Children

Vinod Kumar

ISBN 1 874 579 08 3

Published by the National Children's Bureau
8 Wakley Street
London EC1V 7QE

Registered Charity Number 258825

Telephone 071 278 9441

Typeset, printed and bound by Saxon Graphics Ltd, Derby

The National Children's Bureau was established as a registered charity in 1963. Our purpose is to identify and promote the interests of all children and young people and to improve their status in a diverse society.

We work closely with professionals and policy makers to improve the lives of all children but especially young children, those affected by family instability, children with special needs or disabilities and those suffering the effects of poverty and deprivation.

We collect and disseminate information about children and promote good practice in children's services through research, policy and practice development, publications, seminars, training and an extensive library and information service.

The Bureau works in partnership with Children in Scotland and Children in Wales.

To the millions of poverty-stricken children in this country whose voice is too amorphous and diffused to be heard by the powers-that-be!

Contents

List of tables   viii

List of figures   xi

Glossary   xiii

Acknowledgements   xix

Foreword   xxi

Introduction   1
    Poverty, deprivation and inequality   1
    Scope and methodology   4
    The framework of the study   5

Part 1

1. Trends in child poverty in the UK   7
    Introduction   7
    National trends in child poverty   7
    Regional trends in poverty   17
    Income of the poor   20
    Widening inequality in income and wealth   29
    Conclusions   37

2. Factors underlying child poverty   39
    Introduction   39
    Economic trends   39
    Unemployment and the British economy   51
    Poverty and employment   53
    Demographic trends   61
    Social policies in recession   69
    Conclusions   88

Part 2 Effects of child poverty   91
   Introduction   91

3. Social class, deprivation and children's health   94
   Introduction   94
   Definition of health   94
   Importance of children's health   95
   Measurement of health   95
   Access to health services and equity   116
   Social inequalities in child health   118
   Conclusions   121

4. Poverty, deprivation and children's health   122
   Introduction   122
   Deprivation and social class   122
   Income, diet and health   123
   Unemployment and health   123
   Poverty and housing deprivation   125
   Multiple deprivation and health   138
   Conclusions   141

5. Poverty, deprivation and education   144
   Introduction   144
   Parental poverty and deprivation – effect on a
   child's education   145
   Primary education   148
   Summary   153
   Secondary education   154
   Summary   166
   Truancy and deprivation   167
   Summary   170
   Education policy and expenditure – implications for
   provision   171
   Adequacy of expenditure to needs?   172
   Summary   175
   Access to further and higher education   176
   Summary   183
   Conclusions   184

6. Conclusion   187
   Rise in child poverty   187
   Underlying factors   187
   Limitations of the study   188
   Deprivation and ill-health   189
   Deprivation and education   191
   Government response to rising poverty   192
   Policy implications   196
   An alternative political morality?   199

Appendix
Tables I.1 to I.6 – see list of tables   201

Bibliography   206

Index of names   230

Index of subjects   235

List of tables

1.1   Number of children in families receiving family income supplement/family credit or supplementary benefit/income support in the UK 1979-1991   9

1.2   Children in families with low incomes - various multiples of Supplementary Benefit (SB)/Income Support (IS) in the UK 1979-1989   11

1.3   Percentage of individuals in different family types with income below 50% of the contemporary average in the UK 1979-1990/91   13

1.4   Number of children and adults in varying degrees of poverty in Britain 1983-1990   17

1.5   Proportions of children below various income thresholds analysed by region in the UK 1980/82-1983/5   18

1.6   Children below various fractions of the income distribution - analysed by region in the UK 1980/82 – 1983/85   20

1.7   Percentage contribution of social security benefits to the incomes of those below various percentiles of the income distribution 1979-1988   21

1.8   Supplementary Benefit/Income Support scales for a couple with two children under 11 (a) at constant prices and (b) as a proportion of the median disposable income of a couple with two children 1979-1992   22

1.9   Real increase in benefit rates following the introduction of income support (£ per week)   24

1.10   Fluctuations in the share of the total of low income groups in the UK 1979-1988/89   30

1.11   Percentage shares of total original, gross, disposable and post-tax incomes by quintile groups of households in the UK 1979-1989   33

2.1   UK unemployment and vacancies 1979-92   42

2.2   Unemployment by region in the UK 1979-92 (% unemployed, seasonally adjusted)   46

2.3   Unemployment among 16 to 19-year-olds in Great Britain 1979-92: Comparison of DE Claimant Count and the Labour Force Survey   49

2.4 Percentage change in Real General Government Expenditure (GGE) and Real Gross Domestic Product (GDP) in the UK 1979-80 to 1991-92   71

2.5 General Government expenditure on Welfare Services £billion (£b) (real terms 1990-91) and as a share of total government expenditure (TGE) in the UK 1979-80 to 1991-92   72

2.6 Expenditure on education in England in real terms £million at 1990-91 prices   75

2.7 Net Institutional Expenditure in England 1980-81 to 1989-90 (1990-91 real terms)   76

2.8 Trends in UK Education Expenditure (Volume) 1979-80 to 1986-87   77

3.1 UK Vital Statistics for children under one year 1971-1991   97

3.2 Infant mortality by region and by mother's country of birth in the UK 1990   98

3.3 Deaths during the first year by father's social class for the period 1978-90 England and Wales (for births within marriage only)   102

3.4 Infant deaths by father's social class – England & Wales - 1987 -1990 (within and, jointly registered outside, marriage)   103

3.5 Relative risk of child mortality by social class and age England and Wales 1979, 1980,1982,1983   106

3.6 Trend in disability (estimated) among children at home and in institutions by age and sex in Great Britain 1976-88   107

3.7 Trends in parentally-reported morbidity in children in Great Britain 1979-90   109

3.8 Childhood morbidity (parentally reported) 0 to 15 in Great Britain 1985-89   109

4.1 Deprivation and child mortality by age in England and Wales 1989   139

4.2 Deprivation and child health in London 1985-86   140

4.3 Probability of child having poor or fair health in London 1985-86   141

5.1 School leavers in England – Achievement at GCSE/ 'O' level/ CSE examinations 1979/80 -1990/91   155

5.2 Those leaving secondary school with five or more CSE grade 1, and/or 'O' level grades A-C, and/or GCSE grades A-C in England 1979/80 – 1989/90   157

5.3 Those leaving secondary school with no graded results in England 1979/80 - 1989/90   159

5.4 Participation of 16 to 18-year-olds in education in England 1979/80 - 1991/92   178

5.5 Participation in full-time education by young people aged 17 in England 1980/81 - 1989/90   179

5.6 Participation of 16 to 18-year-olds in education and training by age and type of study: international comparison, 1987   181

Appendix

I.1   Proportion of adults and children below half of contemporary   201
      average income in the UK
I.2   Proportion of dependent children with incomes below various   201
      thresholds which change with average income (AHC) in the UK
      1979-1990/91
I.3   Distribution of wealth in the UK 1979-89   202
I.4   Dependent children in the UK below various income thresholds   203
      of contemporary average income (AHC) by economic status
      1979-1990/91
I.5   Education and day care of children under five in the UK 1981   204
      -1990
I.6   Education and day care of children under five by age and region in   205
      the UK 1989

Information from DFE Statistical Bulletins, Autumn Statement 1992, Distribution of Wealth in the UK, Employment Gazette and Households Below Average Income is Crown copyright and reproduced with the permission of the Controller of Her Majesty's Stationery Office.

Numbers in Table 2.8 reproduced by permission of Oxford University Press.

List of figures

1.1   Number of children in families on FC/FIS or IS/SB   8
1.2   Children in low income families - various multiples of Supplemen-   10
      tary Benefit (SB)/Income Support (IS)
1.3   Percentage of individuals in different family types with income   13
      below 50% of the contemporary average
1.4   Proportion of dependent children with income below 50% of   14
      average 1979 real terms. After housing costs
1.5   Proportion of dependent children below 50% of average income   14
      for each year. After housing costs
1.6   Proportion of dependent children with incomes below various   16
      thresholds which change with average income. After housing
      costs
1.7   Fluctuations in income share of low income groups 1979-89   31
1.8   Share of income of the bottom and top quintiles of equivalised   35
      post tax income
1.9   Distribution of wealth in the UK 1979-89   36

2.1   UK unemployment 1979-1992   43
2.2   UK unemployment by region 1979-1992   45
2.3   Unemployment among 16 to 19-year-olds in Great Britain   48
2.4   Composition (%) of lone parent families in GB 1971-1989   63
2.5   Economic activity among women with dependent children under   65
      18 - 1987-1989
2.6   Economic activity among women with dependent children under   66
      five - 1987-1989
2.7   Economic activity among lone fathers with dependent children -   68
      1987-1989
2.8   Government expenditure on welfare services 1979-92   73
2.9   Education of children under five 1981 to 1990   80
2.10 Day care of children under five 1981   81
2.11 Education and day care of children under five: by age and region   81
      1989

3.1   UK vital statistics   97
3.2   Infant mortality 1990 regional trends   98
3.3   Infant mortality 1990 by country of birth of mother   99
3.4   Mortality rates among under one-year-olds by mother's country of   101
       birth
3.5   Relative risk of child mortality by social class and age: 1979, 1980,   105
       1982, 1983 England and Wales
3.6   Trends in parentally-reported morbidity in children 1979-1990   108

5.1   Participation of 16 to 18-year-olds in education 1979/80-1991/92   177
5.2   16 to 18-year-olds in full-time education and training – Interna-   182
       tional Comparison, 1987

Glossary

ACC	Association of County Councils
AHC	After housing costs
AMA	Association of Metropolitan Authorities
B&B	Bed and Breakfast
BHC	Before housing costs
BMA	British Medical Association
CAG	Controller and Auditor General
CB	Child Benefit
CIPFA	Chartered Institute of Public Finance and Accountancy
CMO	Chief Medical Officer
CPAG	Child Poverty Action Group
CRE	Commission for Racial Equality
CSE	Certificate of Education
CSO	Central Statistical Office
CVCP	Committee for Vice Chancellors and Principals
DE	Department of Employment
Decile groups	These are groups of the population defined by the *decile points*. The lowest decile group is the ten per cent of the population with the lowest incomes.
Deciles	These are income values which divide the population, when ranked by income into ten equal-sized groups. The decile is the same as the lowest or the bottom 10th *percentile*.
DES	Department of Education and Science
DFE	Department for Education
DH	Department of Health
DHAs	District Health Authorities
DHSS	Department of Health and Social Security

Disposable income	*Gross* income minus income tax, national insurance contributions, local taxes, rates (the Community Charge or the Council Tax).
DoE	Department of Environment
DSS	Department of Social Security
Early neonatal mortality	Deaths in the first six days of life
EC	European Community
EEC	European Economic Community
EHCS	English House Conditions Survey
EOC	Equal Opportunity Commission
EPA	Educational Priority Area
Equivalence	The process by which household income is adjusted to account for variations in household composition and size.
ERM	European Exchange Rate Mechanism
ESL	English as a Second Language
ESWI	English, Scottish, Welsh and Irish
Family (or a Benefit Unit)	It is synonymous with the term 'Benefit Unit': A single *adult* or a *couple* together with any *children* dependant on the adult(s).
FC	Family Credit
FE	Further Education
FECs	Further Education Colleges
FES	Family Expenditure Survey
FHE	Further and Higher Education
FIS	Family Income Supplement
FPSC	Family Policy Studies Centre
FSM	Free School Meals
FT	Full Time
GB	Great Britain
GCE	General Certificate of Education
GCSE	General Certificate of Secondary Education
GDP	Gross domestic product
GGE	General Government Expenditure
GHS	General Household Survey
GP	General Practitioner
Gross income	Equals *original* income plus social security benefits
HAs	Housing Associations
HB	Housing Benefit

HBAI	Households Below Average Income
HE	Higher Education
HEA	Health Education Authority
HEC	Health Education Council
HMI	Her Majesty's Inspectorate
HMIs	Her Majesty's Inspectors
Household	A household is one person living alone or a group of people living at the same address having meals prepared together and with common housekeeping arrangements.
HVA	Health Visitors Association
IFS	Institute for Fiscal Studies
ILEA	Inner London Education Authority
ILO	International Labour Organisation
Infant mortality	Deaths under one year of age
IS	Income Support
KS	Key Stage
LA	Local Authority
Late neonatal mortality	Ages 7-27 completed days of life
LBA	London Boroughs Association
LC	Low cost
LEAs	Local Education Authorities
LFs	Lone Fathers
LFS	Labour Force Survey
LIFs	Low Income Families
LMs	Lone Mothers
LMS	Local Management of Schools
LPFs	Lone Parent Families
LPU	Low Pay Unit
Mean (or arithmetic mean)	The mean income is the *average* calculated by summing up all the incomes in a population and dividing the total by the number of incomes.
Median	The median income is the income value which divides the population when ranked by income, into two equal groups.
MITR	Mortgage Interest Tax Relief
MMs	Married Mothers
Morbidity	Prevalence or incidence of disease used as one of the indicators of health outcomes.

Mortality	Incidence of 'mortality' in the population – the number of deaths in a defined period – is used as one of several indicators of health outcomes
NACAB	National Association of Citizens' Advice Bureaux
NACNE	National Advisory Committee on Nutrition Education
NAO	National Audit Office
NAS/UWT	National Association of School Masters/Union of Women Teachers
NC	National Curriculum
NCDS	National Child Development Study
NCH	National Children's Homes
NCIE	Net Current Institutional Expenditure
NCWP	New Commonwealth and Pakistan
NEDO	National Economic Development Office
NES	New Earnings Survey
NFER	National Foundation for Educational Research
NFHA	National Federation of Housing Associations
NHS	National Health Service
NIC	National Insurance Contributions
North	Consists of Northern Ireland, Scotland, Wales, and the following regions of England: Northern, Yorkshire and Humberside, North West and West Midlands. The traditional dividing line linking the Severn Bridge and the Wash is used to distinguish it from the 'South' (see also 'South').
NSHG	National Study of Health and Growth
OECD	Organisation for Economic Cooperation and Development (European)
OFSTED	Office for Standards in Education
OPCS	Office of Public Censuses and Surveys
OPD	Out-patients department
Original income	Means *all* income from employment, pensions, investment and other sources
PAC	Public Accounts Committee
PCAS	Polytechnics Central Admission System
Percentiles	These are income values which divide the population, when ranked by income, into 100 equal groups. Thus ten per cent of the population have income below the 10th *percentile* or the bottom *decile*.
Perinatal mortality	Includes *still* births and deaths in the first week of life.

Personal Disposable Income	This is income net of Income Tax and National Insurance Contributions, local government taxes and certain other deductions such as contributions to occupational pensions and repayments of Social Fund loans. It does include social security benefits, including rent and rate rebates.
PHCDS	Public Health Common Data Set
Post-tax income	*Disposable* income minus indirect taxes such as Value Added Tax
Postneonatal mortality	Deaths at ages 28 days and over but under one year.
PSBR	Public Sector Borrowing Requirement
PSI	Policy Studies Institute
PSS	Personal Social Services
PT	Part Time
Quintiles	These are income values which divide the population when ranked by income into five equal groups. The lowest quintile is the same as the 20th percentile.
RDA	Recommended Daily Amount
RG	Registrar General
RHAs	Regional Health Authorities
Sampling error	The uncertainty in the estimates which arises from taking a *random* sample of the relevant population.
SB	Supplementary Benefit
SEG	Social-economic Group
SF	Social Fund
SHIL	The Single Homeless in London Working Party
SMR	Standardised Mortality Ratio is the ratio of the observed death rates at difference ages within a particular social group to the expected death rates, based on the age-specific death rates of a standard population. It is yet another commonly used indicator of health outcomes.
South	Comprises East Midlands, East Anglia, Greater London, South East and South West (see also 'North').
SSA	Social Security Act
SSAC	Social Security Advisory Committee
SSC	Social Services Committee
Still births	Late foetal deaths after 28 weeks of gestation
TECs	Training and Enterprise Councils

GLOSSARY

TES	Times Educational Supplement
UB	Unemployment Benefit
UCCA	Universities Central Council on Admissions
UK	United Kingdom
UU	Unemployment Unit
UUYA	Unemployment Unit and Youthaid
VAT	Value Added Tax
VR	Verbal Reasoning
WHO	World Health Organisation
YT	Youth Training

Acknowledgements

I am happy to acknowledge with grateful thanks the contribution of a number of other people to the successful conclusion of this study. My thanks to the Joseph Rowntree Foundation whose grant made this study possible; and to Barbara Ballard in particular for her interest and encouragement. Thanks also to the Bureau for financing the latter part of this study.

I owe a special debt of gratitude to David Berridge, Research Director at the Bureau, whose advice and support was invaluable throughout this study. He ploughed through several drafts and made useful comments, while also helping with the arduous task of proofreading. Given the wide sweep of this study, I benefited greatly from discussions at the two meetings of the Steering Group of specialist consultants set up for this project, as well as from individual consultations with Jonathan Bradshaw, Fran Bennett and Zarrina Kurtz who were particularly generous with their time, and painstaking and meticulous in their comments on an earlier draft of this manuscript. Thanks also to Roger Grimshaw and Nicola Madge, my colleagues at the Bureau, for their helpful comments on the first draft.

Special thanks are due to Ken Judge and Michaela Benzeval of the King's Fund for making material from their unpublished work available for my use. Thanks are also due to Peter Townsend for consultation on the synopsis of this study; to Beverley Botting of OPCS for her helpful comments on part of the first draft; and to analysts at the Department of Social Security (Analytical Services Division) for helpful advice on HBAI statistics and supply of additional data.

I am particularly grateful to Nicola Hilliard and other colleagues in the Bureau's Library (especially Iain Murray and Lisa Payne) for their enormous help in the collection of a wide variety of materials required for this study. Many thanks are also due to Fiona Blakemore, Publications Manager; Ebah Eshun and Bernadette Blair for typing the manuscript; and to Mark Currie for producing the Figures included here.

Naturally, the responsibility for the contents of this book remains entirely mine, as also for any shortcomings which remain.

Finally, I must express my gratitude to my family – especially my wife, Indira – for their patience and understanding in the face of prolonged neglect, and for their warm support throughout this endeavour.

Vinod Kumar
February 1993

The Joseph Rowntree Foundation has supported this project as part of its programme of research and innovative development projects, which it hopes will be of value to policy makers and practitioners. The facts presented and views expressed in this report, however, are those of the author and not necessarily those of the Foundation.

The author

Vinod Kumar carried out this study whilst he was a Senior Research Officer at the National Children's Bureau. He is now Head of Social Policy and Research at the Royal National Institute for Deaf People. He has wide experience of social policy research and has produced a number of papers on the problems of immigration, discrimination and disadvantage.

Foreword

...children must come first because children are our most sacred trust.
(Margaret Thatcher, George Thomas Society Inaugural Lecture, 17 January 1990).

This book reveals that during the period that Margaret Thatcher was Prime Minister of this country children did not come first. The latest official statistics - Households Below Average Income (1993) show that the number of children living in families with incomes below 50% of the average increased from 1.4 million to 3.9 million between 1979 and 1991. While on average the living standards of families improved in real terms, it is now incontrovertible that many families with children were not merely worse off in real terms but absolutely as well. There has been no trickle down. Britain has beome a sharply more unequal society and the most common victims of this trend have been children. The 'sacred trust' has been misplaced.

Responsibility for this cannot all be laid at the door of the Government. Children were also the victims of national and international economic forces and demographic changes. While these are not beyond the influence of government they are beyond its control. Nevertheless Government policy has exacerbated the effects of these trends or failed to mitigate their consequences. The fact that poor families have become worse off during a period when average living standards improved by over a third is the fault of the fiscal and social policies that the Government has pursued. In particular it can be blamed for policies that have produced a more regressive form of taxation and the failure to maintain the level of benefits and services for children. These policies have not been pursued reluctantly but with considerable ideological fervour and in the face of repeated evidence that they have been hurting children. And they are still being pursued. In the context of a budget deficit there are calls for better 'targeting' of public expenditure. Targeting is too often a euphemism for withdrawing benefits from people already hard pressed as an alternative to increasing taxation on those who are already well off.

Of course, many children would be better off if their parents could find work and the Government could and should be doing more to stimulate labour demand. But also we are a rich enough country to be able to afford more generous, more effective child centred social policies. At any one time only a minority of adults are carrying the burden of child rearing and they need help from the rest of us - not after some future economic miracle but now.

In this book, Vinod Kumar identifies where policy has failed children. We know for example that the income support scales for children are too low, that child benefits and family credit are not high enough to compensate adequately for low wages, that the school meals service has been emasculated, that the public sector house building programme is inadequate to cope with the terrible problem of homelessness and so on. We know what is wrong. We have the resources to put it right. What we lack is the moral courage and political commitment to put children first.

Professor Jonathan Bradshaw
University of York
July 1992

Introduction

Child poverty has been rising relentlessly in the UK since 1979 and, by 1991, it was affecting nearly one in every three children. Proportionately more children were then living in poverty than adults. Does this matter? Why has child poverty risen so dramatically? What impact does it have on children's lives?

Children are our 'precious inheritance' as well as our future: our hopes, aspirations and ambitions as a people and as a country reside in, and depend on, them. Yet children are highly vulnerable. That is why 'the rearing of the young is the fundamental issue in a human society – and why the quality and philosophy of health, education and other care available to the child and his family are so important' (The Court Report, 1976, p.3). The way a society treats its children is an acid test of its civilisation. Both morality and self interest, therefore, dictate that conditions are created which are conducive to children optimising their potential as individuals and as citizens, playing their full part in the social, economic and political life of the country.

Yet child poverty can severely inhibit the realisation of individual potential while diminishing the quality of personal and social life, involving as it does both material and social deprivation of various kinds. This study, therefore, looks at how sharply rising child poverty since 1979, in the wake of enormous changes in society – demographic, technological, socio-economic and political – has affected the lives of children, particularly as regards their housing, health and education.

Poverty, deprivation and inequality

There is no official definition of poverty in the UK, nor any generally accepted poverty standard. In fact, the debate on poverty has been long drawn out, frequently controversial, and so far inconclusive. One reason why debates on poverty often shed more heat than light is that people tend to use terms such as poverty, deprivation and inequality interchangeably, thereby causing considerable confusion and misunderstanding. It may be helpful, therefore, to clarify for the purpose of this study the meaning of poverty and to distinguish it from deprivation and inequality.

Poverty does presuppose the existence of an unacceptable degree of inequality and one cannot understand poverty except in the wider context of inequality in society (Wedderburn, 1974). However, poverty, whether defined in absolute or relative terms, is not synonymous with inequality. Poverty is concerned with a lack of adequate resources to satisfy certain **essential minimum** human needs. The critical question is how this notion of the 'minimum' is defined, that is, which human needs and essential for what. It may be defined narrowly, as 'absolute' or 'primary' poverty, or it may be defined more widely as 'relative' poverty, but the notion of the minimum is present in one form or another in both sets of definitions.

To illustrate the point, let us look at some of the ways poverty has been defined in the past. Thus for Rowntree, families were in 'primary' poverty if their 'total earnings...(were) insufficient to obtain the minimum necessaries for the maintenance of merely physical efficiency...' (1901). Sen (1978) has tried to push the boundary of the 'minimum' to '...an irreducible core of absolute deprivation...' at the starvation level, as still applicable to large parts of the Third World.

The proponents of 'relative' poverty define needs more widely. Thus for Adam Smith, the father of modern capitalism, poverty embraced the notion of the 'decent minimum', encompassing '...not only commodities which are indispensably necessary for the support of life but whatever the custom of the country renders it indecent for creditable people, even of the lowest order, to be without' (Smith, 1812, p693). Charles Booth defined the very poor as those whose means were insufficient 'according to the normal standards of life in this country' (Booth, 1888). It was this notion of exclusion from the 'norm' due to inadequate resources that was picked up and further developed by Townsend in his major study, *Poverty in the United Kingdom*, published in 1979. In his view, people can be said to be in poverty when '...their resources are so seriously below those commanded by the average individual or family that they are, in effect, excluded from ordinary living patterns, customs and activities' (1979, p31).

It seems that here too the notion of the minimum is present, but in a different form. In distinguishing inequality from poverty, Townsend says that '...some criterion of deprivation is required by which a poverty line may be drawn...' (Townsend, 1979, p57), otherwise even those people possessing, say, the lowest 10 per cent of resources in a country are not necessarily poor. Here he introduces his concept of a deprivation threshold whereby the severity and/or the depth of deprivation due to inadequate resources reaches a '...point at which withdrawal (from normal social life) "escalates" disproportionately to falling resources...' (Townsend, 1979, p57).

Mack and Lansley (1985), who have adopted the Council of Europe's definition of poverty as exclusion from '...the minimum acceptable way of life...' (EEC, 1981), take a different view. They argue that 'Reference to a minimum, rather than the norm, is implicit in the definition of poverty as lack of necessities'. The difference between them and Townsend appears to us to be a matter of degree – it all depends on how necessities are socially perceived. Where they seem to differ significantly from Townsend is in their approach to measurement of poverty, that is, by gauging public perception of necessities, rather than inferring these from a study of behaviour.

It is clear from the foregoing discussion that, for poverty to exist, inequality has to be severe enough to push deprivation beyond the 'minimum'. Here Townsend prefers the term 'deprivation' to mean '**conditions** of deprivation relative to others', rather than '**feelings** of deprivation relative to others', as Runciman has used it (Runciman, 1966). Townsend has since developed the concept to encompass material as well as social aspects of deprivation (1990a). Used in this sense, deprivation is a consequence of poverty, as well as its defining characteristic – when it reaches a certain level, that is. This is the usage we prefer in this study. However, since the term 'disadvantage' is frequently employed in the literature as a substitute, these two terms will be used interchangeably.[1]

It is because the notion of the 'minimum' is implicit in the term 'poverty' that it '...carries with it an implication and moral imperative that something should be done about it' (Piachaud, 1981, p421). In principle, 'the motivation for doing something about poverty can be quite separate from that of doing something about inequality' (Mack and Lansley, 1985, p40), though, depending on how poverty is tackled, it can have implications for the degree of inequality in society, but there is no automatic link between the two.

It is sometimes argued that the distinction between 'primary' and 'relative' poverty is now largely of heuristic[2] value, for, in practice, it does get blurred (Ringen, 1988). It is true that apart from what Sen calls 'an irreducible core of absolute deprivation...' (Sen, 1978) at the starvation level, both these concepts are affected by the standards prevailing in society at any one time (Veit-Wilson, 1986), and liable to change with the passage of time as norms and needs change (Donnison, 1982). However, the distinction still holds good in at least two respects: the notion of the 'minimum' tends to be defined more narrowly in 'primary' than in 'relative' poverty. Moreover, the poverty standard tends to be adjusted in line with prices in the former, whereas in the latter case, it tends to be dynamic, that is, it moves with average earnings.

There is a large measure of agreement, among academics at any rate, that poverty is meaningful only as a relative and a dynamic concept. This means that the definition of poverty may also vary between countries at any one time as values and living standards differ, and not just within the same country over time as needs and norms change. (This is also our own preferred position on this matter.) However, a major difference of view has surfaced in recent years concerning the nature of poverty with serious implications for its measurement. For Townsend, as we have already seen, 'Poverty can be defined objectively and applied consistently only in terms of the concept of relative deprivation...The term is understood objectively rather than subjectively' (1979, p31). This view is almost the polar opposite of the one advanced earlier by Orshansky, for whom 'Poverty, like beauty, lies in the eye of the beholder' (1969, p37). Townsend's view has, in turn, been challenged powerfully by Piachaud, among others. For Piachaud, the determination of the level of poverty by a society collectively 'will always be a value-judgement. Social scientists have no business trying to pre-empt such judgements with "Scientific" prescriptions' (1981, p421). The problems of definition and measurement have been debated extensively, especially in the Journal of Social Policy, and it is not proposed to go into the minutiae of this debate here.[3] Since this is essentially a policy-relevant study, we shall employ a variety of measures of poverty to portray an overall picture.

Scope and methodology

While studies on poverty in general abound, child poverty is a relatively neglected subject. This gap was partly filled when the National Children's Bureau published, in 1990, a study by professor Jonathan Bradshaw of York University – *Child Poverty and Deprivation in the UK*, which was undertaken as part of a wider, UNICEF sponsored, international, comparative study of child poverty and deprivation in the industrialised countries.

This study of child poverty in the UK, covering the period 1979-92, is a follow-up to that one. In some ways, it continues and extends the analysis in Bradshaw's study, using more recent data, to see if the trends identified by him are continuing, or have been modified. In other ways, its scope is somewhat different. Whereas Bradshaw's study was a comprehensive survey of the state of children in the UK in the wake of major economic and social changes which had occurred in this country during the last decade, the main focus of the present study is limited to examining in some detail the relationship between the rising child poverty and outcomes in children's education, health and housing. It therefore excludes consideration of poverty as a factor, for instance, in child abuse, family breakdown, juvenile delinquency or teenage pregnancies. In other respects, the coverage is somewhat wider – it includes, for instance, a brief discussion of the regional dimension of poverty and unemployment – or more detailed, as for instance, the treatment of changes in the welfare state provision. Data does not exist to enable one to measure the extent of poverty among minority ethnic groups, women and people with a disability. However, where possible, these dimensions are taken into account when deprivation affects the life chances of children from these groups.

For the purpose of this study, the term 'ethnicity' is used to describe the 'ethnic origins' of the minority (or majority) communities. However, the term 'race' is used as a shorthand when referring to the phenomenon of 'racism' or discrimination in society due to 'colour', 'race', 'nationality' or 'ethnic' or 'national origins' – that is, the 'racial grounds' as defined in the Race Relations Act 1976.

Likewise a 'child' is defined in this study as being under 18. It may seem odd to include the 16 to 17-year-olds in this category, since it is more usual these days to refer to them as 'young persons', many of whom in the last two decades have increasingly been living independently. The principal reason for their inclusion in this study is not simply that 18 is the legal age of majority, and happens also to accord with the National Children's Bureau practice, but because many of today's 16 to 17-year-olds are among the young single homeless sleeping rough on streets and, obviously, very poor. Ever since April 1988 when the Government abolished Income Support (IS) for them, their capacity to live independently of their parents has been eroded, if they cannot find a job or a training place.

Given the close relationship between child poverty and family poverty, and the paucity of data on children, some material has been included on family poverty as well to give a fuller picture.

This study is based on an analysis and interpretation of a wide range of official statistics and documents, and a review of evidence in *Hansard* and reports of the House of Commons Select Committees, research and other publications, journal articles and press reports. However, this review is neither definitive, nor comprehensive. Given the wide scope and the short span of this study, and considering the nature of the audience, one has of necessity to be selective in the face of a mass of material, which was not always easily accessible. Consequently, only important references are included in the synthesis for this study.

It should be noted that the latest edition of the Households Below Average Income statistics was published (30 June 1993) **after** the completion of this manuscript. Consequently, the most recent data has been included in some of the tables and the accompanying text, but it has not been possible to change the graphics at this late stage.

The framework of the study

The study is in two parts. Part I contains two chapters. The first deals with three main issues: one, a variety of measures are considered to chart trends in child poverty; two, we examine the impact of changes in the tax and social security systems on the income of the poor, and its adequacy; third, as a contrast, and to provide a fuller picture, we look at the trend towards a widening of income and wealth inequalities in the UK, which became apparent in the eighties. In chapter two, we examine some of the factors underlying the increase in child poverty, such as economic trends, including unemployment and low pay, demographic changes affecting the family, and changes in welfare spending.

In Part II, in chapters three and four, we examine developments in children's health and housing and attempt to relate these to changes in deprivation, as far as possible. In chapter five, we consider the relationship between deprivation and education in the context of other factors such as race, social class, the school, and changes in the Government policy on education and provision.

In the concluding chapter, we pull together various strands emerging from this study, and draw out some implications for policy. We also consider briefly some of the deficiencies of evidence and their effect on this study's conclusions.

Tables are numbered sequentially in each chapter. For instance, table one in chapter one is numbered 1.1, table two as 1.2, and so on; tables which are placed in the appendix are numbered I.1, I.2 and so on. Figures may not always add up because of rounding. Charts and graphs are also numbered likewise.

A glossary of abbreviations and technical terms appears at the beginning of the book, as does a list of tables and figures.

Notes

1. For an attempt to distinguish between these two terms, see Rutter and Madge (1976); they prefer to use the term 'disadvantage' in this context.

2. Even Rowntree, according to Veit-Wilson (1986), used it as a heuristic device to convince others that people were poor because of low income, not fecklessness.
3. For a critique of Townsend's attempt to operationalise the concept of poverty, see in particular Piachaud (1981, and 1987), Ashton (1984) and Townsend (1981). For a discussion of the work of Mack and Lansley, see Ashton (1984), Piachaud (1987), Veit-Wilson (1987) and Walker (1987) among others. Piachaud (1987) discusses all three main approaches to the measurement of poverty. See also a recent study by Roll (1992) which came out too late for consideration here.

1. Trends in child poverty in the UK

Introduction

In the first two sections of this chapter we examine trends in child poverty since 1979, at national and regional levels, using a variety of measures. In the next section we trace the impact of changes in social security benefits in the eighties on the incomes of low income families with children, and question the adequacy of income of such families on social assistance. Finally, we consider changes in the taxation system in the eighties, together with those in social benefits, and relate these to the trend towards a widening of inequality in incomes and wealth, which became apparent in the eighties.

National trends in child poverty

Income support as a measure of poverty

In the absence of an official definition of poverty, one way is to infer poverty from a variety of official statistics. One surrogate measure of poverty which is widely used is the National Assistance scales (since replaced first by Supplementary Benefit (SB) in 1966 and, in 1988, by Income Support (IS)). These were introduced in 1948 as part of the reform of the Social Security System envisaged in the Beveridge Report (1942). These rates were based on a 'subsistence standard', adapted from Rowntree's work among others, representing poverty in the pre-war era, and provided for very basic dietary requirements plus modest allowances for clothing, fuel and certain other household costs (Bradshaw, Mitchell and Morgan, 1987). These rates also took into account differences in family composition and have been uprated from time to time. This 'subsistence poverty' is prescribed by Parliament for people without other resources, and has come to be seen by most people as '...a "national minimum" – a floor to living standards below which no-one need fall' (Donnison, 1982, p.6).

Table 1.1 gives details between 1979 and 1991 of children living in families dependent on SB/IS because their parents are sick, have disabilities, are unemployed or lone parents, and on Family Income Supplement (FIS)/Family Credit (FC) because their parents' earnings are low. It shows that the number of

Figure 1.1   Number of children in families on FC/FIS or IS/SB

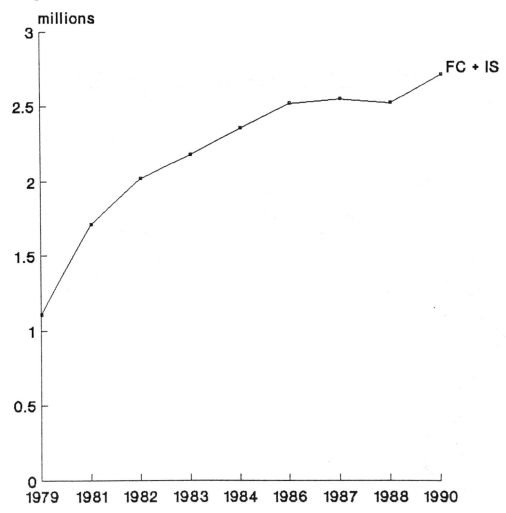

Source: DSS Social Security Statistics

children living in families dependent on these benefits has increased two and a half times during this period. Figure 1.1 shows how the numbers have fluctuated over the years. Only a very small part of this increase is due to an increase in the real value of these benefits – this was estimated by the Institute for Fiscal Studies (IFS) to be around 30 thousand between 1979 and 1989 (Social Security Committee 1993). Of particular interest is the threefold rise among the unemployed between 1979-86, and more than twofold rise in the number of lone parents.

Table 1.1 Number of children in families receiving family income supplement/family credit or supplementary benefit/income support in the UK 1979-1991

Thousands

Year (1)	FIS/FC (2)	SB/IS (3)	of whom unemployed (4)	of whom lone parents (5)	All (SB/IS+FIS/FC) (6)
1979	184	918	339	538	1102
1980	NA	1084	494	547	NA
1981	222	1485	810	620	1707
1982	306	1711	948	700	2017
1983	396	1781	977	760	2177
1984	417	1938	1053	825	2355
1985	405	NA	NA	NA	NA
1986	405	2113	1087	946	2518
1987	446	2100	965	1036	2546
1988	428	2092	778	1167	2520
1989	NA	2030	574	1250	NA
1990	663	2045	476	1333	2708
1991	NA	2370	640	1490	NA

Source: DSS Social Security Statistics.
Answer to Parliamentary Question 16.7.92.
NA = Not available.

Low income family statistics

Another important source which is often used to assess the incidence of poverty is the official series, Statistics on Low Income Families (LIF). It is based on the annual Family Expenditure Survey (FES) with a sample of about 7,000 households, and uses as a benchmark of 'low income' the current SB/IS scales, together with various multiples of them. These statistics were produced every year between 1974 and 1979, and then every two years until 1985 when the series was discontinued by the Government. Since then, the IFS has extended this series up to 1989 on behalf of the House of Commons Social Security Committee who published it in 1993.

Table 1.2 gives details of the number of children in families with low incomes at various income levels related to the SB/IS level during 1979-1989. It shows that the number of children in families at or below SB/IS, that is the 'national minimum' level, has almost doubled during this period from 1.5 million to 2.8 million; and exactly doubled as a proportion of all children from one in eight to one in four in the same period. Looking now at children in families living in or on the margin of poverty, that is at incomes below 140 per cent of SB/IS, one finds that their number has increased during this period by almost 50 per cent from 2.6 million to 3.8 million children, constituting 35 per cent of all children in 1989 (see Figure 1.2). In fact this was a significant decline from the peak of 38.5 per cent in 1983.

Figure 1.2   Children in low income families – various multiples of Supplementary Benefit (SB)/Income Support (IS)

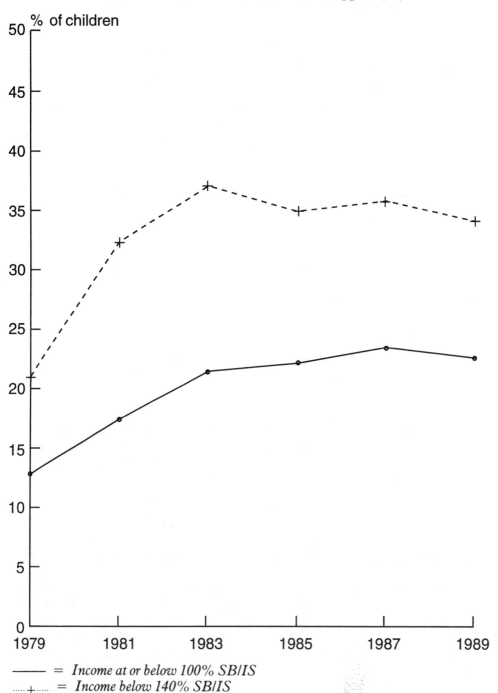

—— = *Income at or below 100% SB/IS*
·····+····· = *Income below 140% SB/IS*
Source: SSC (1993) *Low Income Statistics 1979-89*

Table 1.2   Children in families with low incomes – various multiples of Supplementary Benefit (SB)/Income Support (IS) in the UK 1979-1989

	1979	1981	1983	1985	1987	1989	% change 1979-89
Income at or below SB/IS level (1,000s)	1,500	2,140	2,600	2,710	2,760	2,760	+84
% of all children	(12.4)	(18.1)	(22.5)	(23.9)	(25.7)	(25.8)	
Income below 140% of SB/IS level (1,000s)	2,580	3,910	4,440	4,150	4,000	3,780	+47
% of all children	(21.4)	(33.0)	(38.5)	(36.5)	(37.2)	(35.4)	

Source: SSC (1993) *Low Income Statistics, 1979-1989*
(Derived from various tables)

A part of this increase is due to a rise in the real value of benefits.[1] However, even if the real value of SB/IS were held constant in 1979 terms, there was a substantial increase in the number and proportion of children in low income families: the number of children in families at or below SB/IS increased by one and a three quarters times between 1979 and 1989, still numbering one in four of all children; and those in families at the margin of poverty increased by over half a million to 3.1 million, or 29 per cent of all children. The number of children in both these categories is likely to be a good deal higher in 1993 in view of the largerscale increase in unemployment since then.

Households below average income (HBAI)

This is a new series introduced by the Government to replace LIF statistics. There have been several editions and the one published in July 1992 covered the period between 1979 and 1989; the data for the calendar years 1988 and 1989 was combined (1988/89) to improve the accuracy of the results. The coverage was extended from Great Britain to the UK. Because of this, and some important methodological changes[2] introduced in this edition (HBAI, 1992), its results are not comparable with those in earlier editions. With the discontinuation by the Government of LIF Statistics, HBAI series has come to be seen as an important surrogate measure of poverty.

The HBAI provides estimates of the distribution of personal disposable income, and of changes over time. It does not cover the whole population – only those living in private households are included; but people in residential institutions, nursing homes and barracks, for instance, and homeless people in Bed and Breakfast (B & B) accommodation or living rough are excluded. As its name implies, it provides data only on the lower half (50 per cent) of the income distribution, broken down into five equal groups of ten per cent each ('deciles'). The measure of income used – 'personal disposable income' – is net of Income Tax and National Insurance Contributions (NICs), local government taxes (the Community Charge or the

Council Tax from April 1993) and certain other deductions. It does include Social Security benefits, including rent and rate rebates.

Like the LIF statistics, the HBAI is also based on the FES (mainly), and its results are therefore estimates only, subject to sampling errors. However, unlike the LIF, it is not linked to the IS level. Instead, it provides data on the number and proportion of individuals below various levels of income below the UK average. The unit of income in HBAI is the 'household', as distinct from 'family' in the LIF. All members of a household are assumed to share its income equally. When comparing income between households, HBAI allows for differences in their size and composition by adjusting their incomes, using 'equivalence' scales to produce income levels which are intended to achieve broadly similar living standards. However, results vary significantly, depending on the kind of equivalence scales used.

Analysis based on this series can be particularly sensitive to the choice of definition: how average is defined (for instance, HBAI 1992 uses arithmetic mean for the national average, but median for the decile groups); which fraction of the average is taken as a measure of poverty (whether 50, 60 or 70 per cent or any other fraction below average); whether income is calculated before or after housing costs; and, finally, whether the average is related to changes in prices or earnings.

In HBAI 1992, the results are presented both **before** the deduction of housing costs (BHC), and **after** such deductions (AHC). The justification provided by the Government for adopting this procedure is that the available data does not show to what extent variations in the cost of housing reflect variations in its actual quality, thereby justifying BHC treatment; and to what extent such cost variations, at a point in time and over time, are unrelated to the quality of housing, and therefore share '...some of the characteristics – from the view point of income analysis – of a tax, which should perhaps be deducted from income' (HBAI, 1992, p.13).

To appreciate the difference that a choice of definition makes, let us look at Table 1.3, reproduced from HBAI 1992 and 1993 (Table F1). It shows how individuals in different household types below 50 per cent of the average income (BHC and AHC), when adjusted in line with earnings, have moved over the 1979-90/91 period. Figure 1.3 illustrates this graphically in relation to the period 1979-88/89.

Looking at the difference made by housing costs, one finds that, in 1979, eight per cent of the population was below half the national average income **before** housing costs (BHC), and nine per cent **after** housing costs (AHC); by 1990/91, both had increased by two and a half times: 21 per cent BHC, and 24 per cent AHC. The difference between BHC and AHC is significantly greater in the case of lone parents with children: from 16 per cent BHC to 19 per cent AHC in 1979; the corresponding figures for 1990/91 are 50 and 60 per cent respectively. HBAI 1992 recognises that, comparing income over time, BHC tends to overstate the incomes of low income households – such as lone parent families – when a rise in housing costs, accompanied by a corresponding rise in social security benefits, will produce a rise in income BHC, even though such

Figure 1.3   Percentage of individuals in different family types with income below 50% of the contemporary average

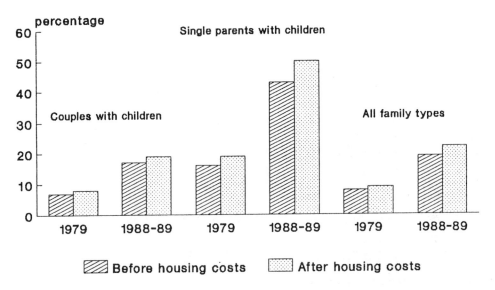

Source: DSS: *HBAI 1992* (Table F1)

Table 1.3   Percentage of individuals in different family types with income below 50% of the contemporary average in the UK 1979-1990/91

Year	Couple with children		Single Parents with children		All family types Before housing costs		All family types After housing costs	
	BHC	AHC	BHC	AHC	%	No (m)	%	No (m)
1979	(7)	(8)	(16)	(19)	8	4.4	9	5.0
1981	(11)	14	(12)	(20)	9	(4.7)	11	6.2
1987	(17)	(20)	(29)	(39)	16	8.7	19	10.5
1988/89	(17)	19	(43)	(50)	19	10.4	22	12.0
1990/91	(19)	(23)	(50)	(60)	21	11.6	24	13.5

Source: DSS: *HBAI 1992, 1993* (Table F1).
NB: Estimates in brackets ( ) are particularly uncertain.

households may not, in fact, be any better off. Their position is much worse, however, when sharply rising housing costs are only partially compensated for by increases in the Housing Benefit (HB), as happened in the eighties with tenants of council housing. In their case, the BHC figures '...may show an improvement which is not present in the after-housing cost figures' (Atkinson, 1990, pp. 2-3). In view of this, most other data in this series are presented AHC.

The next two sets of data (Figures 1.4 and 1.5) are presented (AHC) to illustrate the difference it makes whether the average is held constant in real

Figure 1.4   Proportion of dependent children with income below 50% of average 1979 real terms. After housing costs

Source: SSC: *HBAI 1991* (Table E3)

Figure 1.5   Proportion of dependent children below 50% of average income for each year. After housing costs

Source: SSC: *HBAI 1991* (Table F3)

terms, or it moves with average earnings. These data relate to the proportion of dependent children during 1979-88[3] below half the average income analysed by economic status. Figure 1.4 shows the average held constant in 1979 real terms, while Figure 1.5 shows it moving with average earnings. The differences between the two are striking not only for the proportion overall, but also for all the status groups: in Figure 1.4 there is hardly any movement except mainly in the case of lone parents; in Figure 1.5, on the other hand, there are significant differences in all the status groups, and the overall figure of dependent children below 50 per cent of **contemporary** average income has doubled from 12 per cent in 1979 to 25 per cent in 1988. However, according to the latest figures (HBAI, 1993, Table F3), this figure increased threefold from ten per cent in 1979 to 31 per cent in 1990/91 (see also Table I.4).

Children are significantly over-represented among the poor compared with adults. As poverty increased during the eighties, the disparity between adults and children increased too. In 1979, ten per cent of children were living in households with incomes 50 per cent below the contemporary national average (AHC) as against nine per cent of adults. By 1990/91, the corresponding figures had risen to 31 per cent and 24 per cent respectively (see Table I.1).

Finally, Figure 1.6 illustrates how the choice of income below various thresholds can affect the proportion of dependent children. For instance, at income 50 per cent below national average, the percentage of dependent children increased from 10 in 1979 to 25 in 1988-89; and to 31 in 1990/91 (see Table I.2). And at 60 per cent below average, it doubled from 20 to 40 in the same period. It is worth noting here that half the national average income is the poverty standard adopted by the European Commission for its poverty programme (Atkinson, 1990). It roughly corresponds to the UK national assistance scales; likewise, income 60 per cent below average broadly corresponds to income below 140 per cent of the SB/IS level - generally referred to as the 'margin of poverty'.

Consensual approach to measuring poverty

A different approach to measuring poverty in the UK was adopted by the *Breadline Britain* documentary series. It commissioned MORI to conduct a general survey of the population to find out what most people consider should be the minimum acceptable standard of living in the UK these days. Two surveys have been done so far, in 1983 and in 1990, so that it is possible to compare the results over time. In each of these surveys, respondents were asked to classify items from a list into two categories: one 'which (items) you think are necessary, and which all adults should be able to afford and which they should not have to do without'; second, items 'which may be desirable, but are not necessary' (Frayman, 1991). The process was repeated for items which relate only to families with children. In the second part of the survey, people were asked among other things which items from these lists they possessed, which they lacked, and which ones they lacked because they could not afford them. Those items on the list of necessities, which gained at least 50 per cent support in interviews, formed the basis on which *Breadline Britain* compiled their data on poverty. The detailed results of the 1983 survey have already been published (Mack and Lansley, 1985); but at the time of writing those for the 1990 survey were only available in outline (Frayman, 1991).

Figure 1.6   Proportion of dependent children with incomes below various thresholds which change with average income. AHC

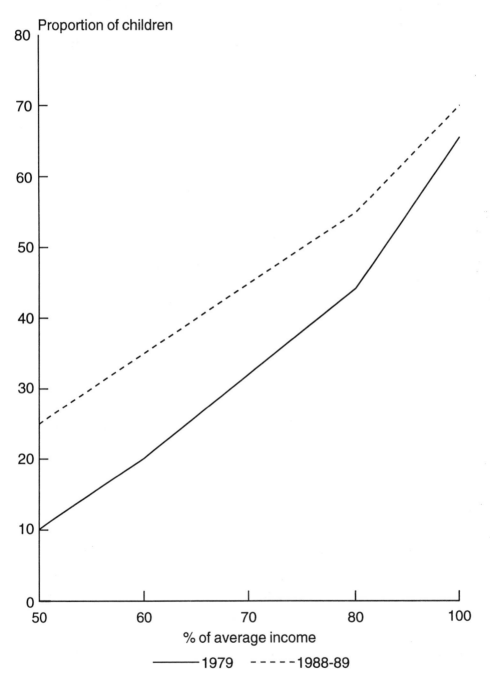

Source: DSS: *HBAI 1992 (Table F3)*

Table 1.4   Number of children and adults in varying degrees of poverty in Britain 1983-1990

Degree of Poverty	Children		Adults		Total	
	1983 Number (%)	*1990* Number (%)	*1983* Number (%)	*1990* Number (%)	*1983* Number (%)	*1990* Number (%)
In or on the margins	4.2 (NA)	NA	7.9 (NA)	NA	12.1 (22.2)	NA
In poverty	2.5 (NA)	3 (NA)	5.0 (NA)	8 (NA)	7.5 (13.8)	11 (NA)
Sinking deeper	1.4 (NA)	NA	3.3 (NA)	NA	4.7 (8.6)	6 (NA)
In intense poverty	0.9 (NA)	NA	1.7 (NA)	NA	2.6 (4.8)	3.5 (NA)

Source: Mack and Lansley, 1985 (Table 6.4)   NA = Not available.
Frayman, 1991.

People lacking three or more of these socially approved necessities, which they could not afford, were deemed to be poor; those who could not afford five or more were 'sinking deeper' into poverty; and those who could not afford seven or more were in 'intense' poverty. On the other hand, people who could not afford one or two of these items were on the margin of poverty. The results are shown in Table 1.4. These indicate that in 1983 there were 2.5 million (22 per cent) children living in poverty, 1.4 million (12 per cent) were 'sinking deeper' into it, while nearly a million (0.9) (eight per cent) were in intense poverty. By 1990 the number of children in poverty had increased to more than three million (about 28 per cent); the figures for the severity of poverty are not available for children. But the figures for adults show that the number in poverty has doubled from five to 11 million between 1983 and 1990, with corresponding increases for those 'sinking deeper' and those in 'intense' poverty.

Regional trends in poverty

It will be useful to look now at the picture from the regional perspective. Table 1.5 shows how poverty is distributed regionally, and how it changes over time. This table is based on an analysis of the latest available data, that is Households and Families Below Average Income (HFBAI, 1990) statistics for the period 1980-85, done by the IFS at the request of the Social Services Committee because the Government had earlier refused to do so. Because the sample size of FES (7,000 households) gets small at the regional level, the IFS got around this problem by combining the three-year data for the period 1980-82 and comparing it with data for the period 1983-85, thereby enlarging the sample. Even so, the data needs to be interpreted with care.

The various regions are so arranged in the Table that the top half (above the line) can be characterised as the 'North' and the bottom half as the 'South',

**Table 1.5 Proportions of children below various income thresholds[1]
analysed by region in the UK 1980/82-1983/85**

Family income	1980-82 % with income (AHC)[2]		1983-85 % with income (AHC)[2]	
Region	Below 50%	Below 60%	Below 50%	Below 60%
Northern Ireland	42	53	42	54
Scotland	20	31	21	30
Wales	19	33	25	38
Northern	22	35	28	41
Yorkshire and Humberside	26	36	23	36
North West	20	31	25	36
West Midlands	16	30	22	34
East Midlands	15	26	16	24
East Anglia	14	28	16	25
Greater London	14	26	19	29
South East	14	23	11	20
South West	14	26	16	27
England (Total)	17	28	19	29
UK (Total) (Per cent)	18.5	29.6	20.3	30.9
UK Total (numbers, 000s)	2,490	4,000	2,630	4,000

Source: Social Service Committee, *HFBAI, 1990* (Table C8).
Notes: 1. Income thresholds change with average income (AHC).
         2. AHC = After Housing Costs.

corresponding to the traditional dividing line between the Severn Bridge and the Wash, following Borooah, McGreggor and McKee (1991).

Looking first at the 1980-82 period, one can see that nearly two and a half million children were living in families below half the national average income – the poverty line in the European Community (EC). One can also see a glaring difference between the two halves of the country: in the South, the proportion of dependent children is considerably below the UK average of 18.5 per cent, but it is well above this figure in the North with the exception of West Midlands – even there it is greater than in every single region in the South. In the North the number of children living in families below this poverty line vary from one fifth in Scotland and Wales to two-fifths in Northern Ireland.

Let us see how this picture looks when we compare the two periods. In the North, especially in Wales, West Midlands, the North West and the Northern regions, there have been steep increases in the proportion of children living below half the national average for this period. On the other hand, the increase in the South has been modest by comparison except for the Greater London region, in parts of which the deprivation levels are comparable to those in the North and where the recession of the early eighties seems to have had a similar effect. This picture may be modified somewhat, as the recent economic recession has been bearing down much harder in the South East (see chapter 2).

However, let us now consider children living in families with income 60 per cent below the national average which, as we saw earlier, roughly corresponds to income below 140 per cent of the SB/IS level. There are in all four million children living in families below this income level: around a quarter of them in the South, but anything from nearly a third (in West Midlands) to over half (in Northern Ireland) in the North. This trend was considerably strengthened during the 1983-85 period.

Table 1.6 shows another way of looking at the North-South divide. It indicates the proportion of children in families below the lowest decile against corresponding population figures. Whereas 64 per cent of the children in the North are in families below this level of income – 10 per cent more than their proportion in the population – the situation is reversed in the South where 35 per cent of children live below this level, that is ten per cent less than their population proportion. Once again the situation is much worse in Northern Ireland than anywhere else. The change from 1980-82 to 1983-85 is less dramatic here: generally, modest increases in the North, but in the South there is little change except for a slight increase in the South West, but a striking reduction of five percentage points from 14 to 9 per cent in the case of the South East.

It is interesting to note that an econometric analysis of regional poverty based on 1985 FES data came to the following conclusion: at every poverty line (SB, 120 per cent and 140 per cent of SB level) the North had a greater proportion of individuals who were poor, but this was qualified by the finding that '...the depth of poverty was greater in the South...than in the North', that is, people in the North were, on average, less poor as compared with those in the South. (Borooah, McGreggor and McKee, 1991, p85).

Summary

Despite significant differences in the measurement of child poverty in the results presented above, there is a remarkable similarity and consistency. The trend is clearly upward – the number of children estimated to be living in poverty varies from 1.1 million to 1.4 million in 1979; by 1990/91, it had risen to almost four million, or nearly one in every three children in the country. The number in or on the margin of poverty varies between 2.4 million and 2.8 million (20 per cent) in 1979, and rises to five million (40 per cent) by 1990/91. This corresponds to the overall increase in poverty from five million (8 per cent) in 1979 to 13.5 million (24 per cent) in 1990/91. Regional breakdown of data suggests that child poverty is not evenly spread across the country – it is concentrated more in the North with traditionally higher rates of unemployment. However this position may have been modified somewhat by the recent recession (since March 1990), which appears to have affected the South more than the North (see chapter 2).

Table 1.6   Children below various fractions of the income[1] distribution – analysed by region in the UK 1980/82-1983/85

Region	Proportion of children Percentile of the Income Distribution below 10% 1980-82 (average)	All children Total Population	Proportion of children Percentile of the Income Distribution below 10% 1983-85 (average)	All children Total Population
Northern Ireland	7	3.6	8	3.7
Scotland	10	9.4	8	8.8
Wales	5	5.3	7	5.8
Northern	7	5.7	9	5.5
Yorkshire & Humberside	13	9.1	12	9.7
North West	14	11.8	14	11.3
West Midlands	8	9.5	11	10.4
'North' Total	64	54.4	69	55.2
East Midlands	6	6.9	6	7.2
East Anglia	2	3.9	2	3.3
Greater London	8	9.9	8	8.3
South East	14	18.0	9	18.9
South West	5	6.8	6	7.2
'South' Total	35	45.5	31	44.9
England	77	81.7	76	81.8
UK Total (%)	100	100	100	100
UK Total (No) (000s)	1,790	13,490	1,720	12,940

Source: Social Services Committee, *HFBAI, 1990* (Table A8)
Notes: 1. Ranked by family income, after housing costs.

Income of the poor

Increasing dependence on social security benefits

One effect of the rapidly rising poverty in the eighties was to greatly increase the dependence of people on low incomes on social security benefits. This has taken two forms: one, to greatly increase the number of people claiming benefits; the other, to increase the contribution made by benefits to their total income. Table 1.1, as we saw earlier, illustrates the first trend: the number of dependent children in families claiming IS or FIS/FC increased two and a half times between 1979 and 1990.

The other aspect of dependence on social security benefits, that is how these constitute an increasing proportion of the income of those on low incomes is illustrated in Table 1.7. For those on half average income, the proportion increased from 35 per cent in 1979 to a peak of 45 per cent in 1985, where it stayed until it came down in 1988 to 39 per cent. Second, this dependence greatly increases as one goes down the income scale. For instance, for those on incomes below 10 per cent of average, social security benefits accounted for nearly three-quarters of their income during much of the eighties; and two-thirds of the income of those below 20 per cent of the average.

Table 1.7 Percentage contribution of social security benefits to the incomes of those below various percentiles of the income distribution 1979-1988

| Year | Social Security Benefits | Percentile of the income distribution | | | | |
		below 10%	below 20%	below 30%	below 40%	below 50%
1979	All Social Security Benefits	72	62	51	42	35
	of which					
	Supplementary Benefit	18	13	9	7	6
1981	All Social Security Benefits	71	65	56	48	40
	of which					
	Supplementary Benefit	24	18	14	11	9
1985	All Social Security Benefits	75	69	62	54	45
	of which					
	Supplementary Benefit	28	20	16	12	9
1987	All Social Security Benefits	73	69	62	53	44
	of which					
	Supplementary Benefit	27	20	16	12	9
1988	All Social Security Benefits	76	68	60	49	39
	of which					
	Supplementary Benefit	24	17	13	9	7

Source: SSC, *HBAI, 1991* (Table G)

Impact of changes in social security benefits

Given the increasing dependence of low income families with dependent children on social security benefits, any changes in the value of these benefits have an important bearing on their living standards. We shall, therefore, review below some of the main changes in these benefits since 1979 which particularly affect such families.

Link between benefits and earnings severed

One significant development was the Government's decision in 1980 to sever the link between earnings and level of benefits as provided for in the 1980 Social Security Act (Edwards, 1987). Since then the main benefits have been uprated broadly in line with prices.

As Table 1.8 shows, the value of SB/IS for a couple with two children slipped from 37 per cent of the median disposable income in 1979 to 29 per cent in April 1990 – the latest date for which official information is available[4]. In the eight year period between 1979 and 1987, the real value of SB, for a married couple

Table 1.8 Supplementary Benefit/Income Support scales for a couple with two children under 11 (a) at constant prices and (b) as a proportion of the median disposable income of a couple with two children 1979-1992

Uprating date	Actual Benefit Rate[1]	Benefit Rate at April 1992 Prices[2]	Benefit as a Percentage of Median Disposable Income[3,4]
Supplementary Benefit:			
November 1979	42.20	89.32	37.2
November 1980	49.20	91.85	36.5
November 1981	53.55	90.39	36.6
November 1982	59.20	93.79	37.1
November 1983	61.80	93.50	35.9
November 1984	64.75	94.34	35.6
November 1985	68.05	94.54	34.2
July 1986	68.80	93.08	31.4
April 1987	70.15	93.16	30.2
Income Support:			
April 1988	79.10	101.25	30.5
April 1989	84.80	103.05	29.4
April 1990	89.65	102.46	28.7
April 1991	98.15	103.38	NA
April 1992	105.00	105.00	NA

Source: Department of Social Security in answer to a Parliamentary Question 16.7.92.
         NA = Not available.
Notes: 1. The calculation of the Actual Benefit Rate is based upon a couple who are householders, with two children aged 10-years-old, claiming benefit on the grounds that they are unemployed.
2. Benefit rate is calculated using the Rossi index (that is, RPI less housing costs).
3. Income is for households comprising a couple with two children of any age. Source for this figure is the *Family Expenditure Survey* published reports 1979 to 1990.
4. No allowance has been made for housing costs.

with two children under 11, increased by only four per cent – in 1986 and 1987 it actually fell. This was followed by a one-off increase of around nine per cent in April 1988 as part of the implementation of the 1986 'Fowler' reforms. In the subsequent four years (1988-92) its value increased by around four per cent in real terms. In other words, the uprating pattern of the 1980s – of increasing SB broadly in line with prices – was resumed.

Changes affecting the unemployed

A second significant development concerns a series of changes in benefits adversely affecting the unemployed, who constitute a high proportion of people with dependent children on half average income (see Figure 1.4 and Table 1.1[5]). Some of these changes have a particular bearing on children. For instance, in November 1984 the Government abolished the child dependency additions to Unemployment Benefit (UB) which, together with child benefit, would be worth £13.10 per child in 1992, if uprated in line with prices. Against that, unemployed people in September 1992 received only child benefit: £9.65 for the first child, £7.80 for others (Lynes, 1992).

To appreciate the effect of various changes on the income of unemployed families with dependent children, let us see how the value of UB has changed since 1979. For instance, in 1979 an unemployed man previously on average earnings, with a non-earning wife and two children, would have received £127.70 (1992 real terms) per week. In 1992-93, he would get £73.21 if he is liable to pay tax, and £87.15 if he is not. This indicates a fall in real terms in benefit income after tax of 43 per cent since 1979 (Lynes, 1992). It is fair to add that some of this loss would in many cases be made up by reliance on means-tested benefits. As for the cumulative impact of various changes on the unemployed generally, a study by Atkinson and Micklewright (1989) demonstrates that the unemployed claimants stand to lose £2.92 per week (1988 prices), while the Government gains £465 million annually.

Shift from universal to means-tested benefits

A third development of note, which affects both the income and the rights of low income families, concerns a significant and rapid shift in emphasis in the 1980s from universal, contributory, benefits available as of right, to selective, means-tested, benefits. For instance, the proportion of unemployed claimants receiving SB, which is a means-tested benefit, rose from 65 per cent for men and 48 per cent for women in 1979, to 85 per cent and 66 per cent respectively in 1989 (*Social Security Statistics* 1982 and 1989). Correspondingly, as we saw earlier (Table 1.1), the number of dependent children in unemployed families claiming SB increased threefold between 1979 and 1986; it came down as unemployment fell in the next four years, but has started to rise again since 1990.

Among the factors contributing to this considerable growth in dependence on means-tested benefits are: one, a largescale increase in unemployment in the 1980s generally, and long-term (over one year) unemployment in particular (see chapter 2), since UB is payable for only one year; two, the various reductions in unemployment benefit, and changes in its entitlement; three, lack of eligibility for UB due to a failure to build up enough NICs.

The Social Security Advisory Committee (SSAC) expressed their concern that 'a major shift from contributory to means-tested non-contributory benefit appears to be taking place without public debate on its implications' (1981, para.3.6). Some of the implications are that means-tested benefits tend to be complex and costly to administer; they are personally intrusive and stigmatising for the claimants; and consequently tend to have a low and variable take up. For example, the take-up of Family Credit (FC) in Great Britain in 1991 was 70 per cent by value, and 64 per cent by caseload (*Hansard*, 16 December 1992, col. 326). The corresponding figures for 1989 for IS were 87 per cent and 75 per cent respectively; and for HB, 91 and 83 per cent respectively (DSS, 1993b).

Reform of the social security system

Finally, a major development in the 1980s was the introduction of the 'Fowler' reforms in the 1986 Social Security Act (SSA), which came into operation in April 1988. It streamlined the structure of, and the relationship between, the three most important income-related benefits: Income Support (which replaced the SB), Family Credit (which replaced FIS), and Housing Benefit (HB). Entitlement to these benefits was put on the same basis with common definitions of income and needs allowances. A central feature of these reforms was '...the emphasis on targeting and on using means tests to direct resources to those people "most in need"' (Millar, 1991, p.30). In its 1986 White Paper on Social Security Reform, the Government had stated its intention to concentrate additional help on low income families with children. How successful has the Government been in doing this?

Help for families with children

Given that reforms were to be achieved at nil cost, their financial impact was limited – it is summarised in Table 1.9.

Table 1.9   Real increase[1] in benefit rates following the introduction of income support (£ per week)

Lone parent plus a child aged 3	− £2.52
Lone parent plus children aged 4 and 6	− £2.56
Couple plus child aged 3	+ £0.72
Couple plus children aged 4 and 6	+ £0.68
Couple plus children aged 13 and 16	+ £2.91
Couple plus children aged 3, 8 and 11	+ £0.60
Couple plus children aged 6, 8, 11 and 16	+ £2.83

Source: Social Services Committee (HC 437-1 para. 32 1989)
Notes: 1. This does not take into account the loss of single payments available under SB.

While modest gains were made by many families with children, especially older ones, many one parent families were distinctly worse off. According to the Government's own estimate, about half a million low income families with children would be losers but one million would be gainers (DHSS, 1987). However, these limited gains need to be set against other losses: people on Income Support have to pay 20 per cent of their Rates (now Community Charge[6]), all of their water rates, and lose single payments for meeting major expenses such as replacement of furniture or bedding in exceptional need. This was worth £200 million in 1987, compared with expenditure of £335 million for single payments in 1985-86 (Millar, 1991). Instead, they have now to apply for a largely loan-based, cash-limited and discretionary social fund.

The Government claims that the extra help it has provided for low income families since the 1988 reforms will, from April 1993, be worth around £1 billion (*Hansard*, 16 December 1992, col. 325). Although the Government did not provide any breakdown of how this money was being spent, one can nevertheless identify some improvements in certain benefits for low income families with dependent children, even if it is difficult to quantify them, and to balance them against losses in other areas. For instance, the family credit is considerably more generous than FIS, and potentially more than twice as many families would be eligible as FIS (*Hansard*, 18.11.87, col. 1172). But its take up is still low, although it has improved. As compared to FIS, the take up of FC in 1991 was 64 per cent of eligible people and 70 per cent of value (*Hansard*, 16.12.92, col. 326), as compared to 51 per cent and 60 per cent respectively for FIS in 1987 (DSS, 1991b).

However, it is estimated that nearly a quarter of all those getting FC may find their gains offset by large losses in HB - an estimated 40,000 would lose more than £5 per week (*Hansard*, 13.2.88, cols. 737-742). In addition, FC claimants getting HB may also lose varying amounts of compensation (allowance in FC of £2.55 per week) for free school meals and welfare milk (*Hansard*, 16.11.87 col. 442).

Another area where there has been a significant improvement recently is in child benefit, which was frozen for three years from April 1988 to April 1990, thereby losing 24 per cent of its April 1987 value (*Hansard*, 18.4.91, col. 238). Since October 1991, CB is paid at two levels – a higher rate for the eldest child (£9.65 per week from April 1992) and a lower rate (£7.80 per week) for others. The higher rate has now more or less caught up with its 1987 value, but the lower rate still falls short of that level. The Government has decided that, as from April 1992, CB would be index-linked to the Retail Price Index (RPI) (Ditch, Pickles and Whiteford, 1992; *Coalition for Child Benefit*).

Moreover, these increases in CB were also matched by increases in the means-tested benefits for children in October 1991, such as IS and FC, thus directly benefitting low income families with children.

However, the critics maintain that these improvements were achieved by diverting resources from other areas such as housing benefit, which was cut by about £900 million in the 1980s (Lister, 1989; Alcock, 1991). According to one estimate, the Government would have saved about £600 million in the first year of the implementation of the 1986 Social Security Act, if some other cuts in expenditure in the run-up to the Act were taken into account (Oppenheim, 1988). According to another assessment, over four-fifths of couples with children and about three-quarters of lone parent families emerged as losers financially when IS replaced SB (Svenson and MacPherson, 1988).

Effectiveness of Social Fund

Of particular concern to families with children was the replacement in 1988 of single payments under SB (sharply reduced in the two preceding years) by the Social Fund.

Five in every six of these payments were claimed by parents with children (House of Commons Standing Committee E, 10.12.87, col. 510), and grants to them averaged out at £4.15 per week (Berthoud, 1986). How has the SF operated in practice? Recent research by the Social Policy Research Unit at York University, sponsored by the DSS, has concluded that '...the fund does contribute substantially to the meeting of **some** needs of **some** applicants, on **some** occasions' (emphasis added) (Huby and Dix, 1992). However, they could not say that '...those who got awards were in greater general need than those who did not; nor...that the social fund is meeting its objective "to concentrate attention and help on those applicants facing greatest difficulties in managing on their income" (DSS, 1991c)' (Huby and Dix, 1992). This is not surprising, in view of another study's finding that the demand for help is far outstripping the volume of cash available. While the number of applications increased by 70 per cent between 1988-89 and 1991-92 when it reached almost three million, the rate of refusal jumped from 49 per cent to 73 per cent in the same period. This study points out that 'there is a fundamental contradiction between the notion of a weekly minimum subsistence benefit widely regarded as inadequate to provide for major items of expenditure, and the idea of extra help given as loans' (Craig, 1992). If the SF can meet only some needs of some people some of the time, what can others, especially low income families with children, do except to turn to charities and, failing that (given their limitations[7]), to add to their credit commitments, and thereby run the risk of increased indebtedness? A recent study of indebtedness has identified low income families with children, lone parent families (on low income) with children, and unemployed families with children, as at greatest risk of debt (Berthoud and Kempson, 1992).

Adequacy of benefits

The foregoing discussion raises the question about the adequacy of SB/IS to meet the needs of a growing number of people, especially of families with children. In his study on child poverty, Bradshaw, while appreciating that this was recognised by the Government in its intention to concentrate extra help on families with children, observes that 'It is not at all certain that this objective was achieved in practice and certainly no attempt was made to define adequacy' (1990, p25; Cohen and colleagues, 1992).

However, as Beveridge himself recognised, the original standard on which these rates are based did not '...constitute a reasonable living wage', and was meant to be used only as an emergency measure in the short term (1942). The 'subsistence standard' underpinning the SB has been criticised for its spurious objectivity; that it concentrated too much on the physical needs of survival, but paid insufficient attention to social needs (Abel-Smith and Townsend, 1965; Rein, 1970). These social needs have grown in the wake of enormous economic and social changes in the UK since then. Although the rates of benefit have more than kept pace with the rise in prices – in fact, they have more than doubled in real terms since 1948 - their value in relation to earnings (which have risen much faster than prices) is lower now than it was in 1948 (Bradshaw, 1990). More recently, between 1979 and 1992, as we have seen, the value of SB/ IS for a couple with two children under 11 as a proportion of net disposable income actually fell by well over a fifth (22.9 per cent) (Table 1.8)[4]. There is also considerable evidence that the RPI 'is not a good indicator of movements in the living standards of claimants' (Godfrey and Bradshaw, 1983).

Despite some improvement recently in the benefit level, there still remain serious questions as to its adequacy in relation to needs, as discussion in Parliament (*Hansard* 23.1.92 col. 532) and a number of recent studies have demonstrated.

The most recent research by Bradshaw, Hicks and Parker (1992) at the Family Budget Unit at York University shows that the IS level of income is barely enough to meet three-quarters of the cost of what they call a 'Low-cost' (LC) standard of living for two adults with two children under 11, or a lone mother with two children under 11. In other words, the former requires £36 per week, and the latter £25 per week, in **addition** to IS to achieve the LC standard. The LC standard includes only those items which two-thirds of people described as 'necessities' in the 1990 Breadline Britain Survey, plus any items which more than three-quarters of the population have. All items were priced on the basis of 'cheaper brands'.

The following two studies give a more graphic account of what it is really like living on income at or around the SB level. The first is by Bradshaw and Morgan, based on an analysis of data on living standards derived from a survey of 76 families, using 110 per cent of SB rate in February 1986 for a married couple with two children aged five and ten. They found that:

the living standards of families on SB, particularly those on the ordinary rate of benefit, is harsh: the food component is short on calories and even that diet is only achieved with the most determined of self control in purchasing only the cheapest items and avoiding all waste. Furthermore, it is achieved at the expense of expenditure on all other commodities. We have shown this with clothing but in addition the family cannot afford a holiday away from home – only a day outing a year – cannot afford a newspaper every day and has no money for books and magazines, never go to the cinema, cannot afford to buy bicycles or run a car, cannot maintain a garden, can afford one haircut a year, and so on (1987, p179).

A more recent study in the North East of England of a sample of families with children with an unemployed head living on SB had this to say about the quality of life in such families:

The picture which emerges from this detailed study of family lives is one of constant restriction in almost every aspect of people's activities...The lives of these families, and perhaps most seriously the lives of the children in them, are marked by the unrelieved struggle to manage with dreary diets and drab clothing.

They also suffer what amounts to cultural imprisonment in their homes in our society in which getting out with money to spend on recreation and leisure is normal at every other income level (Bradshaw and Holmes, 1989, pp. 138-39).

Hardship among young people

Finally, another area of concern is the difficult position of young people under 18, whose entitlement to IS has been abolished by the Government except for a restricted range of cases, and they have been effectively debarred from claiming UB by the recent tightening of contribution conditions. The Government had guaranteed a Youth Training (YT) place (with an entitlement to training allowance) to all those under 18 who were not in full-time education and could not find a job. In practice, it has proved difficult to implement fully this guarantee and many young people are left without any source of income (Lynes, 1992; see also chapter 2). A report compiled by the National Association of Citizens Advice Bureaux (NACAB) indicates that many young people cannot find a YT place even after exhausting their Bridging Allowance of £15 per week which is available for eight weeks (1992). Such people can of course apply for severe hardship payment, and many do. In fact, applications have gone up almost four-fold since January 1990 to reach over 8,000 per month. The success rate has also gradually improved from 70 per cent to 85 per cent in the same period (DSS 1992b).

However, the crucial question is what proportion of the 'target' population this benefit is reaching. In the absence of official data on young people without jobs or training and in hardship who do not apply, it is difficult to answer this question satisfactorily. However, an estimate by the Unemployment Unit (an independent body) suggests that in January 1992, only one-fifth of unemployed young people (16 to 17-year-olds) without a YT place had access to state benefits; and only one in every 14 of the remainder (11,000 out of 80,000) received severe hardship payments (*Working Brief*, April 1992). In view of this evidence, and on the basis of cases of hardship reported by CABx, the NACAB report concludes that 'this discretionary scheme cannot provide a consistent and comprehensive substitute for the benefits that have been with-drawn...'(1992, p39).

Summary

With a rapid rise in poverty in the eighties, the dependence of low income families on social benefits increased both in terms of the number of claimants, and benefits as a proportion of their income. Their living standards have been adversely affected as a result of four main changes in the value of these benefits: the shift from universal to selective, means-tested, benefits whose take-up is variable; the severing of the link between benefits and earnings; significant cuts in UB; and changes in the social security system under the 1986 SSA.

Whilst the effects of the last measure were complicated, and there were more winners among low income families with children than losers (the latter were more numerous among lone parent families), the gains were modest, and offset by losses in other benefits (such as HB). These losses were considerable – people on IS had to pay a fifth of local government taxes, all of water rates, and lose single payments for exceptional need. Research indicates that the largely loan-based, cash-limited, Social Fund which replaced these grants has failed to meet the needs of the 'target' population.

Despite some recent improvements by the Government in CB and the child component in means-tested benefits (IS and FC), there are serious questions as to the adequacy of these benefits to meet the growing needs of low income groups, especially those of families with children, in the face of enormous economic and social changes in the UK since the 'subsistence standard' represented by these rates was first fixed in 1948. Although the rates of benefits have considerably increased in real terms since then, their value in relation to earnings is lower now than it was in 1948; it has also slipped by more than a fifth since 1979. Whilst a number of studies have testified to the inadequacy of social benefits to support a 'minimum acceptable' living standard, the difficulty remains that successive governments have refused to define 'adequacy'. Finally, it was found that a significant proportion of 16 and 17-year-olds, who were without a job or a training place, were experiencing hardship because of the abolition of IS for them.

Widening inequality in income and wealth

In this section, we shall look at how incomes of low income families with children have fluctuated since 1979, and how these fluctuations are related to changes in the income of population generally; the relative impact of tax changes; and their impact on the wider distribution of income and wealth in the country. This will enable us to see the rising trend of child poverty in the UK since 1979 in a wider perspective and provide a context for the consideration of economic trends in society.

Income gap increase

According to HBAI 1993 statistics, the real income (AHC) of the bottom ten per cent of the population[8] declined by 14 per cent during the period 1979-90/91, and the income (AHC) of the second lowest decile remained unchanged during this period. This contrasts with the growth in the average real income (AHC) of the general population of 36 per cent in the same period (Table A1). At the other end of the income scale, the corresponding rise in the income of the top 20 per cent of the population in the same period was 40 per cent (Townsend, 1991).

The effect of this differential change in the incomes of different groups is reflected in Table 1.10, which indicates how the shares of various low income groups in total income have steadily declined during the period 1979-90/91. Thus the share of income (AHC) of the bottom half of the population has declined from nearly a third (32 per cent) in 1979 to a quarter by 1990/91. Likewise, the share of income of the bottom 10 and 20 per cent of the population has also fallen sharply during this period: from four to two per cent, and from ten to six per cent respectively. Figure 1.7 illustrates this trend graphically.

Table 1.10   Fluctuations in the share of total income of low income groups in the UK 1979-1988/89

	Before housing costs			After housing costs		
Year	Bottom 10%	Bottom 20%	Bottom 50%	Bottom 10%	Bottom 20%	Bottom 50%
1979	4.2	9.9	33.0	4.0	9.6	32.0
1981	4.1	9.7	32.0	3.7	9.0	31.0
1987	3.6	8.6	29.0	3.0	7.6	28.0
1988/89	3.2	7.9	28.0	2.5	6.9	27.0
1990/91	2.9	7.4	27.0	2.1	6.2	25.0

Source: HBAI, 1992, 1993 (Table A.3)

The income (AHC) of the bottom quintile (20 per cent) of married couples with children **fell** by 14 per cent between 1979 and 1990/91, as against an average **increase** of 31 per cent for this group as a whole. The corresponding data for the bottom quintile of the lone parent families with children is not available. However, the income (AHC) of the second and third quintiles between 1979-90/91 **fell** by three and five per cent respectively as against a five per cent average **rise** for the group generally (HBAI 1993, Table A4).

Changes in the tax and benefit system

Official data indicate that the burden of direct taxation on individuals (income tax plus national insurance contributions (NICs)) in the period 1978-79 to 1991-92 has tended to decrease proportionately with the rise in their income. For instance, for a married couple with two children (one partner working on half average income) their tax liability increased from 2.5 per cent of gross earnings in 1978-79 to 6.7 per cent in 1992-93. At the other end, at ten times the average income, the liability fell from about two-thirds to about a half of earnings in this period. The pattern was similar for people with incomes in between, except that the reduction tended to become smaller as one moved from the higher to the lower level of income (*Hansard*, 17.6.92, cols. 531-34).

We shall now look at changes in the tax and benefit systems together as these affect families with children. The IFS (1992) has done this analysis for the period 1979-92, based on uprating the 1979 data to 1992 prices; it also includes changes in indirect taxes. Their analysis indicates that the overall effect of changes has been an average increase of £18 per week, but it is very unevenly spread across different income groups. Only the top 30 per cent have gained this much or more; the top ten per cent gaining £87 per week. In the lower half of the income distribution, the gains have been limited, varying from £9 per week for the fifth decile to £2 per week for the second; the bottom decile actually lost £1 per week.

Figure 1.7   Fluctuations in income share of low income groups 1979–89

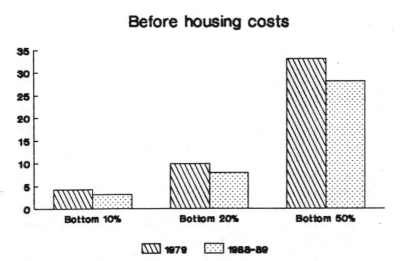

Before housing costs

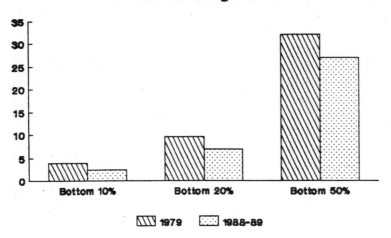

After housing costs

Source: HBAI 1992 (Table A3)

Analysis by family type indicates that an important factor influencing the outcome was whether someone in the family was working or not. Thus a family with two children where two persons were working did best (they gained £37 per week on average) - '...a direct reflection of their higher incomes' (p21). Where only one person was working, the average gain was £18 per week; and where no one was working[9], it was only £2 per week.

Although this analysis does not identify low income families as such, it is known (see Table I.4) that unemployed people form a high proportion in such families. So their gains are likely to be quite small. However, lone parent families did reasonably well – gaining £14 per week on average. Likewise, in families with children, irrespective of whether someone was working or not, the gainers far outnumbered the losers, even though their gains were modest. According to the IFS, this reflects the fact that it was one of the aims of the 1986 Social Security Act reforms that help should be directed at the low income families with children. However, in two respects, the IFS overstates their gains: one, they assume a 100 per cent take-up of benefits which, as we have seen, is far from being the case; two, they also do not take into account the loss of single payments, which is significant.

Discussing the reasons for the large gains made by the rich, the IFS singles out the cuts in income tax rates, particularly at the higher level, as the most important factor. These included the reduction in the basic income tax rate from 33 per cent to 25 per cent; and in the top rate on earned income from 83 per cent to 40 per cent, and on unearned income from 98 per cent to 40 per cent. These were accompanied by an increase in NICs (from 6.5 per cent to 9 per cent) with a regressive effect of the upper limit on employee contributions; and greater reliance on indirect taxation. The share of income tax declined from nearly a third (32 per cent) in 1979 to nearly a quarter (24 per cent) of all tax revenue in 1988-89. Apart from the reduction in mortgage interest tax relief for the higher rate tax payers in 1991, there was no significant broadening of the tax base by, for instance, cuts in the standard mortgage interest tax relief, or the tax expenditure on private and occupational pensions (worth £10 billion in 1991/92, according to Sinfield (1993)). 'The resultant increase in vertical inequity', argues Sinfield, has led to a 'pronounced' shift downwards in the burden of tax (1993). In fact the overall burden of tax increased from 34.3 per cent in 1978-79 to 37.1 per cent in 1990-91, as well as shifted downwards. For instance, in 1978-79, as earnings increased from 0.5 to three times the average, the tax burden increased from 41 per cent to 51 per cent. Ten years later, the corresponding figures were 44 per cent and 48 per cent respectively.

These regressive changes in the tax regime have clearly been an important contributory factor in the widening of income inequality in the eighties, as is evident from Table 1.11, which gives a comprehensive picture for the ten-year period 1979-89, for which the latest information is available. It shows how total household income is shared between households, tracing developments from the **original** income (**all** income from employment, pensions, investment and other sources), to **gross** income (plus all kinds of social security benefits), to **disposable** income (minus income tax, employees' NIC, Rates) and, finally, to

Table 1.11 Percentage shares of total original, gross, disposable and post-tax incomes by quintile groups of households[1] in the UK 1979-1989

	1979	1981	1983	1985	1987	1989
Equivalised original income						
Quintile group						
Bottom	2.4	2.9	3.0	2.5	2.1	2.0
2nd	10	9	8	7	7	7
3rd	18	17	17	17	16	16
4th	27	26	26	27	25	26
Top	43	46	47	47	50	49
All households	100	100	100	100	100	100
Equivalised gross income						
Quintile group						
Bottom	8.5	8.4	8.5	8.3	7.5	7.1
2nd	13	12	12	12	11	11
3rd	18	17	17	17	16	16
4th	24	23	23	24	23	23
Top	37	39	39	40	43	42
All households	100	100	100	100	100	100
Equivalised disposable income						
Quintile group						
Bottom	9.4	9.3	9.5	9.2	8.2	7.6
2nd	13	13	13	13	12	12
3rd	18	17	17	17	16	17
4th	23	23	23	23	23	23
Top	36	38	38	38	41	41
All households	100	100	100	100	100	100
Equivalised post-tax income						
Quintile group						
Bottom	9.5	9.0	8.9	8.6	7.6	6.9
2nd	13	13	13	13	12	11
3rd	18	17	17	17	16	16
4th	23	22	22	23	22	23
Top	37	39	39	39	43	43
All households	100	100	100	100	100	100

Source: Central Statistical Office *Economic Trends* January 1992
Notes: 1. Ranked by equivalised disposable income.

post-tax income (minus indirect taxes such as VAT), all equivalised to take into account variations in the size and composition of households. In 1989, for instance, the top 20 per cent of households (top quintile) received nearly a half of all the original income. Even after allowing for cash benefits, taxes and rates, they still retained 43 per cent of total post-tax income.

Another significant point to note here is that, throughout this period, the share of income received by the top quintile has increased over time, at each stage of the tax-benefit system; its share of the equivalised post-tax income having increased from 37 per cent in 1979 to 43 per cent 1989. In the same period, the share of the equivalised post-tax income of the bottom quintile declined from 9.5 to 6.9 per cent; and that of the second quintile from 13 to 11 per cent. Figure 1.8 illustrates the contrasting trend in the respective shares of the top and bottom quintiles of their equivalised post-tax income.

The rising poverty and increasing inequality in the eighties marked a new departure in post-war social policy, which hitherto was characterised by stability in the relative distribution of income, if not actual narrowing of the gap between the rich and the poor. The Royal Commission on the Distribution of Income and Wealth, noticing little change in the share of income of the bottom half of the population between 1949 and 1976-77, remarked that 'the income distribution shows remarkable stability from year to year' (Cmnd 7595, para. 2.25). In fact, the seventies saw a narrowing of the gap between the rich and the poor. Analysis of income changes in the UK between 1971 and 1986 over five-yearly intervals by Coulter (and others) indicated that, between 1971 and 1976, income growth was much greater for poorer groups than richer ones: 15 per cent for the bottom decile (tenth) as against a fall of about seven per cent for the top decile. However, after 1976, the situation was reversed: the income of the bottom decile fell by one per cent between 1976–81, and rose by ten per cent between 1981–86; by contrast the income of the top ten per cent increased by about a fifth in each of these two periods (1991).

Inequality in the distribution of wealth

At the same time that the gap in incomes has increased, there has also been an increase in inequality in the 1980s in the distribution of wealth. Table I.3 shows the distribution of wealth in the UK during the period 1979-89. In 1989, the top 10 per cent of the people owned over half (53 per cent) of all marketable wealth in the UK, and the top 25 per cent, three-quarters. Except for a slight decline in the wealth of the top one per cent, the wealth of all the other groups in the top half has increased over this period in all three measures of wealth. This means that the share of the bottom half has suffered a drop from eight to six per cent of marketable wealth, from 13 to six per cent if the value of dwellings is taken out, and from 20-22 per cent to 17 per cent of total personal wealth. Figure 1.9 shows the trend in the changing distribution of total wealth (marketable wealth plus occupational and state pension rights – historic valuation). A significant feature of this increase in inequality in wealth is that it occured in the context of a three-fold growth in personal total wealth since 1979 (*Economic Trends*, 1991). Also significant here is the increase in the share attributable to occupational

Figure 1.8   Share of income of the bottom and top quintiles of equivalised post tax income

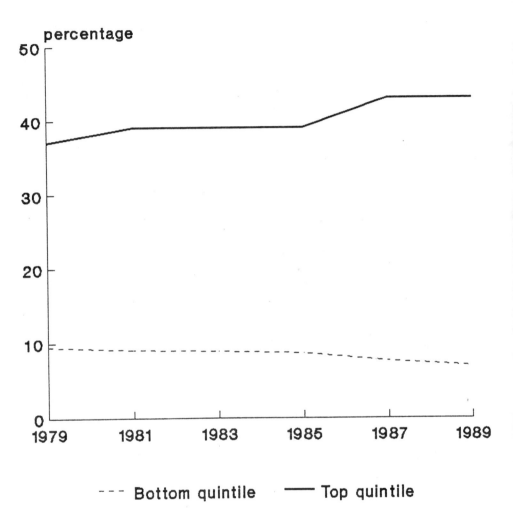

Source: CSO: *Economic Trends* January 1992

Figure 1.9   Distribution of wealth* in the UK 1979–89

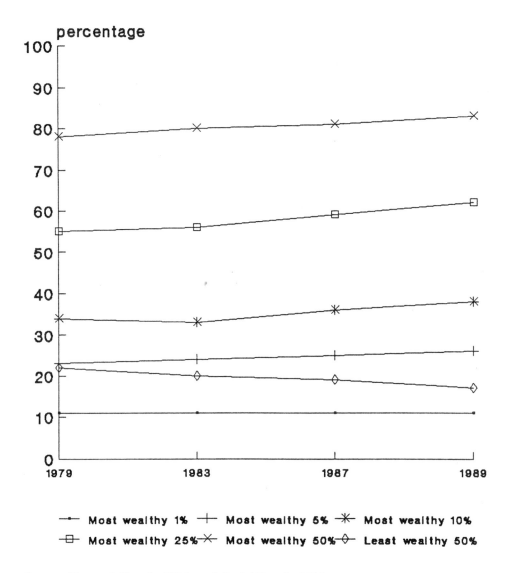

Source: Economic Trends, 1991; and *Social Trends*, 1992.
Note: This figure is based only on a **part** of Table I.3, representing marketable wealth and occupational pension rights, whereas the text is based on the **whole** of this table.
*Historical valuation

pensions, disproportionately subscribed to by the richer half, and a significant fall in the share attributable to state pensions (due to legislative changes in the eighties) on which the overwhelming majority of the poorer half of the population depends.

Conclusions

The foregoing analysis, based on a variety of measures of poverty, indicates the continuation of an unmistakable trend towards sharply rising child poverty charted earlier by Bradshaw (1990). The proportion of children living in poverty has increased threefold in the period 1979-90/91, from ten per cent to 31 per cent of the population; with another ten per cent living on the margin of poverty. This has been accompanied by a widening of the gap between the rich and the poor – because of increasing divergence in their shares of both incomes and wealth – thereby reversing the post-war trend towards stability in income distribution.

The living standards of low income families with children - increasingly dependent on social security benefits because of rising poverty – have, on the whole, been adversely affected by changes in benefits since 1979. Despite some recent improvements in child support by the Government, there is a serious question about the adequacy of social benefits for low income families with children. On the other hand, higher income groups have largely benefited from the tax cuts and other changes in taxation, thereby contributing to the widening of the gap between the rich and the poor. What are the main factors underlying the rapid rise in child poverty in the eighties? This is the question we shall be addressing in the next chapter.

Notes

1. Strictly speaking, the IFS gave an estimated number of families with children (10,000 married couples with children; and 40,000 single parent families with children) who benefited from SB/IS because of an increase in its real value during the period 1979-89 (para 5.3; Table 17). We have therefore estimated the number of children involved on the basis of the *proportion* of children to the total number of persons in these two categories during this period.
2. These are based on recommendations of a stocktaking exercise conducted in 1991 by the Department of Social Security Working Group (1991).
3. The data used in these two figures is derived from HBAI 1991 prepared by the Institute for Fiscal Studies for the House of Commons Social Services Committee, since the HBAI (1992 and 1993) data does not lend itself to be presented in this way.
4. In practice, the fall may be somewhat lower: although Table 1.8 excludes housing costs from both sets of calculations, 'those receiving benefits would normally be entitled to extra assitance with mortgages or rent, while most of those receiving "median disposable income" would have housing costs to meet' (DSS 1.9.92).
5. This Table (1.1) gives a partial picture of children in unemployed families since it covers only those on SB; their total number will of course be much larger.
6. It is understood that IS claimants will not be liable for the payment of the Council Tax when it comes into operation in April 1993.

7. A letter to the *The Times* dated 11.1.88 signed by 54 charities expressed their inability to meet the needs of a large increase (anticipated) in applications in view of the short fall in the SF budget.
8. Strictly speaking, it should be bottom 10 per cent of the 'income distribution', not 'population'; the latter is used only for the sake of convenience, following the HBAI convention.
9. This category included all those under 60 who were not working, students, and sick and disabled.

2. Factors underlying child poverty

Introduction

In the last chapter, it was observed that child poverty had risen rapidly in the UK in the eighties. This chapter will examine some factors related to this increase. However, given the constraints of this exercise, the treatment will necessarily be brief and selective, largely confined to the factors over which policies can, in principle, have a measure of influence. The discussion will revolve around the three interacting factors identified by Bradshaw (1990) as having contributed to the increase in the incidence of child poverty in the UK in the 1980s: economic trends, demographic changes and social policies.

An attempt will be made to relate trends in employment to general economic trends, and the basic tenets of the Government's economic policy. The interaction between low pay, unemployment and poverty will be explored in the wider context of changes in the pattern of employment. Under demographic trends, factors underlying the increase in the number of lone parent families as a high risk factor in child poverty will be discussed, and in particular the reasons for a relatively low level of economic activity among them. Finally, changes in certain social policies will be reviewed in the context of fluctuations in social welfare expenditure, especially on social security, health, education and housing.

Economic trends

Economic policy – commitment to full employment abandoned?

Unemployment is '...a tax levied on the poorest, weakest and most deprived sections of the community to the benefit of the more privileged in the short term and in the pursuit of vague abstractions in the longer term.'
[W. Daniel, Director, Policy Studies Institute. *Unemployment Unit Bulletin No. 1*, 1981]

The British economy had been in long-term decline even prior to the eighties. It was beset with some '...very deeply entrenched adverse trends in evidence for decades...' (Godley, 1992). These were twofold: first, low investment, low productivity, industrial strife, low growth, relatively high inflation and the balance of payments problems; the second was closely related to the first, that is, the 'Stop-Go' nature of the performance of the British economy, whereby short periods of economic growth accompanied by relatively high inflation and trade imbalance would be followed by periods of recession – low or negative growth, lower inflation but higher unemployment (NEDO, 1977). However, despite these endemic problems, for 30 years after the Second World War it had been possible to achieve more or less 'full' employment, that is, to confine unemployment to below three per cent of the workforce. On this aspect of economic and social policy, there had been a high degree of political consensus among the three major political parties in the post-war period, even though it was proving difficult to achieve in the second half of the seventies following the oil-price crisis of October 1973.

The new Conservative Government led by Margaret Thatcher had different ideas about responding to the British economic malaise. It sought to rekindle the British spirit of free enterprise by relaxing state controls and promoting competition. Through a combination of policies of deregulation of financial institutions and increasing privatisation on the one hand, and a tight monetary policy, lower taxes, lower public expenditure and lower public borrowing on the other, it set out to create the conditions for sustained economic growth in a stable, low inflationary environment, free from recurrent balance of payments crises. A high priority would be accorded in the new scheme of things to maintaining low inflation, even if it meant high unemployment in the short run, for this policy, it was argued, would lead to 'real' more durable jobs in the long run.

Despite the change in the leadership of the Conservative Party and the Government in November 1990, there is in many respects a continuity with the basic tenets of this economic philosophy. Specifically, on the question of giving primacy to fighting inflation over unemployment, there is very little to distinguish between the stance of the two governments: as a Chancellor in 1989, John Major said, 'if it (his policy of using high interest rates to curb inflation) isn't hurting, it isn't working' (*Financial Times* 28.8.1990; see also *Hansard* 31.10.89, cols 200–208). In 1991, his successor, Norman Lamont, told the House of Commons, 'Rising unemployment and the recession ... (were) a price well worth paying for the defeat of inflation' (*Hansard*, 16.5.91, col 413). This policy has been reiterated by the Government on a number of occasions – the last one in January 1993, following the release of the unemployment figures for December 1992 (showing it was approaching three million), when Mr Lamont forcefully stressed the Government's '...**central** determination to bring about a lasting reduction in the rate of inflation, the only sound basis on which sustainable growth and secure jobs can be built' (emphasis added) (*The Independent*, 23.1.93).

An era of mass unemployment?

Unemployment and child poverty

Unemployment is arguably the single most important factor related to the increase in child poverty in the UK since 1979. This is due to three interrelated reasons: the increase in numbers affected, cuts in entitlement to benefits, and slippage in the value of benefits for the unemployed in relation to earnings.

Table I.4 indicates the risk of child poverty incurred by different economic status groups. At half average income as the poverty line, in 1979, 73 per cent of children were in poverty in households with an unemployed head, as against four per cent where the head was in full-time (FT) work. With the increase in unemployment in the eighties, the corresponding figures rose to 88 per cent and 15 per cent respectively by 1990/91. The proportion of children in poverty in households of all economic types increased threefold from 10 to 31 per cent in the same period. If the poverty line were to be 60 per cent of average income, the proportion of children in poverty increases correspondingly for all groups, but the basic pattern remains the same.

Trends in UK unemployment

The importance of unemployment as a factor in child poverty clearly depends on its duration, scale and fluctuations over time. A study by Berthoud and Brown (1981) suggests that the risk of poverty is directly related to the extent and duration of unemployment. We shall address this question in this section.

As Table 2.1 shows, unemployment rose rather steeply from 1.4 million in October 1979 to nearly 3 million by October 1981, and remained at this level for the next five years. Having peaked at 3.3 million in June 1986, it began to come down until it was almost halved by March 1990. However, it started climbing up again thereafter and, by October 1992, it had reached 2.9 million – an increase of 78 per cent; and, by January 1993, it had crossed the three million mark once again. Since then unemployment has fallen for four sucessive months by 80,000. However, it is too soon to say if it has finally peaked, until there are clear signs that the economic recovery is likely to be strong and sustained.

It is pertinent to note here that the official Department of Employment (DE) unemployment figures significantly understate the true level of unemployment in the country because of no fewer than 30 changes in the definition of unemployment by the Government since October 1982. These alterations reflect changes in policy and practice; some of them follow from the decision to base the unemployment count on numbers claiming benefits or credits. This means that each time there is a change in the benefit rules, such as removing benefits from 16 and 17-year-olds in 1988, it reduces the numbers on the register. Other changes were of administrative or statistical nature: for instance, more rigorous checks on availability for work, or the removal of those on temporary work and training schemes (nearly half a million up to January 1986) from the register are of the first kind. Statistical changes following from the decision to base the count on benefit claimants resulted in the loss of a significant number of people (around 200,000) who were signing-on earlier but were not entitled to benefits; likewise, leaving out those seeking part-time work removed another 50,000 people (Lynes, 1992).

To appreciate the effect of these changes on the number of unemployed, we have reproduced pre-October 1982 figures in column 3 of Table 2.1 – prepared

Table 2.1   UK unemployment and vacancies 1979-92   Million

Month/Year (1)	Total unemployment		Vacancy[3] Ratio (4)	Long term Unemployment	
	DE[1] Count (2)	UU[2] Count (3)		DE Count (5)	% (6)
Oct 1979	1.4	NA	7:1[4]	0.4	26
Oct 1980	2.1	NA	19:1	0.4	19
Oct 1981	3.0	NA	28:1	0.8	26
Oct 1982	3.3	NA	27:1	1.2	36
Oct 1983	3.1	3.5	18:1	1.1	37
Oct 1984	3.2	3.7	18:1	1.3	40
Oct 1985	3.3	3.7	16:1	1.3	41
Oct 1986	3.2	3.7	12:1	1.3	41
Oct 1987	2.8	3.4	9:1	1.2	43
Oct 1988	2.1	2.9	8:1	0.9	42
Oct 1989	1.6	2.5	7:1	0.6	38
Oct 1990	1.7	2.7	10:1	0.5	30
Oct 1991	2.4	3.5	19:1	0.7	27
Oct 1992	2.9	4.0	29:1	1.0	33

Source: Employment Gazette
Unemployment Unit: *Working Brief*

.. = Not available
NA = Not applicable

Notes: 1. From October 1982 the unemployment count covers benefit claimants only.
2. Based on Pre-October 1982 basis, it takes into account other changes to the system of counting.
3. From 1985 vacancy figures include self-employed in addition to those for employees.
4. Relates to January 1979.

by the Unemployment Unit and Youthaid (UUYA). A comparison indicates that, if no changes had been made during the last ten years, the actual figure of unemployment in October 1992 would have been four million (13.7 per cent), that is 1.1 million higher than the official figure of 2.9 million (10.1 per cent). Figure 2.1 illustrates graphically the trends represented by these two sets of figures.

Apart from the intrinsic justification of these changes – some may be more justifiable than others – the point to note here is that such frequent changes make comparison over time difficult – nationally as well as internationally. They also create anomalies: since the official count now includes only those people who are unemployed *and* claim unemployment related benefits or credits, it therefore excludes all those (60 per cent of them women) who, though unemployed, are not eligible to claim such benefits. Consequently, official figures understate female unemployment. For instance, the Labour Force Survey (LFS) in spring 1992 showed 43 per cent more women unemployed than

Figure 2.1   UK unemployment 1979–1992

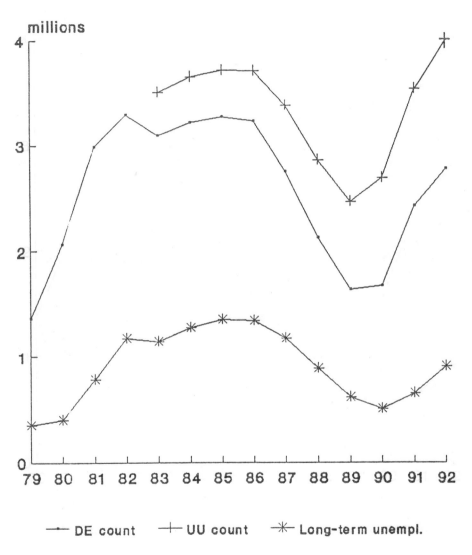

millions

Source: *Employment Gazette*
        Unemployment Unit: *Working Brief*

the corresponding DE figures, even though LFS definition of unemployment is tighter in some ways than that of DE[1].

Long-term unemployment

This is officially defined as the number of people unemployed for over one year. As a proportion of all unemployed people, the number of long-term unemployed increased steadily in the eighties, rising from 26 per cent in 1979 to 40 per cent in 1984; thereafter, it stayed in the 40-43 per cent range up to 1988 before gradually coming down to 27 per cent by October 1991. However, by October 1992, it had risen again to 33 per cent (Table 2.1). There are also significant regional variations - the proportion being about a quarter in East Anglia, but over a half in Northen Ireland. The rise since March 1990 in the general level of unemployment is likely to push up the long-term unemployment too, albeit with a time lag.

Another way to appreciate the severity of unemployment is to look at fluctuations in the vacancy level. One can see from Table 2.1 that, whereas 28 unemployed people were on average chasing each vacancy at the height of the first recession in October 1981, it took another eight years for this ratio to come down to the 1979 (January) level, that is 7:1. By June 1991, it had risen again to 19:1 and, by October 1992, it had surpassed the 1981 level to reach 29:1. Evidence from recent surveys suggests that most vacancies (about three-fifths) appear to be filled by job-changers, with only a minority (varying between 20 and 30 per cent) by unemployed claimants; and even fewer by those unemployed for over six months. In fact, Taylor notes '...a fair degree of employer reluctance to recruit longer term unemployed people' (1989). This is also confirmed by information from official sources. Nearly three-fifths of those on the register at the end of their six-month period will still be on it six months later; nor will all of the two-fifths who came off the register in the meantime necessarily have jobs (*Hansard*, 24.6.92, col.249).

Duration and severity of unemployment are closely related to poverty. A recent survey of living standards of unemployed people by the OPCS found that their average disposable income fell by two-fifths (41 per cent) after three months, leading to cuts in expenditure on essentials such as food and clothing (Heady and Smyth, 1990). This is not surprising, since the reductions in benefits for the unemployed and a fall in their value in the eighties (chapter 1) would have eroded their capacity to weather the effects of unemployment except for a very short period, especially where the family's previous earnings from employment were low in the first place.

Unemployment in families

The DE does not normally publish unemployment statistics concerning families with children. However, according to data in the LFS in 1987, there were well over one million children (1,276,000) living in households with an unemployed head. Of these, over three-quarters of a million (767,000) lived in households where the head had been unemployed for over a year, and over half a million (568,000) where the head had been unemployed for over two years.[2]

These figures were slightly down from 1984 – seven per cent for the overall total, and four per cent for the long-term unemployed (Kiernan and Wicks, 1990).

There is also a noticeable tendency for unemployment to be concentrated in certain families. In 1983, only 30 per cent of unemployed men's wives were employed, as compared to 58 per cent for employed men (Kiernan and Wicks, 1990). Likewise, another study found that, in 30 per cent of families where the head had been unemployed for over a year, one or more members of the family were also unemployed (Hakim, 1982).

Trends in regional unemployment

Traditionally, unemployment has been very much higher in the 'North' than in the 'South'[3]. However, the recent economic recession appears to have hit the South harder than the North. For instance, unemployment more than doubled in the two years between August 1990 and August 1992 in London and the South East, East Anglia and the South West; in the Midlands, it rose by over 75 per cent. However, in areas traditionally constituting the North, the rise in unemployment has been well below the UK average (see Table 2.2 and Figure 2.2). Thus in the North West, Wales and Yorkshire and Humberside, the increase was between 40 per cent and 50 per cent; in the case of Scotland and the Northern region, it was in the 20 per cent to 30 per cent range, while in Northern Ireland it was 'only' 13 per cent.

Figure 2.2   UK unemployment by region 1979–92

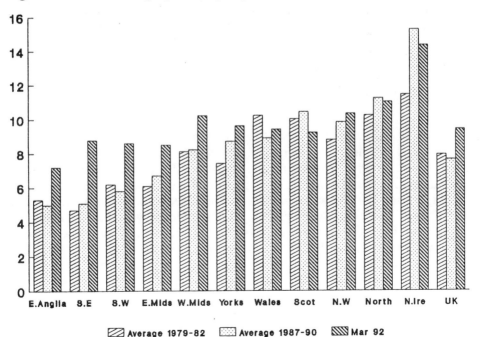

Source: Employment Gazette

Table 2.2   Unemployment by region in the UK 1979-92
(% unemployed, seasonally adjusted)

| | DE Claimant count | | | | | UU Index |
	1979-82 (average)	1983-6 (average)	1987-90 (average)	Oct 92[1]	% Increase Aug 90-Aug 92	Oct 92[1]
SOUTH:						
East Anglia	5.3	8.1	5.0	8.0	109.0	10.7
South East	4.7	7.9	5.1	9.9	133.9	13.1
Greater London	NA	NA	NA	11.2	..	14.3
South West	6.2	9.1	5.8	9.5	107.4	14.4
East Midlands	6.1	9.8	6.7	9.1	76.8	12.7
NORTH:						
West Midlands	8.1	12.8	8.2	11.0	80.3	14.3
Yorks & Humberside	7.4	11.9	8.7	10.1	49.0	14.1
Wales	10.2	13.3	8.9	10.0	47.6	15.2
Scotland	10.0	12.8	10.4	9.7	21.1	13.4
North West	8.8	13.6	9.8	10.7	40.0	14.9
Northern	10.2	15.1	11.2	11.6	29.1	15.2
Northern Ireland	11.4	16.2	15.2	14.7	13.4	21.4
United Kingdom	7.9	10.8	7.6	10.1	69.8	13.7

Source: *Employment Gazette* (various issues)
Working Brief: Unemployment Unit
NA = Not available
Notes: 1. Provisional

However, it is important to set these figures in the context of the traditionally higher level of unemployment in the North and the wider picture of unemployment and poverty in the eighties. Table 2.2 gives a regional breakdown of unemployment, showing how it has changed over the 1979-92 period. During 1979-82 when the first economic recession was at its height, and during 1983-86 when it was easing off, unemployment was generally below the national level in the South, but well above it in the North. During the period of economic expansion (1987-90), the unemployment rates in the South came down rapidly to between five and seven per cent, that is, below the UK rate of 7.6 per cent. However, in the North, unemployment was slow to come down and was still generally above the rates prevalent in the early 1980s. Some areas like West Midlands and Wales did better than others such as Scotland, Northern Region and Northern Ireland, where unemployment was still in double figures despite the economic boom in the rest of the country. If anything, the gap between these areas of the North and the South had, in fact, widened during the eighties. What the recent recession has therefore done is to narrow down the traditional North-South gap, but it has by no means eliminated it. For, as the October 1992 unemployment rates in Table 2.2 indicate, the rates in the South (except for Greater London) are still below the UK level of 10.1 per cent, while the rates in the North are almost at or above the UK rate, and Northern Ireland with an unemployment rate of 14.7 per cent appears to have been little affected either by the economic growth of the 1987-90 period, or by the recent recession.

Unemployment among teenagers

The Government abolished general entitlement to income support for under 18-year-olds in September 1988 (as we noted in chapter 1). Being unable therefore to claim benefit as unemployed, most 16 and 17-year-olds have largely disappeared from the DE claimant count. However, there are two other sources of data on teenage unemployment. One is the Government's LFS, which uses the same definition of unemployment as the International Labour Organisation (ILO) and the Organisation for Economic Cooperation and Development (OECD). It includes everyone who had done no paid work in the week prior to the interview, was free to start a job within two weeks, and had been actively seeking one in the previous four weeks. But it combines all young persons in the 16 to 19 age-group, without identifying separately 16 to 17-year-olds. The latter are so identified in the quarterly estimates of teenage unemployment, produced by UUYA, who point out that, as compared to LFS, their estimates also tend to understate the numbers of 16 and 17-year-old unemployed, though by no means as much as the DE claimant count (*Working Brief*, April 1992).

Table 2.3 and Figure 2.3 show unemployment among 16 to 19-year-olds in Great Britain for the period 1979-92 based on DE data, as adjusted by UUYA, and compare it with LFS data. Between 1979 and 1984, youth unemployment increased two and a half times from around 200,000 to over half a million – the LFS figure was 32,000 higher at 541,000. From this peak, the number was halved by 1990, roughly corresponding to the period of growth in the economy. However, it has since begun to rise again, registering an increase of 20 per cent by April 1991 and an increase of 74 per cent by April 1992, the date for which the latest information is available.

As for unemployment among 16 to 17-year-olds, one can identify three phases, similar to, but not overlapping with, 16-19 unemployment (Table 2.3). In the first phase (1979-83), unemployment rose dramatically among this age-group by almost 275 per cent (from 73,000 to 200,000). In the second phase (1983-90), it began coming down and, by April 1990, it was reduced to under a third (59,000) from its peak. In the last phase (since April 1990), it rose by two-thirds to 99,000 by April 1992, and more than doubled (to 125,000) by October 1992 – the latest date for which this information is available. It should also be noted that there is a large discrepancy between DE figures based on claimant count and the LFS figures – the latter showing consistently higher level of unemployment, around 50 per cent higher on average, but varying from 23 to 86 per cent. Such a large and consistent discrepancy in one direction suggests

Figure 2.3   Unemployment among 16 to 19-year-olds in Great Britian

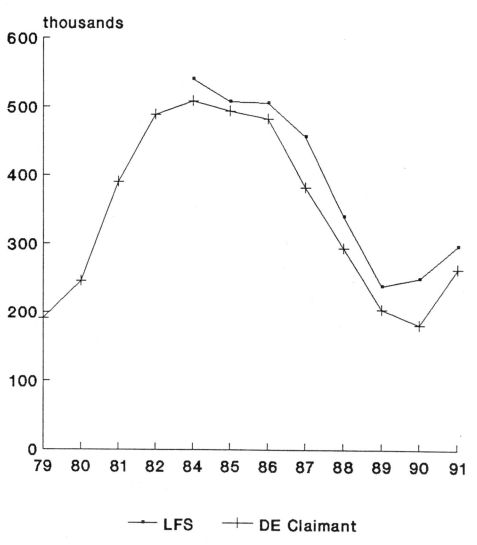

Source: Employment Gazette
*   Labour Force Survey*
       Unemployment Unit: *Working Brief*, Apr. and June 1992

Table 2.3 Unemployment among 16 to 19-year-olds in Great Britain 1979-1992: Comparison of DE Claimant Count and the Labour Force Survey

Year (000s) (1)	16 to 19-year-olds			16 to 17-year-olds		
	LFS[1] (Spring) (2)	DE Claimant[2] Count (April) (3)	% Shortfall in DE data (4)	DE[2] Claimant Count (April) (5)	LFS[1] (Spring) (6)	% Shortfall in DE data (7)
1979	..	191	NA	73	..	NA
1980	..	246	NA	109	..	NA
1981	..	390	NA	149	..	NA
1982	..	489	NA	186	..	NA
1983	..	..	NA	200[4]	..	NA
1984	541	509	6	156	235	51
1985	508	494	3	156	226	44
1986	506	483	5	181	225	24
1987	457	382	16	124	205	66
1988	340	294	14	102	156	53
1989	239	204[3]	15	66[3]	114	71
1990	249	182[3]	27	59[3]	110	86
1991	298	264[3]	11	86[3]	136	58
1992	..	317[3]	NA	99[3]	122	23

* 1983 UK figure   207,500
Subtract the difference between 1982 UK figure and 1982 GB figure, that is   = (−) 7,336
Balance is 1983 GB figure (estimated)   200,164

Source: *Employment Gazette* (various issues)
Unemployment Unit: *Working Brief* April 1992.
NA = Not applicable
.. = Not available

Notes:
1. Based on ILO/OECD definition of unemployment.
2. Based on DE count of claimants of unemployment-related benefits.
3. Figures adjusted by Unemployment Unit.
4. This is an estimate, derived from the **UK** figure for 1983 (Since 1983 **GB** data is not available) as shown **above**:*

the existence of a bias, which is probably related to, but not entirely explained by, the removal of this age-group from general entitlement to unemployment-related benefits and therefore from the official count.

Scarcity of youth training places

The Government's response to the problem of youth unemployment (16 to 17-year-olds) was to guarantee a Youth Training (YT) place with a training allowance to all those not in full-time education or employment. There is evidence to show that difficulties are being encountered in fully meeting this guarantee. According to an analysis of school leavers' destinations carried out by the UK Heads of Careers Services for the Association of County Councils and the Association of Metropolitan Authorities (ACC/AMA), one in 12 respondents was not in youth training, education or work; and there had been a sharp decline in the numbers of 16-year-olds finding work from 18 per cent in 1989 to 10 per cent in 1991; and in the numbers accepted for YT from 22 to 15 per cent in the same period (ACC/AMA, 1992). A recent report published by Youthaid and The Children's Society argues that there are not enough YT places, and that cash is too limited to offer places to all, and to maintain quality (1992).

While the demand for places has increased with rising unemployment, availability is adversely affected by the recession. According to a leaked report of a survey by the UK Heads of Careers Service in December 1991, there was a shortfall of 50,882 YT places (*Working Brief*, April 1992). Waiting lists for places have lengthened, as Patrick McLoughlin, Parliamentary Under-secretary at DE conceded recently (*Independent* 16.6.92).

The Eighth Report from the Social Security Advisory Committee (SSAC) also agreed that the guarantee was not being delivered in full, and that there were no signs that the situation was improving – in some areas it was getting worse. It was concerned that vulnerable youngsters were left with no visible, legal means of support, and referred in this context to problems in getting Severe Hardship payments (see also chapter 1).

Unemployment among minority ethnic groups

Since standard unemployment statistics collected regularly by the DE do not contain information on ethnic origin of claimants, one has to rely on the LFS, but it has a relatively small sample. LFS resolves this problem up to a point by aggregating data for three years. Its findings show that generally unemployment among minority ethnic groups tends to be twice the national rate. During the 1984-86 period, when the average White employment rate was 11 per cent, the minority ethnic group figure was 21 per cent; comparable figures for the period 1988-90 were 7 and 12 per cent respectively; and for 1989-91 period, seven per cent and 13 per cent respectively. There are also significant variations as between different minority ethnic groups. Unemployment amongst people of West Indian/Guyanese origin has tended to be about double the White rate during the 1981-90 period; the corresponding rates for the people of Indian origin for the same period have been one and half times the White rate; and for people of Pakistani and Bangladeshi origin, over two and a half times the White rate. However, by 1991, the gap for people of Pakistani and Bangladeshi origin had widened to three times the White rate. For young people (16 to 24) from minority ethnic groups, the rate is even higher – 22 per cent, as compared to 12 per cent for Whites (LFS, 1984-1990).

Minority ethnic group unemployment in the regions generally reflects the trend for the White unemployment; however, in the West Midlands, for instance, the non-White rate was significantly higher than the White rate by comparison with the national trend, largely accounted for by a considerably higher rate for those of Indian origin. Reasons for this are not clear (LFS, 1984-1990; *Hansard*, 21.5.92, col.247-8).

The long-term unemployment rate is also significantly higher among minority ethnic groups: during 1984-86, when the White rate was 40 per cent, the Black rate was well over 50 per cent; in 1982, according to the PSI national survey, the long-term rate for people of Asian and West Indian origin was one half of all unemployed, as against a third for the White population (Brown, 1984). Results from the LFS suggest that people from minority ethnic groups are likely to experience a higher level of unemployment even when they are as well qualified as the White people. For example, among those with higher educational qualifications, the Black unemployment rate was five per cent, when the White rate was less than three per cent; for those with 'other' qualifications, the corresponding rates were 12 per cent and six per cent respectively (*Employment Gazette*, March 1992).

Unemployment and the British economy

Changing unemployment trends are closely related to fluctuations in the performance of the British economy. What follows is therefore not an appraisal, but a brief résumé of how some of the key economic indicators[4] have moved over time in the period 1979-92, and how these relate to the changing levels of unemployment, which we have identified as a major factor in rising child poverty. We shall look at these trends in four phases: 1979-82; 1983-86; 1987-90; and the period since April 1990.

The first phase was characterised by rapidly rising unemployment, when the economy grew (as measured by the Gross Domestic Product (GDP) at an average of only 0.3 per cent per year, and the workforce in employment in Great Britain fell by about 1.5 million. Inflation, on the other hand, was the one indicator which improved significantly in this period: after more than doubling from 10.3 per cent in May 1979 to 21.9 per cent in May 1980, it fell dramatically to 11.7 per cent in May 1981, and to 3.7 per cent in May 1983.

In the second phase (1983-86), the economy grew at an accelerated rate (3.3 per cent a year on average), thus leading to an increase in the number of people in employment by about 400,000. At the same time, however, inflation doubled to seven per cent by 1985 before coming down to 2.8 per cent in 1986. Unemployment also went on rising, though at a decreasing rate, and peaked in June 1986.

In the third phase (1987-90), there was a further spurt in growth in 1987 (4.4 per cent) and 1988 (4.7 per cent) before the economy began to slow down, registering 2.1 per cent growth in GDP in 1989, and one half of one per cent in 1990. Unemployment was now halved to reach its lowest point in the eighties by April 1990 (1.6 million). However, inflation more than doubled, increasing from 4.1 per cent in May 1987 to 9.7 per cent in May 1990, and to 10.7 per cent in October 1990.

After April 1990, the economy entered a recession with the GDP falling 2.5 per cent in 1991, and about one per cent in 1992. Unemployment increased rapidly and was close to the three million mark by December 1992. Inflation came down, however, and was 2.6 per cent in December 1992, that is, less than a third of the level of October 1990.

A look at indicators of industrial activity suggests that, while employment in manufacturing was down from about seven to five million in Great Britain (GB) by 1990, with a further loss of about half a million in the two years to February 1992, output and investment increased by about 12 per cent and productivity by about 50 per cent between 1979 and 1990. Loss of employment in manufacturing was compensated by expansion of the service sector, but there were also significant losses in other sectors of the economy, notably in Agriculture, Forestry and Fishing, Energy and Water, and Construction. Overall, there was an increase in employment in the economy (GB) of just under a million (0.9 million) between June 1979 and March 1991. But this was offset by an increase in the working population of 1.5 million in this period. This was due partly to a rising number of young people entering the labour market in the first half of the eighties because of earlier birth bulges in the 1960s, and partly to a continuing rise in the proportion of women in employment, especially part-time employment (Bradshaw, 1990).

Two main points emerge from this brief review of economic trends in the period 1979-92. One, there was a clear, but inverse, relationship between inflation and unemployment so that a rise in one was accompanied by a fall in the other, and vice versa. The second point, which is closely related to the first, is that growth in the economy tended to be accompanied by progressively higher inflation, with unemployment coming down with a time lag, depending on the strength of the recovery. In the first phase, the Government's policy of giving priority to controlling inflation was successful, but was accompanied by faltering growth, and a large increase in unemployment. In the second and third phases, as the economy grew faster and unemployment gradually came down, especially in the third phase, inflation climbed up rapidly to reach double figures again by October 1990.

This led to a renewed attempt on the part of the Government to control inflation by increasing interest rates, for example, from 7.5 per cent in June 1988 to 13 per cent by November 1988, and to 15 per cent by October 1989. Once again, the Government did manage to bring inflation down, but at the expense of growth and greatly increased unemployment, as in the early 1980s, but this time with the added burdens of a worsening Public Sector Borrowing Requirement (PSBR), and a deteriorating balance of payments position. This culminated in the Sterling crisis in September 1992 – the 'Black Wednesday' – and the UK's precipitate, if temporary, withdrawal from the European Exchange Rate Mechanism (ERM).

This, of course, is the familiar 'Stop-Go' cycle that has beset the British economy for a long time – only this time the recession has been much longer than before. Some observers have asked, therefore, if the Government has come any closer since 1979 to achieving its principal policy objective of freeing the economy from this constraint by creating the conditions for a sustained growth in a low inflationary environment. The question assumes ever greater urgency since, in the meantime, the price in terms of relatively high unemployment (and rising poverty) throughout this period has not only been very heavy, but also has not been shared equally, as we have seen in the last chapter. In fact, it has fallen on the most vulnerable sections of society, especially low income families with dependent children.

Poverty and employment

We saw in the last section that unemployment was a high risk factor in child poverty, as in poverty generally, depending on its duration, severity and frequency. There is also a close link between low pay, unemployment and poverty (Berthoud, 1981). Low paid workers who are unemployed for part of the year are likely to be in poverty. They also tend to be much more vulnerable to unemployment, particularly in the context of technological change and economic restructuring in the eighties and early nineties, when a new concept of 'flexible' or 'precarious' employment has gained currency (Millar, 1991). In this section we shall look at the prevalence of these two trends, and explore their links with poverty in general, and child poverty in particular.

Incidence of low pay

There is no legal minimum wage in the UK and low pay is widespread and its incidence is increasing: the number of workers earning less than the Council of Europe's 'decency threshold' (defined as 68 per cent of all full-timers' mean earnings (£193.60 per week, £5.15 an hour in 1991) rose from 7.8 million in 1979 to 10 million in 1991 (Low Pay Unit, 1992), constituting almost half (47 per cent) of all those in employment. Fifty-seven per cent of this total (5.72 million) were in full-time employment in 1991, more or less equally divided between men and women; however, over four-fifths of the low paid part-timers were women. In 12 years, the number of adult full-time workers in low pay increased by almost a quarter (23.3 per cent) to 5.72 million, constituting 36 per cent of all full-time workers; in the same period, the number of part-timers on low pay rose by over a third (36 per cent) to 4.3 million – over 70 per cent of all part-timers.

Low pay, families and child poverty

It is possible to estimate the incidence of low pay among households with dependent children from the HBAI statistics. Taking 70 per cent of average income (AHC) as the threshold (nearest to the Council of Europe's 'decency' threshold of 68 per cent), we find that, in 1991, almost three and a half (3.4) million children were living in households where the head was in FT low paid employment, amounting to 37 per cent of all children; their number had increased from a quarter (26 per cent) of all children in 1979 – under three million (2.9) (see Table I.4). It is interesting to note that the risk of low pay varies directly with the number of children in the family. For instance, whereas in families with one or two children, 29 per cent of children were in households with the head in FT low paid employment, the corresponding figure for families with three or more children was 47 per cent. Although the latter figure is prone to a certain margin of error, nevertheless, this does suggest a strong relationship (HBAI, 1993, Table F3 (AHC)).

There is likewise a close relationship between low pay and child poverty. Out of nearly three and a half million children who were living in households with a head in low paid FT employment in 1990/91, nearly one and a half (1.43) million children were living in poverty – defined as income below half national average (Table I.4).

Low pay among women
Two-thirds of Britain's low paid are women, numbering six million. Nearly half of all adult women working full-time, and four-fifths of those in FT manual jobs, are low paid, as are three-quarters of women working part-time (Low Pay Unit, 1992).

In 1991, women's earnings were a little over three-quarters (78.3 per cent) of men's, if overtime is excluded, and seven-tenths, when it is included; the corresponding figures in 1979 were 73 and 63.6 per cent respectively (*New Earnings Survey* 1991, Part A).

According to the Low Pay Unit (LPU), the reasons for the shortfall in women's pay and their disproportionate representation among the low paid are: one, their working pattern is such that they are mostly in part-time or temporary jobs, or homeworking, because of family responsibilities, and are generally concentrated at the lower end of grading structures; two, heavy concentration in industries which traditionally pay low wages – retailing, hotels, catering and personal services; three, unequal access to pay premia (bonuses, incentive and shift payments); and, finally, disadvantage and discrimination – direct and institutionalised – in the labour market (LPU, 1992).

Low pay among young people
Roughly 96 per cent of all young people under 18 are on low pay. Their relative position has worsened in the eighties: their share of average weekly earnings as a proportion of average adult earnings (over 21) has gone down from 42 per cent in 1979 to 37 per cent in 1991. The effect was felt soon after the introduction by the Government of the Young Workers' Scheme in 1981, which subsidised employers paying low wages to young employees.

The lowest ten per cent have been particularly badly hit by the current recession, having lost £5 in real terms since 1989, reducing their weekly pay packet to £66.90. There are two main reasons for low pay among them: one, their heavy concentration in low-paying industries; and, two, the weakening of their bargaining position by heavy unemployment – drying up of apprentice-ships – and abolition by the Government of Income Support for them. Consequently the risk of poverty has also increased considerably for this group (LPU, 1992).

Low pay and poverty among minority ethnic groups

There are no national statistics on earnings and ethnic origin. However, evidence from other sources is accumulating which suggests that people from minority ethnic groups are more likely to work in low paid jobs with poor working conditions than White people.

LFS data suggests that minority ethnic groups tend to be over-represented, as compared to White people, in certain industries where wages have traditionally been low. For example, during the 1989-91 period, in distribu-tion, hotels, catering and repairs, almost twice (30 per cent) as many men from minority ethnic groups were employed as White men (16 per cent). A quarter of men working in this sector were earning below £150 per week, as against 10 per cent of the male manual workforce in all industries. In hotels and catering specifically minority ethnic group employment (of men) was nine per cent, as against two per cent of White men. And nearly half (47 per cent) the workforce earned less than £150 a week (*Hansard*, 21.5.1992, cols. 249-50). Evidence from the LFS also indicates that almost half (48 per cent) of men from minority ethnic groups were employed in three industrial sectors during 1989-91, where a high proportion of workers was on low weekly wages (*Hansard*, 21.5.92, cols. 249-50).

As regards incidence of low pay among minority ethnic women, the main difficulty is that women's employment pattern is less easily differentiated along ethnic lines, except in a few areas. This is so partly because of the concentration of women as a whole in particular sectors such as distribution, hotels, catering and repairs, accounting for a quarter of all women in employment. Partly this is also because the industrial categories used in LFS are too broad to identify differences **within** industries along ethnic lines. For instance, one such difference relevant to prevalence of low pay was highlighted in a recent report on the hotel industry, indicating that people from minority ethnic groups were over-represented in unskilled jobs such as cleaning and portering, but under-represented in managerial and supervisory jobs (*Financial Times*, 11.6.1992). Thus the reasons for the prevalence of low income among Black women would appear to be related partly to their gender – the fact that women's position in the labour market is unequal – and partly to their colour (which they share with Black men), and the disadvantage and discrimination which that implies – both direct and indirect.

Another factor affecting low pay among Black employees is that their rates of pay tend to be significantly lower than those of White workers. For instance, median weekly earnings of Black male employees were typically over four-fifths (85 per cent) of White male employees, according to the PSI national survey;

however, it found that the gap between Black and White women's wages was smaller, though significant (Brown, 1984). A number of other local studies differed from the PSI finding in relation to Black women's wages, while broadly confirming the pattern for Black male wages. They found that Black female pay was typically four-fifths of White female pay. Black women earned about 63 per cent of average Black male earnings, whereas White women's earnings were 72 per cent of White male earnings (Low Pay Unit, 1992; Duffy and Lincoln, 1990; Bruegel, 1989).

Evidence from these and some other research studies indicates that minority ethnic groups are also more likely to face worse working conditions, such as doing shift work, particularly at nights, with longer hours of work, and less access to training and occupational benefits (Brown, 1982; Amin with Oppenheim, 1991). A number of studies also suggest that there are reasons why minority ethnic group women are more likely to be home-working than White women, frequently with extremely low wages and exploitative conditions (Amin with Oppenheim, 1991; Low Pay Unit, 1992).

The picture presented here of the prevalence of low pay among people from minority ethnic groups is necessarily patchy for several reasons. In the first place, the definition of 'ethnic minorities' used in the LFS covers people of **all** ethnic origins. In the second place, the data does not generally allow one to differentiate between different minority ethnic groups, because appropriate breakdown is not available. Finally, data from the *New Earnings Survey* (NES) understates the scale of low pay, since it does not cover employees whose earnings are below the lower earnings limit for NIC thereby excluding some of the lowest-paid employees – most of whom are women, and many of them may well be from minority ethnic groups.

These limitations do not, in our view, invalidate the conclusion that people from minority ethnic groups are over-represented among the low paid; if anything, the available data understates the scale of the problem, and the consequent risk of poverty. The latter is closely related to rates of pay, working conditions and, above all, the level and duration of unemployment which, as we have noted, are significantly higher among these people. This is not surprising since, as Berthoud and Brown (1981) have observed, low paid workers are highly vulnerable to unemployment, and often have little in savings to cope with it; they have less access to fringe benefits, and receive less benefit from official schemes where these are related to pay, length of service and contributions record. People from minority ethnic groups are particularly likely to suffer on this score, because of their need to visit families in the countries of their origin for relatively extended period, especially when the nuclear families are not united in this country, because of delays in the operation of immigration procedures.

Their risk of unemployment is also greater because of their position in the labour market and their pattern of employment, which has changed little since the 1950s and the 1960s (Brown, 1984). Two points are particularly significant in this connection. One, minority ethnic groups, except for people of Indian origin, are over-represented in the manual (especially unskilled and semi-skilled) jobs, as compared to White people; and they are under-represented in non-manual, especially managerial and professional positions. According to LFS (1989-91), 20 per cent of Pakistani and Bangladeshi men held professional or managerial positions, as against 36 per cent of White men; on the other hand, 68 per cent of West Indian and Guyanese men, and 59 per cent of Pakistani and Bangladeshi men, were in manual occupations, as against 52 per cent of White men (*Hansard*, 21.5.92, cols. 249-50). Two, people from minority ethnic groups tend to be concentrated both geographically and economically. Almost three-quarters of the minority ethnic population live in metropolitan counties, concentrated in inner-city areas in poor and overcrowded housing conditions. Their segregation into certain industries such as textile, and manual jobs, has exposed them to the accelerated decline of manufacturing in the eighties, and the accompanying hazards of economic restructuring, with consequently much higher levels of unemployment (Amin with Oppenheim, 1991; Cross, 1978).

It is significant, thought not surprising, that the gaps between Black and White unemployment has tended to widen during the recession of the eighties (Robinson, 1990). These inequalities in the labour market are underpinned by structural problems of discrimination (racial and gender) and disadvantage, which considerably increased both the risks, as well as the incidence, of poverty among people from minority ethnic groups. We cannot go into these problems here – they have already been discussed and documented at some length[5]. As a recent study of poverty among minority ethnic groups concludes, ethnic origin and poverty are closely connected, but the precise ways in which they are linked are complex and multi-faceted (Amin with Oppenheim, 1991).

If, as the above discussion suggests, minority ethnic groups are over-represented among the poor and the low paid, their children are also likely to experience a higher level of deprivation, even though data does not exist either in LIF or HBAI statistics to enable one to make direct links between children from these groups with (income) poverty.

Reasons for increase in low pay and poverty

The rise in precarious employment   One of the most important reasons for the increase in low pay and poverty since 1979 is the changing composition of the workforce in the wake of economic restructuring and the consequent increase in 'precarious' or 'flexible' employment in recent years. This includes part-time work, self-employment, temporary or seasonal work and homeworking. In 1986, about a third of the workforce – about eight million workers – were in precarious employment: of these 5.1 million were part-timers, 2.7 million self-employed, and the rest were temporary workers (Huws, Hurstfield and Holtman, 1989).

Between June 1979 and March 1991 male FT employment in GB shrank by about two million; this was offset by an increase in female FT employment of around 0.2 million; thus there was a net loss in FT employment of around 1.8 million during this period. About a half of this loss in employment (0.95 million) was made up by an increase in PT employment – about 0.7 million among women, and 0.25 million among men (*Working Brief*, 28.11.91). There was also an increase of 1.3 million among the self-employed in GB in the same period. Between 1984 and 1989, the number of temporary workers increased by 12 per cent, as against permanent workers which increased by 10 per cent; 58 per cent of temporary workers in 1989 were women (*Employment Gazette*, April 1990). There are no reliable national statistics on the size of homeworking population, but, according to an estimate by the National Homeworking Unit, there may be between one and two million people involved, the majority of them women (LPU, 1992).

Precarious employment – impact on women   As we have noted above, most of the increase in employment since 1979 has been in precarious employment, in which the majority of workers are women – 80 per cent of part-timers, and around three-fifths of temporary workers, and a proportion of self-employed, which includes homeworkers. Average female, part-time, hourly wage-rates (gross) constitute less than three-fifths of male full-time rates – their differential has actually widened slightly from 59.3 per cent in 1979 to 58.2 per cent in 1991. Their low rates reflect features of female employment discussed earlier. In addition, they have fewer legal rights and poorer promotion prospects (LPU, 1992). A DE survey of employers in 1987 found that part-time and temporary workers were significantly less likely to have fringe benefits such as sick pay, and membership of a pension scheme (Wood and Smith, no date). In view of the above, it is not surprising that 70 per cent of part-timers are low paid, as we noted earlier.

According to the LPU, the plight of homeworkers is the worst of all. Although there are no national statistics on their pay, local studies suggest that they are paid exceptionally low rates (an average hourly rate of 88p in the 1980s) so that they have to work very long hours. They are often given self-employed status by their employers; consequently, they have no rights to sickness, holiday, maternity or redundancy pay. They tend to be isolated and not to know their rights (LPU, 1992).

However, the relationship between women's position among the low paid and poverty is complex. In low income families, their income can mitigate family poverty. However, given uncertainty about its continuity, its loss can mean many families lapsing back into poverty (Millar, 1991).

Deregulation of the labour market   The impact of changes in the profile of the workforce in the eighties, reflecting long-term labour market trends, has been exacerbated by recent Government measures to deregulate the labour market. These include:

- changes to benefit rules disqualifying from benefit anyone refusing a job because of the low rate of pay;
- abolished legal minimum rates to under-21s in 1986 in a number of industries covered by the Wages Councils, thereby removing half a million under-21s from their protection; also weakened the Councils in other ways. A Bill to abolish the Councils was introduced in Parliament towards the end of 1992;

- abolition in 1982 of the Fair Wages Resolution leading to a fall in the wages of a wide range of staff employed by Government contractors;
- the powers and rights of trade unions have been considerably restricted, thereby reducing their ability to protect the lowest paid members from reductions in their living standards;
- increasing the qualifying period in 1979 from six months to two years before one can seek redress from an industrial tribunal against unfair dismissal – many part-time workers fail to qualify at all. As a result of these and other changes in 1980 to unfair dismissal legal procedures detrimental to the interests of employees, over a quarter of adult men and over a third of women in full-time work have no legal protection against unfair dismissal;
- a number of measures introduced in the eighties directly affect women's rights, including removal of restrictions in 1988 on night working for women;
- the Government's firm opposition to signing the European Community's Charter of Fundamental Social Rights of Workers and to the draft directives on, for instance, part-time work and parental leave (LPU, 1992; Millar, 1991; Oppenheim, 1990).

The cumulative effect of these changes has been to reduce, and in some cases remove, state protection from the most vulnerable workers – the young, the unskilled, and those in traditionally low paid industries. This, together with relatively high levels of unemployment throughout the 1979-92 period, and increased job insecurity, has reinforced labour market trends towards the widening of wage differentials and the depression of wages, thereby significantly contributing to the increased incidence of low pay and poverty (LPU, 1992).

Wage differentials and low pay Widening wage differentials in the 1980s have not only increased income inequality, but also contributed to the increase in the incidence of low pay of many families whose income has slipped below the low-income threshold as a consequence. The principal conclusion of a DE study of earnings distribution in the period 1973-86 was that the trend towards the narrowing of the distribution between 1973 and 1979 was reversed in the 1979-86 period when differentials began to widen. Its other conclusions were that:

- the earnings of manual workers grew faster than non-manual until 1979, after which they declined;
- the earnings of higher paid occupational groups grew much faster than those of lower paid ones after 1979, thus reversing the trend in the earlier period;
- until 1979, female workers made significant gains relative to males with the introduction of the 1975 Equal Pay Act, but there has been little change in relativity since (Adams, 1987).

The conclusions of this study are also substantiated by evidence from other sources.

The relativities among the manual workers have also widened. Using official data sources, a Low Pay Unit study shows that the earnings of the lowest paid one-tenth of men have dropped from 69 per cent of the median in 1886, and 68 per cent in 1979 and 1982, to 64 per cent in 1991. On the other hand, the earnings of the top ten per cent of male manual workers have gone up from 143 per cent of the median in 1886 to 149 per cent in 1979, and to 160 per cent in 1991. As a result, the ratio of the lowest to the highest has gone up from 1:2.1 in 1886 to 1:2.5. The same study claims that differentials are even wider among non-manual male works: this shows that 'inequalities in pay are larger now than at any time in the past century' (LPU, 1992).

Summary and conclusions

This review of economic trends has identified two main developments: one, unemployment rose rapidly in the eighties and remained at a relatively high level throughout the 1979-92 period, despite some fluctuations; two, the number of low paid workers increased by over a quarter to 10 million workers in 1991 – almost a half of all employees.

Both these trends were closely related to child poverty. As unemployment increased threefold from one to over three million in the first half of the eighties, the number of children in poverty in a household with an unemployed head increased three and a half times from 0.37 to 1.3 million (SSC, HBAI, 1991, Table F3). Likewise, corresponding to an increase in the incidence of low pay by over a quarter between 1979-88, the percentage of children living in households with a low paid FT worker as head, increased from 26 per cent to 33 per cent in the same period; and to 37 per cent by 1990/91, involving nearly three and a half million children – over a quarter of all children in the country. Significantly, two-fifths of children (1.4 million) in low paid families were also living in poverty (defined as half national average income), thereby suggesting a close link between low pay and child poverty.

There was a net loss of 1.8 million FT jobs between 1979-92, mostly at the expense of men; this was offset partly by an increase in part-time (or temporary) employment (about one million), largely benefiting women, and partly by an increase in the number of self-employed (1.3 million), together constituting 'flexible' or 'precarious' employment. This was the single most important reason for the increase in the number of low paid workers, two-thirds of whom are women. The second reason was the Government's policy of deregulating the market which, by weakening the protection for the employment rights of the low paid, together with a high level of unemployment and job insecurity, strengthened labour market trends towards the widening of differentials in salaries and wages, thereby increasing not only inequality, but also pushing a proportion into the lower-paid category.

Income from these recently created jobs, though mostly low paid, and largely held by women, would help to mitigate family poverty for some, while the loss of these 'precarious' jobs in other cases would tend to push them back into poverty. This illustrates the nature of the relationship between low pay, unemployment and poverty: '...the strong correlation between unemployment, occupation, and earnings is symptomatic of a socio-economic position in which unemployment and low pay alternate to produce chronic poverty' (Berthoud and Brown, 1981, p.102). Thus manual, especially semi- and unskilled, jobs were relatively more vulnerable in the recession than non-manual, especially managerial and professional jobs. This meant that a significant proportion would either have to be unemployed for a long time, and/or to accept jobs at significantly lower wages, since the new jobs were mostly low paid and/or part-time. This was particularly so in the case of people from minority ethnic groups, whose unequal position in the labour market, combined with geographical and economic segregation in traditionally low paid industries and jobs, made them much more vulnerable to unemployment, including long-term unemployment, as well as to being trapped in poverty and/or low pay.

Age is another factor in the equation. Thus 16 to 17-year-olds, lacking in skills and their bargaining position, weakened by high unemployment and the withdrawal of IS by the Government, found their position in pay relativities slip further behind that of adults (21 plus). As Millar points out, class, gender, race, age and location all interact to benefit some while disadvantaging others in an increasingly polarised labour market which characterised the eighties, as part of the wider restructuring of society (1991). Moreover, the position of women and Black people is exacerbated by the operation of gender and race inequalities.

Finally, as regards the Government's policy of giving a priority to controlling inflation, it was successful in the 1979-83 period, but with faltering growth and a tripling of unemployment. During 1983-86 and especially during 1987-90, there was an accelerated growth in the economy with significant gains in productivity; a rapid fall in unemployment after 1986, but accompanied by a sharp increase in inflation. In the period since April 1990, the Government has managed to reduce inflation to a third, but only at the expense of the longest recession since the 1930s, nearly three million unemployed, an escalating PSBR, and a large balance of payments deficit, precipitating a Sterling crisis in September 1992, and leading to the UK's withdrawal from the ERM. In other words, the 'Stop-Go' nature of the malaise, from which the British economy has been suffering for decades, does not seem to have changed. What has changed is that the price in terms of rising unemployment (and poverty) is being increasingly paid by the most vulnerable sections of the society, especially low income families with children.

Demographic trends

Poverty among lone parent families

Another major cause of escalating child poverty in the eighties has been a rapid increase in the number of lone parent families (LPFs); combined with their low rate of economic activity, and high reliance on social security benefits – which (as already observed in chapter 1), are hardly adequate to meet the needs of a family with dependent children. Children living in LPFs are at a high risk of poverty, next only to those in unemployed families. Whereas in 1979, 28 per cent of children in this category were living below half average income, by 1990/91 this had gone up to 74 per cent; the corresponding change for the general population in this period was from 10 per cent to 31 per cent (Table I.4).

As for reliance on social security benefits, the number of children in LPFs in receipt of SB/IS increased almost three-fold between 1979 and 1991 (Table 1.1). In addition, a significant proportion would be in receipt of FC/HB. In 1990, two-thirds (67 per cent) of all LPFs had a gross weekly income of less than £150, and over a half of them (51 per cent) had income of less than £100, as against the IS level of £102.42 (General Household Survey (GHS) 1990, Table 2.4).

Another measure of their poverty is that their representation in the bottom quintile of equivalised disposable income increased from six per cent in 1979 to ten per cent in 1989; and, in the second quintile, it increased from three per cent to six per cent. By contrast, the representation of households having two adults with children in the two bottom quintiles actually decreased substantially from 48 per cent to 35 per cent in the same period (*Hansard*, 11.1.93, col. 545-46).

Rise in lone parent families

The number of LPFs is estimated to have increased by over two-fifths from about 850,000 in 1981 to over one million by 1990[6], constituting about one-sixth of all families with dependent children. In the same period, the number of dependent children growing up in these families increased by a third from 1.45 million to 1.9 million (Haskey, 1989a; 1991; Bartholomew and colleagues, 1992); by 1991 the number had gone up to 2.2 million (*Population Trends*, March 1993). It is estimated that, if recent divorce patterns continue, nearly a third of all children borne in the early eighties are likely to have lived in a lone parent family before they are 16-years-old (Clarke, 1989).

Ninety per cent of LPFs are lone mothers, 55 per cent of whom are divorced or separated, 35 per cent single, six per cent widowed, and the remainder (four per cent) married/cohabiting. The number of single (never married) mothers has grown the fastest, having increased from 23 per cent in 1981 to 35 per cent in 1990 (Bartholomew and colleagues, 1992). Figure 2.4 illustrates the changing composition of lone parent families in the period 1971-90[7]. There are also significant geographical variations from the national trend: inner city areas show a heavy concentration of LPFs – 26.6 per cent for inner London, according to the 1981 census, as against 14 per cent for the country. Whether, and how far, this has changed will not be known until the results from the 1991 census are available, although LFS estimates suggest that there has been a decrease in Greater London as a whole (Bartholomew and colleagues, 1992).

About one in 13 LPFs are of minority ethnic origin – 85,000 families in all with 140,000 dependent children. Of these, about one in two is of West Indian origin, one in eight of Indian, Pakistani/Bangladeshi and mixed origins, and one in nine of African origin (Haskey, 1991).

The increase in the number of LPFs is the result of two interrelated developments; a greatly accelerated divorce rate since 1971, and an increased incidence of births outside marriage. The divorce rate has increased from 11.3 per thousand marriages in 1981 to 13.3 in 1991 (*Population Trends*, autumn, 1992). Although the underlying rate of increase has slowed down in the eighties, if divorce were to persist at recent levels, just under four out of ten

Figure 2.4 Composition (%) of lone parent families in GB 1971–89

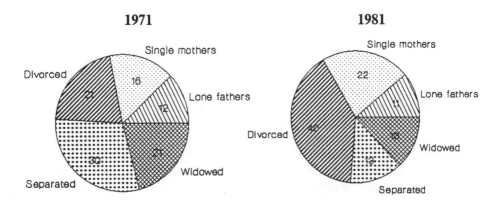

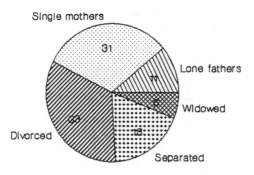

Source: Population Trends, Autumn 1991
Employment Gazette, November 1992

marriages (37 per cent) is likely to end in divorce (Haskey, 1989b). It has been estimated that, in 1985, of all children not living with their natural parents because of divorce, just over one-third live with their lone mother, and about one in 30 live with their lone father; most of the remainder live with their mother who has either remarried or is cohabiting (Haskey, 1990).

Parallel with a steady decline in marriage (from 49.4 per thousand in 1981 to 37.9 in 1990) and an increase in divorce rates, there has been a corresponding increase in cohabitation, greatly accelerated in the eighties. As a result, standard marriage and divorce statistics have become less reliable as indicators of demographic reality, as we do not know the rates at which the consensual relationships (cohabitation) are being formed, broken and reformed; nor how much they contribute to the increase in lone parenthood, for instance. One recent attempt to fill this gap has estimated that there were 1.2 million cohabiting couples in GB in 1989, that is, one in 12 of all couples. The rate of cohabitation greatly accelerated in the eighties, rising overall from 10 per cent of all non-married women in 1979 to 20 per cent in 1989 – the rate among divorced women had reached 30 per cent by then. Likewise, the rate of cohabitation was the highest among divorced men, followed by separated men and then bachelors; the divorced and separated men were one and a half times more likely to cohabit than divorced and separated women (Haskey and Kelly, 1991).

With a continued decline in marriage, and increase in divorce and cohabitation, it is not surprising that births outside marriage should rise as well. These were rising steadily from an average of about four to five per cent of all live births annually in the early 1960s to 10 per cent annually until the late 1970s; however, between 1980 and 1992 (March), the percentage jumped from 12.5 to 30, and the number also increased by more than 150 per cent from 91 to 237 thousand a year. The number of births outside marriage registered jointly by both parents in England and Wales have increased from 58 per cent in 1981 to 74 per cent in 1991, and those giving the same address formed a majority (54.6 per cent) by 1991. Correspondingly, the sole registrations of these births have progressively fallen through the eighties from 41.8 per cent in 1981 to 25 per cent in 1991 (*Population Trends*, autumn 1992). This suggests that only a quarter of births outside marriage are occurring in the context of lone parenthood. Among births which are jointly registered, those from the same address may be assumed to be from cohabiting couples, and the remainder may be intending to cohabit.

Economic activity among lone parent families

Unemployment has already been identified as a major risk factor in child poverty, as in poverty generally. Does this factor, or more generally the level of economic activity among LPFs, help to explain their over-representation among the poor? Neither of the two principal sources of income data (LIF and HBAI) provide a breakdown of economic activity among this category. However, information is available from a number of Government surveys (GHS, LFS, FES), but it is generally thought advisable to combine information from several sources, and for several years, to produce reasonably reliable estimates (Haskey, 1991). The latest information available on this basis is for the period 1987-89[8].

Figure 2.5 compares the level of economic activity between lone mothers (LMs) and married mothers (MMs) with dependent children under 18 for the period 1987-89[9]. There are two significant differences between them: unemployment is higher among LMs (nine per cent) as compared to MMs (six per cent); there is no difference in FT employment but, in part-time (PT) employment, MMs' participation at 38 per cent is considerably higher than LMs' at 21 per cent.

Since economic activity among women depends partly on the number and age of dependent children, Figure 2.6 compares their relative participation only for those women with children under five. Once again, there is a substantial difference in PT employment: participation of MMs (27 per cent) is more than

Figure 2.5   Economic activity among women with dependent children under 18 1987–1989

Source: Population Trends, Autumn 1991

Figure 2.6   Economic activity among women with dependent children under five – 1987–1989

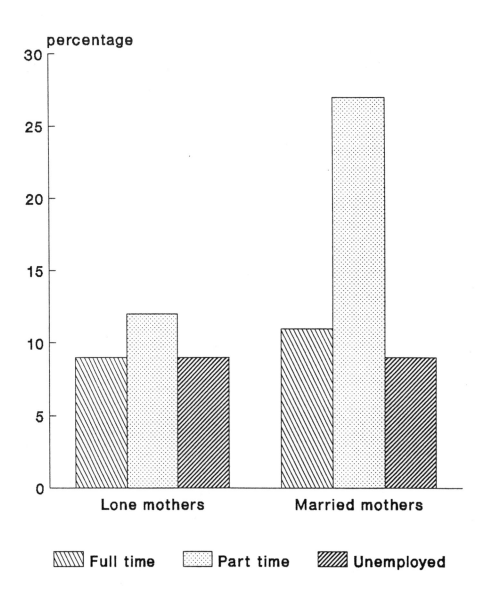

Source: Population Trends, Autumn 1991

twice that of LMs (12 per cent), and a small difference (two percentage points) shows up in FT employment, while the difference in unemployment disappears. However, data based on the GHS for the period 1988-90 does indicate a significant difference in FT employment: eight per cent for LMs, as against 13 per cent for MMs; but the difference in FT employment disappears for those with children over five even in this data set, but remains substantial in PT employment (30 per cent for LMs, as against 48 per cent for MMs (GHS 1990, Table 2.39).

How does one explain such a large gap in participation in PT employment between these two groups? A national sample survey of LMs by Bradshaw and Millar (1991) suggests that there is no difference in employment aspirations between these two groups, but childcare, especially its cost (Millar, 1989; Moss, 1989), does emerge as an important factor, having been mentioned by over half (54 per cent) of non-employed LMs who want to work or would if it were available (1991). A shortage of good quality childcare at a reasonable cost has been identified as a problem by a number of recent studies (EOC, 1990; Cohen and Fraser, 1991; Holtermann, 1992). This problem is also shared by MMs, though, except in so far as their husbands share in the care of their children, and their ability to pay for childcare is greater. Fear of loss of benefits on taking up work influenced the employment decisions of only a small proportion (10 per cent) in the Bradshaw-Millar study; however, the most important factor explaining reluctance to seek work in this study was '…their perceptions of the needs of, and their responsibilities towards, their children' (1991, p.43). Once again, LMs share with MMs the society's expectation – a belief which is becoming weaker over time – that mothers with young children under five should stay at home to look after them. However, as LMs are apt to be stereotyped as irresponsible, the dilemma is particularly acute for them as '…being the only parent, trying to be a "good" mother, and also providing for their children through employment' (Edwards, 1991a). Distress of relationship breakdown is another factor mentioned in this connection (as is illness), to explain the disparity, but are these factors, including the society's attitudes to women with young children working, enough to explain the gap between LMs and MMs in taking up PT work?

It may be useful to look at this point at the experience of lone fathers (LFs). Figure 2.7 indicates that 55 per cent with children under 18 are employed FT, and four per cent part-time. It has been argued that the vast majority of them do not have children under five (Bradshaw and Millar, 1991). This is true but, as Figure 2.7 also shows, participation in FT employment among those LFs who do have younger children, is only slightly lower (48 per cent). However, what is different here is the high level of unemployment among LFs (twice the rate for married fathers (Haskey, 1991)), particularly for those with children under five (20 per cent) – and this at a time when the economy was at the height of the boom. In times of economic recession, such as in the first half of the eighties, or since April 1990, the rate of unemployment for this group is likely to have been even higher, but the Government does not maintain employment statistics for this group on a regular basis. It is significant to note here that LMs have also

**Figure 2.7   Economic activity among lone fathers with dependent children
1987–1989**

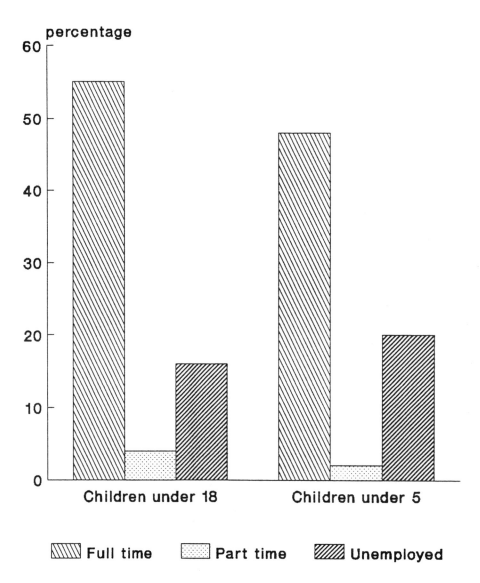

Source: Population Trends, Autumn 1991

experienced considerable fluctuation in the level of their economic activity in the eighties: it declined from 49 per cent in the late 1970s (1977-79) to 42 per cent in the mid-eighties (1985-87) (with a corresponding decline in FT employment from 22 to 18 per cent), only to recover the original level by the late eighties (1987-89); in the same period, the rate increased for MMs from 52 to 56 per cent (Haskey, 1991; FPSC, 1990). The decline in LMs' employment seems to correspond broadly with the changes in the economic cycle. **Potential** employment among LMs is quite high though – over a quarter (26 per cent) of those on IS were willing to start work immediately or in the very near future (Bradshaw and Millar, 1991), provided adequate wages and childcare were available.

A significant difference between LMs and LFs (in addition to the former looking after the majority of children under five), is the latter's earning power (Haskey, 1991), reflecting a higher standard of education and skills (Bradshaw and Millar, 1991). The reasons for this are structural, as we have already seen: women were largely concentrated in low paid, part-time or temporary, jobs in traditionally low-wage industries – and it is these types of jobs which had increased in the eighties. As the Bradshaw-Millar study points out, almost all LMs on IS and working PT were low paid, and did not work long enough to get employment protection rights. Even among those working FT, three-quarters were low paid, including two-thirds (65 per cent) who were **not** on IS, and their pay was **lower** than average female pay (which is three-quarters of men's pay). Even full-time employment, they conclude '...was no guarantee of financial security' (1991, p.97).

Summary

It has been argued in this section that LPFs are a high risk factor in child poverty due to a considerable expansion in their numbers in recent years, a relatively low level of economic activity, and heavy dependence on social security benefits. A rapid rise in their numbers is related to increased level of marital breakdown and births outside marriage. It is argued that the level of economic activity is lower among LMs in particular, as compared to MMs, due to the interaction of three factors: LMs' unequal position in the labour market, together with the scarcity of affordable good quality childcare, and the socialisation of women into child rearing responsibilities – which poses a particular dilemma for LMs because of the existence of stereotypical attitudes in society against them.

Social policies in recession

This chapter has been devoted so far to an examination of the main economic and demographic trends in the UK since 1979. As a result, the principal factors underlying the rapid rise in child poverty in this period have been identified: a substantial increase in unemployment, a considerable increase in the incidence of low pay, and a large rise in the number of lone parent families. In this section, changes in certain social policies will be reviewed to see how these have impinged on families with children. As the changes in the Government's taxation and social security policies were examined in the last chapter, the scope here will be limited to reviewing trends in public expenditure in general, and in the four areas of housing, health, education and social security (constituting the core of the welfare state) in particular, to see how services for families with children have been affected in the period 1979-92. It should be borne in mind though that the data are generally not disaggregated to a level that allows an assessment of the effect of changes in expenditure on children, let alone children in low income families. Unless otherwise stated, all figures in this section are in real[10] terms (1990-91 prices).

Public expenditure and the welfare state

As was noted at the beginning of this chapter, the Government in the eighties was committed to reducing public expenditure, for it was seen as a drain on the economy, stifling private investment and consumption. The welfare state, moreover, was often portrayed by Government representatives as '...wasteful, dominated by a self-serving bureaucracy and that help should be concentrated where it was needed most' (Bradshaw, 1991). The 'nanny' state was also viewed as fostering a dependency culture and harming personal incentives to work. How has this policy worked out in practice?

The general government expenditure (GGE) rose, in fact, in real terms, in the period 1979-92 at an average of 1.27 per cent per year. Most of the increase is confined to the first five years, when unemployment was rising and the economy was still reeling under the impact of the 1979-81 recession. For both these reasons, real GGE as a proportion of the real gross domestic product (GDP) rose from 43.3 to 46.1 per cent. During the last five years of Margaret Thatcher's government (1985-86 to 1989-90), when the economy grew at an accelerated rate (18.5 per cent), public expenditure grew by just over two per cent (2.2), and declined to 39.3 per cent of the GDP. In the last two years, it has risen to 41.5 per cent, once again due to rising unemployment and the effects of recession (Table 2.4).

This general picture masks wide variations in different sectors of the welfare state (see Table 2.5 and Figure 2.8), which in turn help explain the reasons for this modest increase, instead of the sharp fall which was the Government's intention. Indeed, a large part of the increase in welfare expenditure is explained by the spurt in social security payments, which rose from £43.5 billion in 1979-80 to a peak of £60.9 billion in 1986-87 (40 per cent increase), before falling to £57.5 billion in 1989-90. Since then, it has risen again to £64.8 billion in 1991-92 – an increase of nearly 50 (48.9) per cent over 1979-80 (Table 2.5). Consequently, social security expenditure as a percentage of GGE grew from a quarter (25.9 per cent) in 1979-80 to just under a third by 1991-92 (31.7 per cent).

Reasons for the rise in social security expenditure are primarily related to a large increase in the number of those who are unemployed, and to a lesser extent prematurely retired, sick and disabled; and, partly due to the higher cost of meeting rising demands from an expanded population of the elderly.

General government expenditure

Table 2.4 Percentage change in Real General Government Expenditure (GGE) and Real Gross Domestic Product (GDP) in the UK 1979-80 to 1991-92

| Year | Percentage Changes | | Real GGE as % of real GDP |
| | Real GGE | Real GDP | |
(1)	(2)	(3)	(4)
1979-80	-	-	43.3
1980-81	1.8	−3.8	45.8
1981-82	1.4	0.2	46.4
1982-83	2.7	2.1	46.6
1983-84	1.7	3.7	45.7
1984-85	2.7	1.9	46.1
1985-86	−0.1	3.7	44.4
1986-87	1.7	4.2	43.3
1987-88	0.0	4.9	41.3
1988-89	−2.4	3.8	38.8
1989-90	3.0	1.9	39.3
1990-91	−0.3	−0.2	39.9
1991-92	3.0	−1.0	41.5

Source: HM Treasury, *Autumn Statement* January 1992 (Table 1A.1).
Note: The GGE:GDP ratio figures for 1989-90 and before are shown as they were published at the time, and not adjusted upwards by 0.7 per cent because of the switch from rates to community charge as they are shown in current Treasury figures.

Expenditure on health and Personal Social Services

Expenditure under this heading increased by 45 per cent from £24 billion in 1979-80 to £34.9 billion in 1991-92. As a proportion of GGE, it increased from 14 to 17 per cent in this period. Of this total, the expenditure on Personal Social Services (PSS) increased from £3.7 billion to £5.5 billion – an increase of nearly 50 (48.6) per cent – while that on health increased from £20.3 billion to £29.4 billion – an increase of 45 per cent in real terms, or an average of 3.75 per cent per year (Table 2.5).

What additional volume of goods and services did this extra money buy? And, was it enough to meet the additional need generated, for instance, by a large increase in the elderly population during this period, or by increased morbidity due, among other things, to a sharp rise in unemployment? Or an increase in demand for health care as a result of the rise in personal incomes? Or increased demand for services emanating from additional statutory responsibilities such as those stipulated in the Children Act 1989? A study by Le Grand, Winter and Woolley (1991) tried to answer some of these questions up to 1986-87. They show that, whereas in terms of volume of goods and services, the value increased by 7.3 per cent between 1978-79 and 1986-87, or at an annual average rate of 0.9 per cent, the corresponding real term increase in

Table 2.5   General government expenditure on Welfare Services £billion (£b) (real terms 1990-91) and as a share of total government expenditure (TGE) in the UK 1979-80 to 1991-92

	79-80	80-81	81-82	82-83	83-84	84-85	85-86	86-87	87-88	88-89	89-90	90-91	Est 91-92
Social Security (£b)	43.5	44.4	49.3	52.3	54.9	56.6	58.4	60.9	60.3	57.7	57.5	58.8	64.8
% of TGE	25.9	26.3	28.5	28.8	29.9	30.2	31.3	31.8	31.5	30.9	29.7	30.1	31.7
Health & Personal Social Services (£b)	24.0	25.9	26.5	26.9	27.3	27.9	27.9	29.0	30.3	31.2	32.0	33.0	34.9
% of TGE	14.3	15.4	15.3	14.8	14.9	14.9	14.9	15.2	15.8	16.7	16.5	16.9	17.1
Of which Health (£b)	20.3	22.0	22.6	22.9	23.2	23.7	23.8	24.7	25.6	26.4	26.8	27.7	29.4
% of TGE	12.1	13.0	13.0	12.6	12.7	12.7	12.7	12.9	13.4	14.1	13.8	14.2	14.4
Education & Science (£b)	24.4	25.1	24.9	25.0	25.2	24.9	24.4	25.9	26.8	27.0	28.4	28.4	29.0
% of TGE	14.5	14.9	14.4	13.8	13.7	13.3	13.1	13.5	14.0	14.5	14.6	14.5	14.2
Housing (£b)	12.3	10.5	7.2	6.1	6.7	6.5	5.6	5.3	5.2	3.8	5.7	4.9	5.5
% of TGE	7.3	6.2	4.1	3.4	3.7	3.5	3.0	2.8	2.7	2.1	2.9	2.5	2.7

Source: HM Treasury: *Public Expenditure Analyses to 1994-95. Statistical Supplement to the 1991 Autumn Statement*, January 1992.

Figure 2.8   Government expenditure on welfare services 1979–92

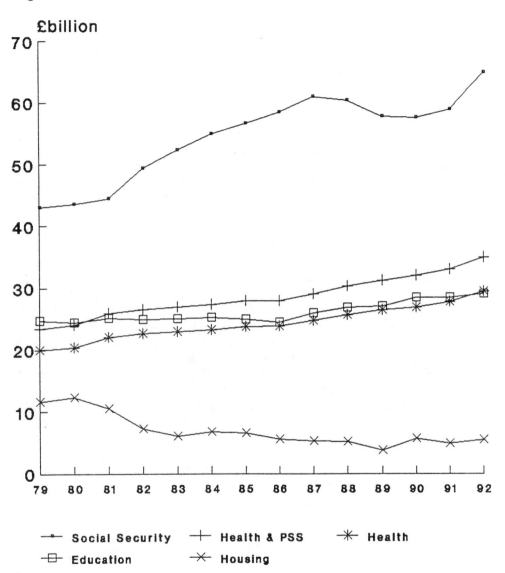

Source: Public Expenditure analyses to 1994–95: Statistical Supplement to the 1991 Autumn Statement, January 1992.

was 22 per cent. In other words, the real terms expenditure figures inflated the actual increase in services by a factor of three[10]. Using the index of 'need' based on the Department of Health (DH) calculations of changes in the demographic structure of the population, Le Grand and colleagues estimate that the growth in the volume of services during the eighties '...was only slightly higher than the growth in need (0.9 per cent as against 0.8 per cent at annual rates)' (p.100). But, after taking the increased **demand** into account, they conclude somewhat tentatively that '...balance between the growth in volume and the growth in need and demand was not maintained' (p.101). This conclusion is, however, reinforced by the following considerations: one, the DH index, by consensus, '...provides the lowest possible figure for the effects of the changing demographic structure on the NHS' (Le Grand and others, 1991, p.100); two, it also ignores the effects of any increased morbidity which may have arisen because of the rapid rise in unemployment in the 1980s. In sum, the increase in NHS expenditure was not enough to meet the increase in need.

In addition, continuing the earlier policy of redistributing resources to reduce regional disparities, at a time when demand was exceeding supply, created its own tensions and led to the closure of some hospital wards and a reduction of beds in acute services, mostly in the South East. Overall, though the average number of hospital beds available daily was reduced from 172 thousand in 1981 to 146 thousand in 1989-90, the throughput in terms of the **rate** of in-patients per available bed improved from 30.7 in 1981 to 46 in 1989-90 (*Social Trends*, 1991, Table 7.31). This was achieved by reducing the average length of stay in hospital. However, during the ten year period 1981-91, hospital waiting lists lengthened by nearly 100,000 to 830,000 (*Social Trends*, 1992, Table 7.33).

In a significant departure from previous practice, the Government has progressively increased charges for a range of services: prescription charges have gone up by a factor of 19 from 20p in 1979 to £3.75 in 1992; new dental treatment charges were introduced in April 1988, amounting to between 50 and 75 per cent of actual cost; this was followed by charges for dental examination in January 1989, and eye tests from April 1989. This was presumably done to dampen demand, since their intrinsic contribution to NHS expenditure is limited, rising from two per cent of NHS expenditure in 1978-79 to 2.7 per cent in 1987-88[11]. It has been a long standing concern of successive governments as to how to prevent the demand for NHS services from outstripping supply (Le Grand and colleagues, 1991).

Expenditure on education

Between 1979-80 and 1991-92, public spending on education increased by 19 per cent in real terms, most of this increase taking place over the five year period 1986-87 to 1991-92; prior to this, there was virtually no change. This is reflected also in education as a proportion of GGE: it was more or less stable for the first three years, then declined for the next four years, before showing a modest improvement over the next five years, settling around 14.5 per cent (Table 2.5).

Table 2.6 Expenditure on education in England in real terms £million at 1990-91 prices

Outturn	1979 -80	1981 -82	1982 -83	1983 84	1984 -85	1985 -86	1986 -87	1987 -88	1988 -89	1989 -90	1990 -91[2]	1991 -92[3]
Total[1] Expenditure												
Capital	1131	941	899	872	847	844	843	785	844	1194	1132	1222
Index (79-80=100)	100	83	79	77	75	75	75	69	75	106	100	108
Current	17,549	18,166	18,275	18,387	18,194	17,817	18,980	19,783	19,839	20,461	20,593	21,151
Index (79-80=100)	100	104	104	105	104	102	108	113	113	117	117	121
Total Expenditure												
Index (79-80=100)	100	102	103	103	102	100	106	110	111	116	116	120
Local Authority Expenditure												
Capital	809	661	645	633	601	582	576	528	568	766	688	730
Index (79-80=100)	100	82	80	78	74	72	71	65	70	95	85	90
Current	15,593	16,164	16,046	16,151	16,007	15,676	16,833	17,524	17,541	17,142	17,445	18,314
Index (79-80=100)	100	104	103	104	103	101	108	112	112	110	112	117
Total Index (79-80=100)	100	103	102	102	101	99	106	110	110	109	110[4]	116

Source: DES (1992) Statistical Bulletin 10/92 (Table 4)
Notes: 1. Includes central and local governments' expenditure combined
2. Provisional
3. Estimated
4. As per DFE letter dated 21.6.93

However, one gets a different picture when one looks at the breakdown of this expenditure into capital and current headings (Table 2.6). Although this breakdown is available only for England, and not for the UK as a whole, it does not matter too much, since the trend for the total education expenditure for England (which is roughly four-fifths of the UK education expenditure) during this period is almost identical to that for the UK.

As Table 2.6 indicates, the **current** educational expenditure for England runs in a fairly close parallel to the **total** expenditure, showing a modest increase in the first six years, but a more significant one in the second half of the eighties. By contrast, the **capital** expenditure was cut back by almost a third in the period 1979-80 to 1987-88. Increases in the next three years helped to make up the lost ground so that, in 1991-92, the figure stood eight per cent above its 1979-80 level. The cut back in the **local authority** capital expenditure was even more severe and sustained – and it had still not regained its 1979-80 level by 1991-92.

So far we have looked at education expenditure in the aggregate at the national level. Table 2.7 provides a breakdown of the net (current) institutional, or school based, expenditure (real terms) for the primary and secondary

Table 2.7 Net Institutional Expenditure in England 1980-81 to 1989-90 (1990-91 real terms)

Expenditure category	1979-80	1980-81[1]	1983-84	1987-88	1988-89	1989-90
A. Nursery and Primary Schools						
Teaching staff	..	2945	2798	3225	3368	3478
Other staff	..	250	268	396	454	471
Premises	..	840	818	816	777	825
Books and Equipment	..	123	125	140	140	157
Other	..	61	60	84	86	131
Total	4,068	4,219	4,069	4,661	4,825	5,062
Index 1980-81=100	(100)	(104)	(100)	(115)	(119)	(124)
B. Secondary schools						
Teaching staff	..	3803	3880	4093	4096	4030
Other staff	..	259	285	346	367	318
Premises	..	1032	1040	979	921	932
Books and Equipment	..	206	211	240	239	248
Other	..	137	145	205	204	263
Total	5,094	5,437	5,561	5,863	5,827	5,791
Index 1980-81=100	(100)	(107)	(109)	(108)	(115)	(114)

Source: Data derived from: DES (1991, 1992) *Statistical Bulletins* 21/91 and 10/92.
Information received from DFE (a letter dated 18 December 92).
Notes: 1. These figures are slightly higher (about half of one per cent) than they should be because November 1992 GDP deflator was applied by DFE in adjusting the cash figures, instead of March 1992 deflator used in other cases.
.. = not available.

Table 2.8 Trends in UK Education Expenditure (Volume) 1979-80 to 1986-87

Index 1979-80 = 100	1979-80	1980-81	1981-82	1982-83	1983-84	1984-85	1985-86	1986-87
Current								
Nursery	100	95	93	96	98	96	96	102
Primary	100	96	93	92	91	89	90	95
Secondary	100	98	98	98	99	98	96	99
Capital								
Nursery	100	75	50	38	63	63	75	63
Primary	100	103	72	64	67	65	70	57
Secondary	100	91	69	67	62	53	53	44

Source: Derived from Glennerster and Low (1991), Table 3A.2

Notes: 1. The table from which this one is derived is based NOT on GDP deflator normally used by the DFE to adjust cash prices to real terms; instead, it is based on CIPFA education and a variety of other deflators which are thought to more accurately measure the effects of inflation. This table is therefore a measure of the changes in the volume of goods and services that expenditure at different levels can buy.

levels for the period 1980-81 to 1989-90 for which the latest figures are available (unfortunately, separate breakdown is not available for the nursery and primary sectors). These figures should be seen alongside Table 2.8, which gives a measure of the changes in the **volume** of goods and services that expenditure at different levels can buy. Table 2.8 indicates that expenditure on primary schools actually declined in the first half of the eighties by ten per cent; that it was still five per cent below the 1979-80 level in 1986-87. The increases shown in Table 2.7 in 1980-81 and 1987-88 were, according to Glennerster and Low, accounted for by salary increases to primary teachers to enable them to 'catch up' with other comparable occupations, thereby effectively wiping out the apparent rise in expenditure (1991). For instance, in 1980-81 there was an actual four per cent reduction in primary schools expenditure (Table 2.8), instead of a four per cent increase (Table 2.7). The expenditure on premises in primary schools declined by 7.5 per cent between 1980-81 and 1988-89, before rising in 1989-90, but was still two per cent below its 1980-81 level. As for expenditure on books, there was little change in the first half of the eighties, but it fared better in the second half; there was a 13.8 per cent increase between 1983-84 and 1987-88; and 12 per cent between 1988-89 and 1989-90. However, it is not clear whether this level of increase would be sufficient to absorb a generally higher level of inflation in books (see chapter 5).

The picture is not very different at the secondary level. The increases in the total expenditure of between seven to nine per cent between 1979-80 and 1983-84 (Table 2.7) disappear in Table 2.8, which shows a small decrease in expenditure over the eighties. The reasons for the increases in 1980-81 and 1987-88 are the same as for the primary level, that is higher teacher salaries. There was a decrease of over ten per cent in expenditure on premises in the eighties. Again, there was very little change in the provision for books until 1983-84; followed by 14 per cent increase in the next four years (up to 1987-88), and then very a small increase in 1989-90. The actual value of this 20 per cent increase in expenditure on books in the eighties is likely to be much less, since as is generally recognised, inflation in book prices tends to be very much higher than the general inflation level which the RPI reflects (see chapter 5).

As regards the capital expenditure, a glance at Table 2.8 will reveal major cuts in all three sectors; 37 per cent in the nursery, 43 per cent in the primary and 56 per cent in the secondary schools.

The previous discussion on public expenditure on education needs to be related to the context of falling school rolls, on the one hand, and to changing (rising) needs on the other, even though this is a very complex matter. Primary pupil numbers continued to fall in the first half of the eighties from five million in 1980-81 to 4.5 million in 1985-86; there was a slight increase between 1986 and 1989 so that by 1990 the figure had reached 4.7 million. The number of secondary school pupils continued to decline throughout the 1980s from 4.6 million in 1980-81 to 3.5 million in 1989-90, but it is projected to rise from 1992 till at least 1999 (*Education Statistics*, 1991; *Social Trends*, 1992). As a result of declining pupil numbers, the average class size fell slightly in the eighties. In primary schools, it dropped from 28 in 1977 to 26 in 1981, and was still at the same level in 1990. There was also some improvement in the percentage of classes exceeding 30 pupils in that it declined from 22 to 18 in the same period. However, there are some indications that the situation may be worsening in the early 1990s. A survey of over 1,000 primary and middle schools in England and Wales by the National Association of School Masters/Union of Women Teachers found that over a quarter of classes at these schools exceeded 30 pupils (*The Times*, 8.8.92). This is corroborated by what has been happening to pupil-teacher ratios in the primary school. Having declined in the eighties from 22.3 in 1980-81 to 21.7 in 1989-90, these have begun to rise again, in England at any rate, for which the latest evidence is available. This indicates that the ratio has been rising steadily from 21.9 in 1987 to 22.2 in 1991 (*Statistical Bulletin*, 2/92).

At the secondary school level too, the average size of class has come down slightly from 22 in 1981 to 21 in 1990, and the percentage of classes exceeding 30 pupils fallen from eight in 1981 to four in 1990. Likewise, the pupil-teacher ratio in the UK also declined in the eighties from 16.4 in 1980-81 to 14.8 in 1989-90. Lately, it is beginning to rise again – in England at least. After falling from 15.65 in 1987 to 15.25 in 1990, it rose to 15.55 in 1991 (*Education Statistics, 1991*; *Statistical Bulletin* 2/92).

Provision for under fives
With the rapidly rising labour force participation of married women with children, the education and day care of under fives become very important. Figure 2.9 provides a graphic presentation of data on education for the under fives. Full-time nursery places declined from 22,000 in 1981 to 17,000 in 1990; part-time places increased from 67,000 in 1981 to 80,000 in 1988, only to fall back to 67,000 by 1990. Nursery classes in primary school have expanded significantly in this period – full-time places by almost a quarter, and part-time places by almost three-quarters. However, as a percentage of all children under three and four years in the UK, provision overall increased from 44.3 per cent in 1981 to 51.2 per cent in 1990 (Table I.5). This is still far short of the target of 90 per cent of four-year-olds and 50 per cent of three-year-olds set in 1972 by Margaret Thatcher, the then Secretary of State for Education, to be achieved by 1982.

Nursery classes in primary schools is the only element of under fives' education in the public sector to expand significantly in the eighties, facilitated by falling rolls. Ironically, it was the Government White Paper, *Better Schools* which was sceptical about this form of provision: it maintained that it was 'unrealistic to expect a teacher simultaneously to provide an appropriate education for younger four-year-olds and for children of compulsory school age' (DES, 1985a). There are two main reasons why this is so: infant teachers mostly lack the training and experience in dealing with younger children; staffing and other resources are significantly more generous in nursery schools as compared to infant classes (Bennett and Kell, 1989). Evidence from other research also supports the view that nursery schools and classes are more beneficial to younger children than premature attendance in infant classes. Yet full-time nursery places were cut back by a quarter in the eighties. As Clarke has observed, economic constraints led the Government to reverse its commitment

Figure 2.9   Education of children under five 1981-1990

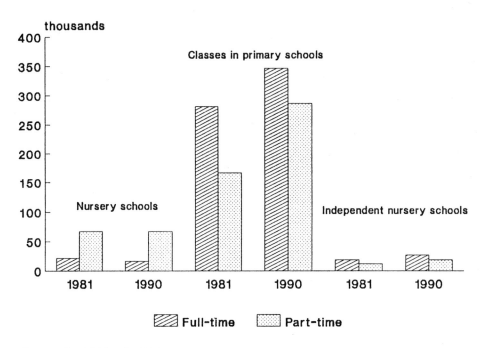

Source: *Social Trends* 1992

to expansion in this non-mandatory sector of education and focus its effort instead on low cost provision (1988).

Whereas nursery provision is free, day care has, in general, to be paid for. As Table I.5 and Figure 2.10 show, local authority provision has been stagnant, but the private nursery places have nearly tripled between 1981 and 1990; and the number of childminders has more than doubled. There are wide regional variations in education and day care provision for children under five, as is clear from Table 1.6 and Figure 2.11. Whereas more than 90 per cent of four-year-olds are provided for in the North, North West and Wales, the figure drops to three-quarters for England, and only three-fifths or fewer are catered for in Scotland and the South East. Likewise, whereas North and Yorkshire and Humberside provide for over 50 per cent of three-year-olds, East Anglia and Northern Ireland provide for only one in six, and the South West provides for only one in eight. Not only is the amount of provision variable across the country, but so is the type and its quality and cost (Clarke, 1988).

Since most of the expansion in under fives' provision in the eighties has occurred in the private nurseries, '...access to services (is) becoming increasingly dependent on the private market and parents' ability to pay ...'(Sylva and Moss, 1992). As already observed earlier in this chapter, the

Figure 2.10 Day care of children under five 1981

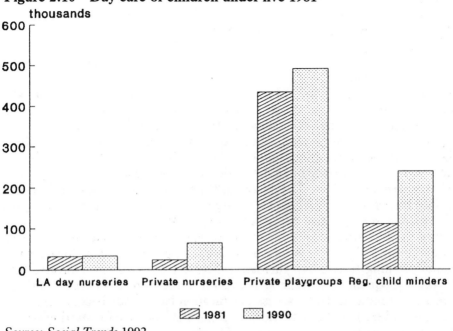

Source: Social Trends 1992

Figure 2.11 Education and day care of children under five by age and region 1989

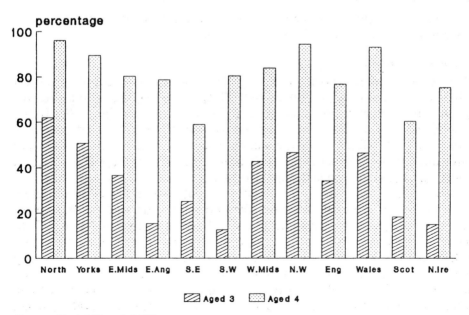

Source: Social Trends 1992

ability of women in general, and that of lone mothers in particular, was constrained by a severe lack of good quality childcare at a reasonable price, to enable them to take on full-time, or even substantial part-time employment. Even if only a proportion of women are successful in obtaining employment as a result of expansion in childcare, others may gain by obtaining access to education and training.

Nor are the benefits confined to the women concerned and their families' living standards. The state stands to gain substantially, by saving on benefits and increasing tax revenue, not counting the beneficial multiplier effects on the economy of extra spending power thus acquired by mainly low income families. In fact, it has been argued by a number of researchers that public expansion of childcare can be self-financing in the medium to long-term (Cohen and Fraser, 1991; Holtermann, 1992). The National Commission on Education has also endorsed this view, while calling for an urgent and wide-ranging review of pre-school provision by the Government (Sylva and Moss, 1992).

However, the strongest argument in our view – and the one which carries considerable moral force – for increasing access to good quality childcare is the benefits accruing to children themselves. Research by Clarke indicates that '...massive inequalities in available provision and resources between areas' has led to a situation whereby '...access to education has already become unequal' for young children by the time they reach the statutory age for starting school (1988, p.276). As the first report of the House of Commons Select Committee on Education, Science and Arts has observed:

the evidence shows little doubt that early educational opportunities can help particularly those...from socially or economically deprived backgrounds and those for whom English is not their first language (1988. para.2.14).

This would, therefore, appear to be an obvious area for the Government to tackle in its desire to raise educational standards.

School meals provision

There was a dramatic drop in the take-up of school meals in England[12] from 4.9 million children in 1979 to 3 million by 1990; as a proportion of pupils present, the take-up declined from 64 per cent in 1979 to 47 per cent in 1988[13]. In the same period, the amount spent by the Government more than halved from £800 million to £359 million, while the amount spent per pupil declined by 27 per cent from £164 to £119 per annum (*Hansard*, 20.5.91, col.361; CIPFA Annual Statistics; Cole-Hamilton and others, 1991).

This is due in the main to the abolition of national price control of school meals by the Government under the 1980 Education Act and the consequent increase in the price of a school meal: it rose from an average of 25p in 1979 to 68p in 1990, with considerable variation between different local education authorities (LEAs), which also helps to explain wide differences in the take-up in different areas (Cole-Hamilton and others, 1991). Since the 1980 Education Act also made it optional for LEAs to provide a school meal, except for those pupils entitled to a free meal, seven LEAs have decided to stop providing school meals for all pupils who want them.

Another factor which has influenced the overall take-up of school meals is the changes in the conditions of eligibility for free school meals. The 1986 Social Security Act restricted entitlement to free school meals to those pupils whose parents received Income Support. Thus, at a stroke, the number of children eligible for a free school meal was reduced by 400,000 to 900,000 as from April 1988 (*Hansard*, 24.7.86, col.450; CIPFA, 1987 and 1988). This was 15 per cent of the school population in England, as compared to 21 per cent in 1979.

This is because the children of low paid families in receipt of Family Credit lost their entitlement, instead they got a cash supplement which was based on the **average** cost of a school meal, which for many people was not enough given wide variations in its price. Moreover, families receiving Housing Benefit as well as Family Credit found that, because of changes in this, the value of their cash supplement for a school meal was reduced to less than 50p per week (Cole-Hamilton and others, 1991). Family Credit is in any case, claimed by only about 64 per cent of those eligible for it, according to the latest official figures. New rules restricting eligibility for IS from April 1992 to those working for less than 16 hours, instead of 24 hours per week prior to this date, is likely to reduce further the number of children eligible for free school meals.

In May 1990 only about three-quarters of children aged between 5 and 16 years, whose families were on IS, were receiving free meals in schools in England (*Hansard*, 10.12.91, col.417). The rate varies between LEAs – it is thought that in some areas the low take-up of free school meals is due to the stigma attached to it, particularly at the secondary level. Other reasons for the low take-up include ignorance of availability or the criteria for eligibility; and, in the case of Muslim pupils, non-availability of 'halal' meat may also be a factor.

LEAs used to have the discretion to offer free school meals to children of low paid families not in receipt of FIS or SB. Prior to 1988, 75 of the 96 LEAs in England did offer a free school meal to such children. Local authority discretion on this issue was abolished by the Government in 1988 when the 1986 Social Security Act came into operation.

Finally, there are concerns regarding the quality of the school meals on offer, following the abolition of national nutritional guidelines (statutory) for school meals, first introduced in 1965 by the 1980 Education Act. This issue will be discussed in the next chapter.

Expenditure on housing

Housing experienced the biggest reduction of all social expenditure in the eighties, having been cut by more than half in real terms from £12.3 billion in 1979-80 to £5.5 billion in 1991-92. As a proportion of total Government expenditure, it was reduced to almost a third from 7.3 per cent in 1979-80 to 2.7 per cent in 1991-92 (Table 2.5).

These figures need to be seen in relation to the changed policy context in the eighties. While the Government adheres to the global aim espoused by successive governments that 'a decent home should be within reach of every family' (DoE 1991a), its approach on how this should be achieved is different, and can be summed up as follows:

Encouragement of self-sufficiency through owner occupation and of increased private investment in the rented sector are major themes of policy... (DoE, 1991a).

Its implications for public sector housing were considerable. The most important of these was the Government's attempt to alter the traditional role of local authorities (LAs) as the main providers of low cost social housing to rent. The 1987 White Paper, *Housing: the Government's proposals* encourages LAs to see themselves primarily as enablers rather than as direct providers of housing services. To this end, the expansion of owner-occupation was to be achieved, in part, by the sale of LA housing. There was also a marked shift away from capital investment in the construction of new town and council houses in favour of renovation of existing LA housing stock. Accordingly, while the spending on new LA dwellings in England was cut by 90 per cent between 1976 and 1989, expenditure on maintenance and repair almost doubled (Hills, 1991). The Government would, in fact, like to encourage the LAs to transfer their dwelling stock voluntarily to the Housing Associations (HAs), which it sees as the main future providers of new homes for rent, together with increased lettings through the private rented sector. Already new capital funding is increasingly channelled by the government through the Housing Corporation and HAs (Audit Commission, 1992; Shelter, 1991).

Finally, the other significant change in policy was a withdrawal by the Government of the general subsidy to council house rents in favour of a more targeted help (Housing Benefit (HB)) to individuals based on need (means-tested). Consequently, the rents of LA tenants went up substantially in the eighties (by over 50 per cent between 1979-80 and 1986-87). The eligibility conditions for HB were so defined that, in the event, only two-fifths of council tenants were eligible for HB in 1979-80. Subsequently, however, the level of HB was substantially cut back in the 1980s, thereby adversely affecting the living standards of low income families (Hills and Mullings, 1991).

The expansion of home ownership had now become the Government's major policy objective. Measures intended to achieve this aim included giving council tenants the right to buy their house or flat at hefty discounts (up to 60 and 70 per cent respectively), tax reliefs on interest payments on house mortgages – mortgage interest tax relief (MITR), and the relaxation of restrictions on house mortgages (for instance, under the 1986 Building Societies Act, not all lending had to be secured against a dwelling). Coming on top of the general financial deregulation, these measures led to an intense competition between the banks and the building societies in providing loans, sometimes, it has been argued, against their better (commercial) judgement (Muelbauer, 1991).

With the help of MITR, home ownership increased from 57.6 per cent in 1980 to 68.8 per cent in 1990 (Audit Commission, 1992) at a cost to the tax payer of £7.8 billion in 1990-91 (Joseph Rowntree Foundation, 1991). Because of the sluggishness of the housing market in the present recession, and a significant fall in interest rates, the MITR bill for 1991-92 was down to £6.1 billion (*Hansard*, 17.6.92, Col. 537-38). By way of contrast, the amount spent on

Housing Benefit in 1989-90 was £4.2 billion (held more or less constant for four years), as against £6.5 billion for MITR (Greve, 1991).

A third of this expansion in home ownership was accounted for by the sale of council housing (one million homes), much of it family properties. Even though this type of housing was greatly in demand by the council tenants, local authorities were not allowed by the Government to replace it with the construction of new dwellings, because of curbs on capital expenditure. Consequently, as we shall see in chapter 4, as homelessness increased in the eighties among families with young children (including a large number of lone parent families), the councils frequently had to put them up in temporary Bed and Breakfast accommodation for long periods at considerable public expense. The cost of keeping a family with two children in such accommodation for one year in London was greater in 1990 than building a new dwelling for them for permanent rehousing (Audit Commission, 1992).

The expansion in home ownership has, moreover, largely benefited the middle and upper income groups, as is evident from the analysis of the General Household Survey (GHS) data by Hills and Mullings (1991) for the period 1979-85. There are reasons to believe that this trend has continued, if not strengthened, since then. There is partial confirmation in the figures for the distribution of mortgage interest tax relief for 1991-92: only 12 per cent was utilised by people earning below £10,000 annually; 41 per cent by those earning between £10,000 and £20,000; and 47 per cent by those earning over £20,000 (*Hansard*, 21.5.91, col. 417-18).

A direct consequence of this expansion in home ownership was greater polarisation (in terms of incomes) between tenures: the sale of council houses in the eighties diminished the representation of upper income groups, and greatly enhanced the representation of lower income groups in council housing (Hills and Mullings, 1991). This was reflected in Government statistics: the average income of local authority tenants as a proportion of *all* households in the country went down from 76 per cent in 1981 to 58 per cent in 1987, and to 56 per cent in 1989 (GHS 1989, Table 8.11). The comparable figure for those renting in the private sector for 1989 was 69 per cent. It appears that the rented sector (public and private) is becoming mostly the preserve of the poor as predicted by Berthoud and Brown (1981).

The rise in owner-occupation has been paralleled by a long-term decline in the availability of privately rented accommodation. Despite recent government measures to attract private investment, the decline has continued unabated, from 14 per cent in 1978, to nine per cent in 1988, and to eight per cent in 1990 (OPCS, 1991a). It is a measure of the demand for privately rented accommodation in relation to supply that rents have risen very much faster than general inflation. For instance, there was a 43 per cent increase (from £30 to £43 weekly) in mean rent for all tenancies between 1988 and 1990. However, the mean rent for the lone parent tenancy group was a good deal higher (£56 weekly). Overall, just under a fifth (19 per cent) of lone parents and couples with dependent children rely on privately rented accommodation (OPCS, 1991a).

The outgoings on housing in relation to income went up substantially between 1979-85, both for tenants and owner-occupiers, though the balance of advantage lay with the latter (Hills and Mullings, 1991). However, in the period 1985-89, the increase in the ratio of house price and income, though cyclical, was particularly steep; it was higher in London and the South East compared to the North of England and Wales (Audit Commission, 1992). This house price inflation was clearly fuelled by high interest rates and easy availability of credit (mortgage lending tripled between 1980 and 1990). As Pearce and Wilcox put it, the MITR is a 'costly and poorly targeted subsidy', which distorts the role of the housing market by raising interest rates and feeding house price inflation (1991). It also tends to distort the economy through personal consumption and in the operation of the macro economy (Greve, 1991).

House price inflation, together with rising unemployment since March 1990 and continuing breakdown in relationships (marital and cohabitational) has led to a 12-fold increase in mortgages in arrears for between six and 12 months, and a 20-fold increase in repossessions (Council of Mortgage Lenders, 1992), thereby greatly exacerbating the problem of homelessness, especially among families with young children, and causing them additional suffering, as we shall see in the next chapter. Some people have clearly benefited from the fall in interest rates and in house prices in the last three years, particularly the first time buyers, and others who were previously finding it difficult to cope. However, the situation has been aggravated by the collapse of the housing market for people facing redundancies or bankruptcies, because they cannot exercise the option of redeeming their debts by the sale of their properties.

The Government's policy on housing, and the downward trend in public expenditure since 1979, are based on the premise that there is a 'diminishing proportion of households who cannot afford the market price of decent housing' (DoE, 1991a). This does not seem compatible with the mounting evidence of increasing unemployment, mortgage arrears, repossessions and homelessness which has been rising since 1978. As the Joseph Rowntree Foundation report noted '...home ownership was not the best housing option for everyone ...it can present financial strains. For many people renting is the only realistic option, and for others it is the most sensible one' (*Inquiry into British Housing*, Second Report, 1991). Housing specialists are inclined to the view that the home ownership level in Britain is now nearing the saturation point (Whitehead and others, 1992). However, as the Audit Commission report points out, 'the private market alone is unable without subsidies to meet the objective of providing a decent home for every family. So the provision of social housing for those households who cannot afford the cost of housing of an acceptable standard in the private sector remains important in national policy. Currently the total demand for social housing is not being met...' (1992, p.6).

The Audit Commission report adds that the need for further social provision is substantial, judging by the increasing numbers of statutorily homeless people in temporary accommodation, let alone people sleeping rough in the streets. Its projections of need suggest that '...even the most optimistic forecast of social housing output implies a shortfall of 12,000 social lettings each year, and little progress can be expected in improving either the public or the private sector housing stock', because the LAs which '...retain primary responsibilities for the maintenance of council housing and some aspects of support for the private sector ...are ill resourced to discharge these responsibilities' (p.1). Other estimates of the gap between availability and need are much higher (around 100,000 dwellings a year) (Shelter, 1991; Whitehead and others, 1992).

Summary

This review of public expenditure trends indicates that the GGE increased by 15 per cent since 1979, despite the Government's intention to reduce it significantly. This was due to a combination of demographic socio-economic and political factors. Given the culture of the welfare state in the UK, the Government '...very quickly came up against the bedrock of public support for the Welfare State' (Borooah, 1988).

While the expenditure on social security increased inexorably, the Government did try to restrict the increase by sizeable cut backs in certain areas, such as the HB or benefits for the unemployed, while making modest improvements in child support.

Health expenditure also increased substantially in response to demographic and political pressures, but not when compared with growing needs. Despite some gains in the efficient use of resources, especially in hospitals, waiting lists have lengthened. The Government's attempt to dampen down demand by imposing large increases in prescription charges and fees for dental and eye examinations is likely to adversely affect many families with low incomes who are not eligible for free prescriptions and examinations because their income is just above the IS level.

Expenditure on education increased by nearly one-fifth, over the period 1979-92, but capital expenditure was cut back by a third – cuts were particularly severe and sustained for LEAs. However, modest increase in the current expenditure was more than offset by salary increases for teachers at both the primary and secondary levels; they had nevertheless slipped further behind when compared to their relative position prior to 1979. There was a significant reduction in the provision for school premises, but modest increase in the provision for books. But it was unclear whether this was enough to meet the generally higher inflation costs of books, and growing needs. There was a slight improvement in class sizes and pupil-teacher ratios at both the primary and secondary levels, but in the last few years there are signs of the situation deteriorating.

Expenditure on education needs to be seen in the context of fluctuations in school rolls on the one hand, and growing needs on the other. This is a highly complex matter, and data is not readily available, or in a form, to disentangle the effects of each. This matter will be discussed at some length in chapter 5.

Under fives provision suffered cuts in full-time nursery education, but there was a significant expansion in numbers in infant classes in the context of falling school rolls, but there are doubts about the beneficial effects of this kind of provision. While private nursery provision has increased significantly, education and childcare provision generally is very variable across the country – in quantity and quality, and access is becoming increasingly dependent on the ability to pay. This is a serious constraint on the ability of many lone mothers and married mothers on low incomes to take up employment (or training) to improve their living standards, and thus lift themselves out of poverty. It also adversely affects equality of access to education even before a child is five-years-old. Yet, there is a lack of a coherent national policy on this issue.

There has been a big drop in the take-up of school meals, as also in expenditure per pupil, due mainly to removal by the Government of national price controls, and resultant increases in its price. Take-up of **free** school meals (FSM) has also suffered a sharp fall – due mainly to changes in eligibility in the 1986 Social Security Act. Moreover, only three-quarters of eligible pupils take up FSM.

Housing expenditure has been more than halved in real terms. Sale of council housing and the Government clamp down on new LA building have resulted in shortages in low cost social housing, while the demand for it has increased, as the supply of privately rented accommodation has declined rapidly over the years, and is now beyond the reach of many low income families with children. Home ownership did expand rapidly in the eighties, relying on easy availability of credit and MITR, to reach a saturation point. However, house price inflation and rising unemployment since March 1990, together with continuing breakdown in relationships, have led to increases in mortgage arrears and house repossessions, thereby aggravating the problem of homelessness, which affects many families with children.

Conclusions

This chapter has identified three main factors underlying the increase in child poverty in the UK since 1979: a relatively high level of unemployment; increase in the incidence of low pay; and a large rise in the number of lone parent families.

It was observed that the level of unemployment was closely related to the performance of the British economy. Two main points emerged from our review of economic trends in the period 1979-92. One, there was a trade off between unemployment and inflation. Second, growth in the economy tended to be accompanied by progressively higher inflation and reduction in unemployment but with a time lag. It was shown that the government policy of giving priority to controlling inflation in the period 1979-83 was successful but at the expense of sluggish growth and largescale increase in unemployment. In the period 1983-90, whereas the economy grew at an accelerated pace, especially after 1986, and unemployment was halved by March 1990, it also led to a sharp rise in inflation. Renewed effort by the Government to control inflation in the late 1980s contributed once again to high unemployment and recession, accompanied by an escalating PSBR and a balance of payments deficit, culminating in the Sterling crisis of September 1992 and the British withdrawal from the ERM.

This raises the question if the Government is any closer to achieving its principal policy objective of ensuring a sustained growth in a low inflationary environment free from the recurrent cycle of 'stop-go' which has beset the British economy for decades. The question assumes ever greater urgency since, in the mean time, the price in terms of a relatively high level of unemployment (and rising poverty) is being paid disproportionately by the most vulnerable sections of society, especially by low income families with dependent children.

Our evidence also indicated a strong relationship between unemployment, low pay and poverty. Reasons for increase in low pay are two-fold: a substantial expansion in 'flexible' low paid jobs largely occupied by women in low wage industries; and, the deregulation of the labour market by the Government, weakening low paid workers' rights and reinforcing trends towards the widening of differentials in a climate of high job insecurity and rising unemployment, thereby increasing inequality as well as poverty. Low pay is closely related to age, gender, race and social class. Manual workers are more prone than non-manual; semi-skilled and unskilled more than skilled; women more than men; young people more than older ones; and Black people more than White people, in an increasingly polarised labour market undergoing profound changes.

Increase in LPFs is attributed to two factors: continuing breakdown in relationships (marital and cohabitational), and increase in births outside marriage. The level of economic activity is low among LPFs, especially LMs and this is due to an interaction between their unequal position in the labour market, the shortage of good quality affordable childcare, and the socialisation of women into child-rearing responsibilities - which pose a particular dilemma for LMs because of society's stereotypical views about them.

Despite the Government's declared intention of reducing public expenditure, it actually increased in real terms by a little over one per cent per year over the period 1979-92, because of the operation of demographic, socio-economic and political factors. Even so, the Government's attempts to restrain public expenditure were more successful in some areas such as housing, than others such as health. Even within individual subject areas, in some aspects they were more successful than others; as for instance there were substantial cuts in HB and in benefits for the unemployed, but the position of low income families with dependent children was less insecure.

Whether fluctuations in expenditure were adequate to meet needs is another matter. This was not obviously the case with social security benefits, whose adequacy was questionable; nor in housing or health. However, this issue is very complex and will be examined to some extent in Part II, particularly as regards education.

Notes

1. For a discussion of these two methods of counting the unemployed, see Employment Policy Institute (1992); and Lawlor and Kennedy (1992).
2. Since LFS is based on a sample survey, these figures are an estimate, not an exact count. Moreover, since LFS uses a different definition of unemployment from that

used by the DE, its figures of overall unemployment tend to differ significantly from those of DE.

3. We are using the same 'North'–'South' dividing line as in chapter 1 when discussing the regional dimension of poverty; see also Tables 1.5 and 1.6.

4. All the statistics quoted in this section are derived from official sources: those on employment and unemployment from the *Employment Gazette*; on growth from the CSO *Blue Book*; the remainder from the *Economic Trends*.

5. There is considerable literature on the problems of discrimination and disadvantage. Apart from official reports from the Commission for Racial Equality (CRE) and the Equal Opportunities Commission (EOC), the following publications are particularly relevant to issues discussed here: Amin with Oppenheim (1991); Brown (1984); Lonsdale (1985); Osborn and Butler (1985).

6. According to Haskey (1991), there is uncertainty about the exact number, as estimates derived from different sources such as GHS and LFS differ considerably, as they do when derived from any **one** source, especially if based on any **one** year. Thus his 'best' estimate derived from a variety of sources for 1989 was 1.15 million, whereas the LFS estimate for 1990 was even less at 1.081 million (Bartholomew, Hibbett and Sidaway, 1992). The same is true of the number of dependent children. Consequently, the most reliable estimates are the ones based on a three-year average.

7. Some of the data in Figure 2.4 may not tally with the text, since it is based on LFS data for one year (1990) – see note 6 above.

8. Information is also available for the period 1988-90 from the GHS, but it is likely to be less reliable for being based on a single source.

9. A sample survey by Bradshaw and Millar based on April 1989 data found that 23 per cent of lone mothers were employed FT and 17 per cent PT; however their response rate was relatively low with wide variations across the country.

10. The Government (The Treasury) uses a common index – the GDP deflator – to convert cash to real term increases in all Government expenditure. The effect of this is to overstate the Government expenditure in particular sectors, such as education, in so far as inflation is higher in those sectors than the rate assumed in the GDP deflator. Consequently, according to the Employment Institute, the Treasury tends to overestimate most types of public expenditure (1991).

11. These expenditure figures do not, of course, take into account some of the increases quoted in this paragraph.

12. Information about school meals is not collected centrally for the UK as a whole: it has been published by the DES from October 1979-1984, and January 1989 and 1990; and for October 1986-1988 by the Chartered Institute of Public Finance and Accountancy (CIPFA).

13. CIPFA statistics were based on the number of pupils *present* on the census day; from 1989, DES figures are based on the number on the *roll* in January each year. This would account for a small decline in the period after 1988; comparison with previous years is also complicated by the fact that figures will be affected by fluctuations in school rolls rather than attendance on the census day.

Part II   Effects of child poverty

Introduction

Rise in child poverty

Our review in Part I of evidence on the nature and scale of poverty in the UK revealed a steep rise in child poverty since 1979, and a widening of inequality in income. The number of children living in poverty increased three times to nearly four million, or one in every three, in the period 1979-90/91, while the number of children living on the margin of poverty increased to five million, or two in every five children.

The real income (AHC) of the bottom 20 per cent of married couples with children declined by 14 per cent, as against an average increase of over 30 per cent in the real income of the general population in the same period; by contrast, the average real income of the top 20 per cent of the population increased by 40 per cent.

Factors related to the rapid increase in child poverty were unemployment, low pay and one parent families. Unemployment was at or above three million during the first half of the eighties, was halved by March 1990, but has been rising ever since and, by January 1993, had crossed the three million mark again. The incidence of low pay has increased by a quarter since 1979 and was adversely affecting the income of ten million workers in 1991 – almost half the workforce; 36 per cent of full-time workers and 70 per cent of part-time workers were low-paid; four-fifths of part-timers in low pay were women.

The number of LPFs also increased significantly during this period – constituting one-sixth of all families by 1990 – as did the number of children to 1.9 million. The risk of poverty was the highest among children of unemployed families, followed by children of LPFs, and lastly those in households headed by low-paid workers.

Increased dependence on benefits

With the increase in poverty, there has been an increase in dependence of low income families with children on social security benefits, which have become less generous as a result of changes since 1979. Research evidence indicates that, despite some recent improvement in child support, social benefits are inadequate to meet the needs of such families. On the other hand, higher income groups have largely benefited from the tax cuts and other changes in taxation, thereby contributing to the widening of the gap between the rich and the poor. It was observed in chapter 2 that children from minority ethnic groups were more vulnerable to poverty and deprivation because of a number of factors. Their parents' unequal position in the labour market (due in part to their experience of racial discrimination and disadvantage), combined with geographical and economic segregation in traditionally low-paid industries and semi- or unskilled jobs, made them much more vulnerable to unemployment, as well as being trapped in poverty, low pay and poor working conditions. Unemployment among minority ethnic groups was considerably higher – general as well as long-term – than among White people.

Effect of rising child poverty

How has the deprivation resulting from this increase in child poverty affected the lives of children in general, and those of minority ethnic groups in particular? We shall attempt to answer this question in Part II with regard to their health, housing and education on the basis of the limited evidence that is available.

The limitations are considerable: the data about the effect of events over time is frequently not collected, let alone up to date or published; the impact of some of the changes may be difficult to assess because of the multiplicity of factors involved, or because their impact may be felt with a time lag over a medium to long-term period. It is also possible that parents may be able to cushion their children up to a point against the effects of deprivation. Finally, there is not much evidence directly linking children's experience of deprivation with outcomes in education, health and housing.

Social class as a proxy for deprivation

For the most part, therefore, one has to rely on evidence based on social or occupational class. This concept has been variously defined by sociologists, but the definition in the *Black Report* seems apt here: 'segments of the population sharing broadly similar types and levels of resources, with broadly similar styles of living...' (1980, p.13).

Two indicators of social class are generally used[1]. The first is the Registrar General's (RG) scale of five social or occupational classes, based on the skills and status of the job, ranging from professionals in class I to unskilled manual workers in class V. The other consists of socio-economic groups (SEG), usually condensed to six or seven categories, where the classification seeks to group together people with similar skills and life-styles. Views differ to what extent these scales are successful in doing this in practice. According to Whitehead, they are 'taken as a rough guide to the way of life and living standards experienced by the separate groups and their families' (1992, p.224). Mortimore is less sure, at least about the RG scale – it '...says little about the type of home, the quality of relationships between parents and children and family interests or life style' (1983, p.7). However, both agree that social class does measure 'something' – the above scales correlate fairly well with other aspects of social status such as education and income. Since the use of this term tends to emphasise similarities between families (and thereby to disguise variation in society), there is a risk of stereotyping. Moreover, as Blackstone and Mortimore (1982) point out, its relationship with deprivation (or disadvantage) is also not exact – not all people belonging to the manual occupations can be described as disadvantaged, but those on social classes IV and V can reasonably be, and generally are, so regarded.

There are, furthermore, some technical objections to the use of this term. For the purpose of this study, the most important are two – periodic changes in the classification of occupations, and the changing size of classes. These changes tend to distort comparison over a long period (Illsley, 1986; Jones and Cameron, 1984). But their effect can be overcome (Wagstaff and others, 1991; Davey Smith and others, 1992; Wilkinson, 1986a and 1986b). They are not a significant problem, though, in the relatively short period of this study.

Outline of Part II

Chapter 3 will examine social class variations in children's health since 1979; it will conclude with a discussion of factors underlying these variations in the context of the relationship between social class and deprivation. Chapter 4 will review the evidence linking discrete aspects of children's experience of deprivation with their health, such as living in unemployed or low paid families in poor housing conditions. Chapter 5 will conclude the discussion in Part II by relating the rise in deprivation since 1979 to children's education, looking specifically at outcomes and access to opportunities.

Note

1. These two indicators are generally used by the OPCS in the classification of data in their surveys, especially in subject areas such as health or housing. However, in educational research, other proxy indicators are more common, such as free school meals or ability (see chapter 5).

3. Social class, deprivation and children's health

Introduction

This chapter will examine social class variations in children's health since 1979, using several indicators of health: mortality, morbidity, 'quality of health' measures such as dental health, growth and nutrition, obesity and diet. It will also review briefly evidence about access to health care services, looking in particular at GP consultations, take-up of immunisation and hospital attendance and admissions. Finally, it will consider various explanations for the generation and maintenance of social class inequalities and their relationship to deprivation.

Definition of health

Health is a state of complete physical, mental and social well-being and not merely the absence of disease or infirmity.
(World Health Organisation)

'Health' is not a simple concept – it means different things to different people, depending on their perspective. But these differences are important, for different definitions carry different implications for policy, approach to measurement and for our understanding of the underlying causes of 'ill-health'. Traditionally, in the medical model of health, this term denotes 'absence of disease'. This is now widely regarded as a fairly limited as well as a negative perspective, when contrasted with the definition of the World Health Organisation (WHO) quoted above.

The WHO definition around which a consensus is emerging, embodies a positive concept of health as a resource for everyday life, emphasising 'social and personal resources as well as physical capacities' (Whitehead, 1992, p223). When so defined, health has '...substantial sociological dimensions and individuals' opinions of their state of health depend greatly on the society they live in and their circumstances within it' (Enfield Health Authority, 1990). This definition also emphasises that attainment of good health depends on a much broader range of activities than the services which health authorities normally provide. It draws attention to the fact that causes of ill-health may lie in the wider socio-economic conditions prevailing in society and the social structure underpinning those conditions. This raises the question whether everyone has a fair opportunity or an equitable chance to attain his or her full health potential, or, are there groups in society who are so disadvantaged that their ability to achieve good health is adversely affected? In other words, does membership of, for example, a particular social class, gender, ethnic or age group affect one's chances of achieving good health? And, do these differences reflect an unacceptable degree of inequality (deprivation) such that some groups fall below the average or below a reasonable minimum?[1] There is a distinction here between inequalities in health on the one hand, and the deprivation threshold of health on the other with quite different policy implications (Whitehead, 1992).

Importance of children's health

The health of children is of major importance not only in its own right but also as a determinant of adult health and of the health of the next generation.
(Department of Health, 1990a)

This view of the importance of children's health is well supported by research, some of it reviewed in the paper from which the above quotation is reproduced. Although deaths in childhood account for only about 1.5 per cent of total deaths annually, its importance is far greater when judged in terms of the total number of years of potential life lost as compared to say someone dying in adulthood, especially after the age of 65. Estimates of 'working life' lost between the ages of 15 and 64 years indicate that deaths in childhood constitute about a quarter of all deaths (26 per cent) (Department of Health, 1990a).

Measurement of health

It is important to distinguish here between (absence of) disease as defined and diagnosed by doctors, and (absence of) illness reported by lay members of the public, since different kinds of data are used to measure health defined in these two different ways (Kings College School of Medicine and Dentistry, 1986). It is possible to be suffering from a disease without feeling any symptoms of distress, just as one can feel ill without having any disease. Traditionally, in the medical model of health, doctors have used several indicators for measuring health outcomes: mortality (death), morbidity (prevalence or incidence of disease) and the Standardised Mortality Ratio (SMR) (the ratio of the observed death rates at different ages within a particular social group to the expected death rates, based on the age-specific death rates of a standard population). Disease may be short-term and acute, restricting one's activities; or long-term and chronic, although the distinction does not always hold in practice (Townsend, 1992). However, during the last ten years attempts have been made to tap other, more positive, dimensions of health, incorporating different 'quality-of-life' measures, such as people's subjective experience of symptoms of ill-health, as, for instance, in the Health and Life-style Survey (Cox and others, 1987). Despite some scepticism from the medical profession about the validity of such health measures based on a lay person's own experience, there is a high degree of agreement between these and the medical assessments using more formal procedures (Whitehead, 1992).

When using mortality data to measure child health, it is usual to present data in different age ranges: under one year of age (infant mortality); 1 to 4; 5 to 9; 10 to 14; and 15 to 19. Infant mortality is subdivided into the following categories:

- **Still births**: Late foetal deaths after 28 weeks of gestation.
- **Perinatal mortality**: still births, and deaths in the first week of life.
- **Early neonatal mortality**: deaths in the first six days of life.
- **Late neonatal mortality**: deaths at ages 7-27 completed days of life.
- **Postneonatal mortality**: deaths at ages 28 days and over but under one year.

Infant mortality

Mortality data are well documented and analysed historically so that one can trace long-term trends; and since 1975, the birth and death registrations have been linked, so overcoming the numerator-denominator bias arising from obtaining information about occupation from two different sources.[2] Although the tip of the iceberg in terms of ill-health, mortality experience '...reflects the cumulative multifactorial interaction of social and biological factors over time' (Balarajan, 1986, p.913). Trends in mortality have been one of the most important indicators of the health of a nation's children (Pharoah, 1986).

This is even more so for infant mortality, which in 1989 accounted for nearly three-quarters (72.5 per cent) of all deaths in childhood (under 15 years of age); and two-fifths occurred in the first four weeks of a baby's life (DH, 1990a).

Trends in infant mortality

There has been a steady decline in infant mortality in the postwar period. However, in the eighties, the rate of decline slowed down somewhat (Figure 3.1 and Table 3.1), especially the rate for perinatal mortality; however, the postneonatal mortality rate remained quite stable between 1976 and 1988, but showed a decline in 1989 and 1990.

It may be that the infant mortality rate is difficult to reduce beyond a certain point (Bradshaw, 1990), but there may be room for improvement still, since the UK rate is significantly above that of a number of other European countries. In 1989, the UK rate (8.4) was higher than that in Austria, Denmark, Finland, France, Germany, Holland, Ireland, Italy, Norway, Sweden and Switzerland (*Hansard* 17.12.1991, col. 126-29). Likewise, other countries are achieving between 20 to 25 per cent better rates in perinatal mortality; on this basis, about 1,200 fewer babies would have died in England in 1987 if it had achieved the Swedish rate (Committee of Public Accounts, 1990; National Audit Office, 1990).

Variations in infant mortality

Despite progress in recent decades in reducing the UK rate for infant mortality, there remain wide differentials between different regions, ethnic groups and social classes.

Regional variations   Figure 3.2 and Table 3.2 give details of infant mortality according to the standard regions and countries of the UK. The lowest rate (6.8)

Table 3.1   UK Vital statistics for children under one year 1971-1991

	Infant mortality rate+	Postneonatal** mortality rate+	Neonatal mortality rate+	Perinatal mortality rate++	Still birth rate++
1971	17.9	NA	12.0	22.6	12.6
1976	14.5	4.4	9.9	18.0	9.7
1981	11.2	4.3	6.7	12.0	6.6
1983	10.2	4.2	5.9	10.5	5.8
1984	9.6	3.8	5.7	10.2	5.7
1985	9.4	3.9	5.4	9.9	5.5
1986	9.5	4.2	5.3	9.6	5.3
1987	9.1	4.0	5.0	9.0	5.0
1988	9.0	4.0	4.9	8.8	4.9
1989	8.4	3.6	4.7	8.3	4.9
1990*	7.9	3.2	4.5	8.1	4.6**
1991* (Sept)	7.5	NA	4.4	8.1	NA

Source: Population Trends 67 Spring 1992; OPCS (1992) Mortality Statistics 1990

+ Per 1,000 live births. ++ Per 1,000 live and still births. * Provisional.
** England & Wales only.
NA= Not Available.

Figure 3.1   UK vital statistics

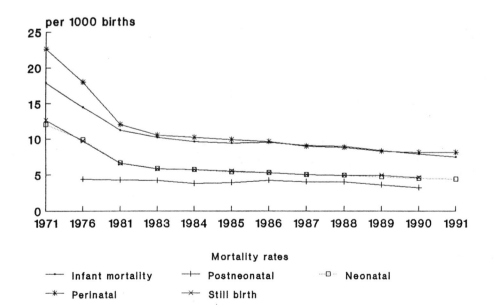

Source: Population Trends Spring 1992

Table 3.2   Infant mortality by region and by mother's country of birth in the UK 1990

a) Infant mortality by region 1990		*b) Infant mortality by mother's country of birth 1990*	
Region	*Rate	Country of Birth of Mother	*Rate
North	7.9	United Kingdom	7.5
Yorkshire/Humberside	8.9	Irish Republic	7.2
East Midlands	7.8	Australia/Canada/New Zealand	7.3
East Anglia	6.9	Bangladesh	5.5
South East	7.2	India	7.4
South West	6.8	Pakistan	14.2
West Midlands	9.9	East Africa	7.6
North West	8.2	Rest of Africa	9.9
Wales	6.9	Caribbean Commonwealth	12.6
Scotland	7.7	Mediterranean Commonwealth	9.8
Northern Ireland	7.5	Rest of New Commonwealth	8.5
		Remainder of Europe	7.9

Source: Regional Trends 1992   *Source: OPCS (1992) Mortality statistics 1990*

* Deaths of infants under 1 year of age per 1000 live births

Figure 3.2   Infant mortality 1990 regional trends

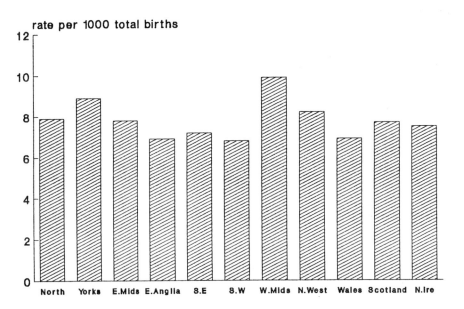

Source: Regional Trends, 1992

is in the South West and the highest in the West Midlands (9.9). In the same vein, the report by the Comptroller and Auditor General (CCAG) had earlier noted wide variations in perinatal mortality in different regional health authorities and Boards during the period 1986-88; it showed that the rate in Bradford (13.5) was more than two and a half times the rate in Huntingdon (5.1) (1990). If the Hungtingdon rate could be achieved in England as a whole, then, according to the Government's own calculations, 5,731 babies' lives could have been saved in the first week in 1988, and another 3,220 lives in the first four weeks (Public Accounts Committee, 1990).

Regional variations in indicators of health outcome reflect in part differences in both the ethnic and social class make up of their populations. Health districts with exceptionally high infant mortality rates tended to have above average proportions of mothers born in the New Commonwealth and Pakistan (NCWP), and above average proportions of fathers in social classes IV and V; they also tended to have a low proportion of social class I or II households (Britton, 1989).

Ethnic variations in infant mortality   Rates of infant mortality vary widely according to ethnic origin based on the mother's country of birth.[3] Trend analysis of this data based on three-year moving averages for the period 1981-89 by the OPCS (1992) shows that infant mortality rates among people of NCWP origins have been consistently and substantially above the UK rates throughout the eighties. There is also considerable variation among the different minority ethnic groups. The infant mortality rate for those of Pakistani origin, for instance, is nearly twice the UK rate, closely followed by the rate for those from the Caribbean Commonwealth (12.5), whereas the rate for those of Indian origin is at par with the UK rate, but significantly lower for those born in Bangladesh (Figure 3.3 and Table 3.2).

Figure 3.3   Infant mortality 1990 by country of birth of mother

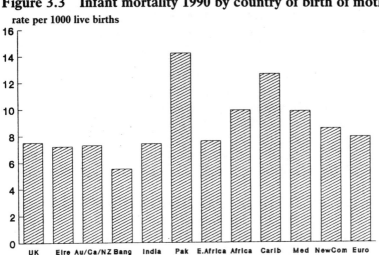

Source: OPCS (1992) *Mortality Statistics* 1990

The reasons for these variations are not clear, for they cannot be explained simply in terms of differences in their relative socio-economic position. However, the picture is quite different if one looks at data relating to different *stages* during the first year of life for the period 1982-85 (Figure 3.4).

Children born to mothers of Pakistani and, to a large extent, Caribbean and West African mothers, have a substantially higher mortality rate in all the four periods of infancy. Among other minority ethnic groups, however, the differences are generally larger in the perinatal period than in the postneonatal period, and not always in the same direction. Whereas in the perinatal, and to a lesser extent, neonatal period minority groups generally tend to have a higher mortality rate than UK-born mothers; in the postneonatal period, several of them (people of Bangladeshi and African origin) have lower than the UK rate. Again, reasons for these differences are not fully understood.

For all groups of NCWP origin, differences in infant mortality are even more marked at the DHA level, with rates ranging from 9.6 to 19 per 1,000 live births (Balarajan and Raleigh, 1990).

Social class variations in infant mortality   There has long been a strong class gradient in health, however measured, in almost all age bands (Power and others, 1991). Table 3.3 gives, for 1990, a breakdown according to father's social class of deaths in the first year of life.

A baby from a household headed by an 'unskilled' father (class V) is twice as likely to die in the first year, as a baby from a household head who is a professional (class I). Stillbirths and deaths in the first month are one and a half times as likely, and postneonatal deaths are two and a half times as likely, in social class V as in professional families. This is likely to be a considerable understatement of the class differential, since it relates to births within marriage only. In 1990, 28 per cent of births took place outside marriage and the infant mortality rate in these babies was one and a half time greater still than that of births within marriage. This is illustrated by the fact that, for the 1988-90 period, the infant mortality rate increased from 7.3 for births within marriage to 7.9 when births outside marriage were included in the analysis (*Mortality Statistics*, 1990, Table B).

Are social class variations in mortality widening?   There are two ways in which the trend in social class related mortality can be examined: the trend in differentials within age-groups, and the trend across age-groups. The policy implications will clearly differ, depending on the persistence or not of inequities in particular age-groups, and/or through the different stages of childhood. One should be aware here of the possible effect on these trends of the changes in the occupational classification from which social class is derived; the last change took place in 1978-79.

In infant mortality, the social class differential (between class V and I) widened from 2.2 during 1949-53 to 2.6 during 1970-72, but by 1978-79, it had come down to 1.8 (Townsend and Davidson, 1982); however, by 1990, it had increased to 2.0 (Table 3.3). But this analysis is based on births **within** marriage and, as shown above, no longer gives a full picture. Table 3.4 gives a breakdown of recent infant mortality data, based on three-year moving averages and covering births within and outside marriage (**jointly** registered). It shows a rise in the class V/I ratio from 1.73 during 1987-88 to 1.89 in the period 1988-90.

Figure 3.4   Mortality rates among under one-year-olds by mother's country of birth

Infant mortality

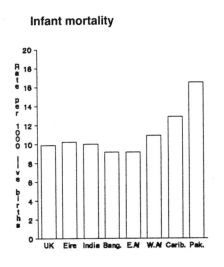

Perinatal mortality

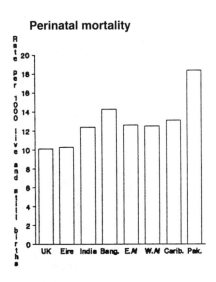

Neonatal mortality

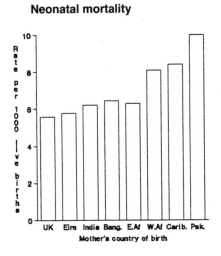

Postneonatal mortality

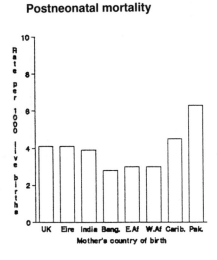

Source: Population Trends 56 1989

Table 3.3 Deaths during the first year by father's social class* for the period 1978-1990 England and Wales (for births within marriage only)

Social class	Still births +Rate	1990				1978-1987			
		Perinatal deaths +Rate	Neonatal deaths ++Rate	Post-neonatal ++Rate	Infant deaths ++Rate	Perinatal deaths +Rate 1978	1987	Neonatal deaths ++Rate 1978	1987
All	4.3	7.4	4.1	2.6	6.7	14.8	8.2	8.3	4.7
I-V	4.3	7.4	4.0	2.5	6.5	-	-	-	-
I	3.6	6.6	3.6	2.0	5.6	11.9	6.8	6.8	3.9
II	3.4	6.0	3.3	2.0	5.3	12.3	7.0	7.0	4.1
III N	4.1	7.1	4.0	2.3	6.4	13.9	7.8	7.9	4.4
III M	4.4	7.6	4.1	2.4	6.5	15.1	8.1	8.1	4.5
IV	5.7	9.5	4.8	3.5	8.3	16.7	9.9	9.3	5.6
V	5.6	9.6	5.8	5.4	11.2	20.3	10.8	10.1	5.9
Other	4.9	9.1	5.9	4.6	10.5	20.4	9.9	14.4	6.8
Ratio V/I	1.56	1.45	1.61	2.7	2.0	1.71	1.59	1.49	1.51

Source: OPCS (1992) *Mortality Statistics 1990.*

* as defined by occupation at death registration
+ Rate per 1,000 total births (live and still)
++ Rate per 1,000 live births

Source: Public Accounts Committee
(1990) *Appendix 1.*

**Table 3.4   Infant deaths by father's social class††† – England and Wales –
1987-1990 (within and, jointly registered outside, marriage)**

Social class	1987-88++ Rate*	1987-89† Rate*	1988-90† Rate*
All	8.5	8.3	7.9
I	7.0	6.7	6.2
II	6.7	6.6	6.2
III N	7.3	7.3	7.1
III M	8.3	8.0	7.6
IV	9.9	10.0	9.5
V	12.1	11.8	11.7
Ratio V/I	1.73	1.76	1.89
Other	13.8	13.7	14.3

Source: OPCS: *Mortality Statistics 1988, 1989 and 1990*
  * Per 1,000 live births
  † three-year average
  ++ two-year average
  ††† as defined by occupation at death registration

These ratios probably understate the differences between babies with the highest and the lowest risk of death as two important categories are not included: babies born outside marriage whose birth is registered by the mother alone, and babies in the 'other' category. Although the mortality rate for babies born outside marriage and registered by the mother alone is 80 per cent higher than for babies born within marriage (*Mortality Statistics*, 1990), no social class breakdown is available. The 'other'[4] category shown in official statistics (Table 3.3 and 3.4) contains several disparate groups such as 'inadequately described' who have 'an exceptionally good mortality record', and others who are 'unoccupied'; the latter is larger in size than social class I or V and has a mortality record 'not only worse than that of social class I by a factor of 3 but...also 42 per cent worse than social class V' (Judge and Benzeval, 1993a).

Two conclusions can be drawn from the above discussion. Firstly, the social class differential in infant mortality is likely to be significantly greater than that revealed by official statistics, if *all* births, within and outside marriage, including those in the 'other' category properly differentiated, are analysed together rather than separately as at present. Secondly, social class differentials (between class V and I) in infant mortality had widened in the eighties for births within marriage; these had also widened in the second half of the eighties when jointly registered births outside marriage are included. The trend throughout the eighties will not be known until the social class breakdown of the relevant data is published.

During the perinatal and neonatal phases of infancy, data for the period 1978-1990 are again available only for **births within marriage** (Table 3.3). The ratio between social classes V and I is shown to decline from 1.71 to 1.45 for perinatal deaths, but for neonatal deaths, it increases from 1.49 to 1.61 – subject to the same limitations discussed above for infant mortality.

For postneonatal mortality, Rodrigues and Botting (1989) have argued that differences between social classes I and V have narrowed for children born within as well as for those born outside marriage and, in the latter case, both whether the birth was registered jointly by the two parents or singly by one.

A number of observations arise from their article. The postneonatal mortality ratio between classes V and I has since increased from 1.8 in 1986 to 2.7 in 1990 (Table 3.3). Even prior to 1986, there was a significant fluctuation: it increased from 2.4 in 1979 to 2.7 in 1984, before falling to 1.8 in 1986; the ratio between 'others' and social class I also increased from 2.1 in 1986 to 2.3 in 1990. The ratio between social classes V and I in postneonatal mortality for jointly registered births outside marriage fell dramatically from 6.2 in 1979 to 1.6 in 1980, jumped to 3.3 in 1981, fell to 0.9 in 1983, rose to 1.9 in 1984, and fell again to 0.7 in 1986.[5] This reflects considerable volatility in the rate for social class I and makes the reliability of these results somewhat suspect. Analysis based on three-year moving average is likely to be more reliable. Rodrigues and Botting (1989) do provide in their article a graph illustrating the combined information on postneonatal deaths for births within marriage and for jointly registered births outside marriage, based on three-year moving averages; however, in the absence of any data accompanying this graph, it is difficult to work out precisely the effect on social class differentials over time. Finally, as already mentioned in our discussion of social class differentials in infant mortality, to gain a full and reliable picture, such an analysis needs to be based, in our view, on *all* births. It is pertinent to point out here that recent evidence shows that, when data relating to births outside marriage is included, the decline in the social class differential in postneonatal mortality in the 1970s disappears (Pamuk, 1988).

Social class variations in child mortality

Social class breakdown of data for child (1 to 15) mortality are yet available only for the years 1979-80 and 1982-83 (OPCS, 1988). A reanalysis of this data by Judge and Benzeval (1993a) is reproduced in Table 3.5. In the original OPCS analysis, 'unoccupied' formed part of the wider category, 'other', which included, in addition, two other groups: armed forces and 'inadequately described'. However, the mortality experience of these three disparate groups differed widely - their age-specific death rates (per 100,000 per year) during this period were 68.8, 28.4 and 13.2 respectively. As already mentioned above, the mortality record of the 'unoccupied' was the worst of all (three times that of social class I and 42 per cent worse than for social class V); that of the armed forces' children was about average, while that of the 'inadequately described' was exceptionally good. (Judge and Benzeval, 1993a).

Table 3.5 shows the effect on social class differentials in child mortality of excluding the 'unoccupied category', constituting six per cent of all children in 1981 census (as has been the OPCS practice to date); and of including it, combining it with social classes IV and V and comparing their experience of mortality with children from social classes I and II. This is illustrated graphically on the left and right hand side of figure 3.5 respectively.

Figure 3.5 **Relative risk of child mortality by social class and age: 1979, 1980, 1982, 1983 England and Wales**

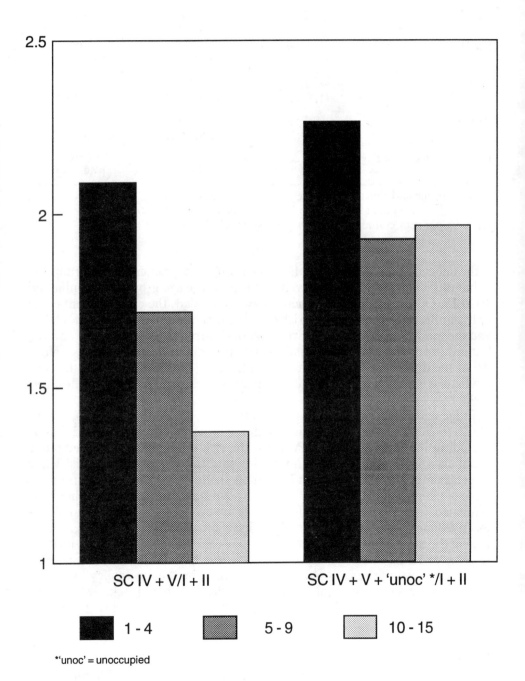

*"unoc' = unoccupied

Source: Judge and Benzeval (1993a)

Table 3.5   Relative risk of child mortality by social class and age England and Wales 1979, 1980, 1982, 1983

Social class	1-4	Age Bands 5-9	10-15
I & II	1.00 (0.83,1.21)	1.00 (0.80,1.25)	1.00 (0.84,1.20)
IV & V	2.08 (1.75,2.49)	1.71 (1.39,2.12)	1.37 (1.14,1.64)
'Unoccupied'	2.58 (2.07,3.22)	2.56 (1.98,3.30)	4.14 (3.43,4.99)
IV, V & 'unoccupied'	2.21 (1.88,2.61)	1.93 (1.59,2.35)	1.98 (1.69,2.32)

Source: Judge and Benzeval (1993a)
(Based on data from OPCS (1988) *Decennial Supplement*)
Note: 95 per cent confidence intervals are shown in brackets.

If the unoccupied are excluded, there is a strong class gradient at age-group 1 to 4, but this is weakened progressively as one moves to age-groups five to nine and 10 to 15. On the other hand, when they are included, the class gradient is not only significantly stronger – the risk of dying for children in social classes IV, V and the 'unoccupied' is at least twice that of children in social classes 1 and II – but is more or less consistently maintained throughout the one to 15 age-range. All of the differences are statistically significant. This indicates that the class gradient is more significant than is generally assumed (West and colleagues, 1990).

Judge and Benzeval argue that it is unhelpful, if not disingenuous, for the OPCS to combine the 'unoccupied' with the other two categories; and that by excluding the 'unoccupied', OPCS run the risk of significantly understating social class inequalities in child mortality, and thereby creating a misleading impression of the class gradient becoming shallower as one moves from one stage of childhood to the next, as argued by West and others (1990). They have estimated that 90 per cent of the people in this category are economically inactive lone parent families who, as we have already observed (chapter 2), are among the most disadvantaged. Finally, they conclude that, if their estimate of the size of LPFs in this group is correct – it is based on a set of apparently reasonable assumptions – 'the implications for health policy are profound...strategies to promote the nation's health should acknowledge the importance of material and social deprivation move explicitly' (Judge and Benzeval, 1993a).

Child morbidity

Mortality data are useful as a **summary** measure of a nation's health but they do not tell us much about ill-health or 'health' *per se* among children. As survival improves, the quality of life assumes greater importance. Although life expectancy for children has improved by about two years in the eighties (*Population Trends*, 69, 1992) there is some indication that this has been achieved at the expense of increased disability and suffering (Bebbington, 1991). Accurate information on the prevalence of disease among children is however hard to come by, and often cannot be related to socio-economic conditions.

Trends in child morbidity

Data based on the General Household Survey (GHS) (Table 3.6) shows an unmistakeable rising trend between 1976 and 1988 in disability reported in boys and girls in the age groups 0 to four and five to 14.

Table 3.6   Trend in disability (estimated)* among children at home and in institutions by age and sex in Great Britain 1976-88

Year	Total Disabled Overall rate of disability	Boys		Girls	
		0-4	5-14	0-4	5-14
1976	No	36,700	248,800	26,800	184,300
	Rate	2.2	6.1	1.7	4.8
1981	No	46,600	293,100	44,100	208,100
	Rate	3.0	8.1	3.0	6.0
1985	No	64,900	263,100	46,300	186,600
	Rate	4.0	8.1	3.0	6.0
1988	No	67,500	284,400	48,200	209,200
	Rate	4.0	9.0	3.0	7.0

Source: Bebbington (1991)
    * Based on numbers in the General Household Survey and in institutions

A more differentiated picture of morbidity among children under 16 in the period 1979-90 is given in Table 3.7 and Figure 3.6. The prevalence of longstanding illness, whether limiting or not, has risen consistently over this period in both the age-groups.

The curve for 'limiting longstanding illness' – that is chronic illness which limits one's activities in any way – is more stable by comparison. The 'restricted activity' curves show no discernible trend.

One reason for the rising incidence of morbidity among children is that major advances in the medical care in the neonatal period have meant that an increasing proportion of infants are now surviving who previously would have died, but with congenital abnormalities (Pharoah, 1986).

Infectious diseases also contribute both to mortality and morbidity among children. 'Recent patterns of morbidity in childhood have been profoundly affected...by changes in incidence, notably of infectious diseases...' (Pharoah, 1986 p.125). Infectious diseases still cause an estimated 10 per cent of deaths in

Figure 3.6 Trends in parentally-reported morbidity in children 1979–90

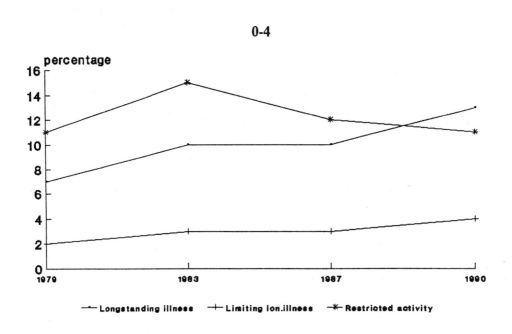

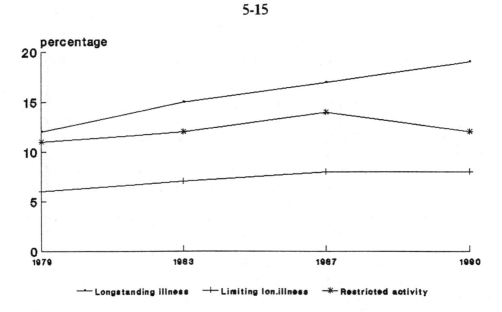

Source: OPCS: *General Household Surveys* 1989, 1990

Table 3.7   Trends in parentally-reported morbidity in children in Great Britain 1979-90

Percentage	0-4				5-15			
	1979	1983	1987	1990	1979	1983	1987	1990
a) Longstanding illness								
Male	8	11	10	14	14	17	19	20
Female	6	9	10	12	10	13	15	17
All persons	7	10	10	13	12	15	17	19
b) Limiting longstanding illness								
Male	2	3	4	5	7	8	8	9
Female	2	2	3	3	5	6	8	7
All persons	2	3	3	4	6	7	8	8
c) Restricted activity								
Male	12	15	13	13	11	12	13	11
Female	10	14	11	10	11	11	14	13
All persons	11	15	12	11	11	12	14	12

Source: OPCS *General Household Surveys, 1989, 1990* (Preliminary results)

Table 3.8   Childhood morbidity (parentally-reported) 0 to 15 in Great Britain 1985-89

Social Class	Males (N=13,949)			Females (N=13,499)		
	Chronic	Limiting	Acute	Chronic	Limiting	Acute
	%	%	%	%	%	%
I	14.7	5.5	10.9	11.8	3.4	14.4
II	15.5	6.3	11.4	13.7	5.0	11.6
III non-manual	17.4	6.4	13.0	13.0	5.0	13.2
III manual	17.4	7.4	12.0	13.8	5.8	12.4
IV	19.3	9.5	13.3	14.5	5.4	11.1
V	21.4	9.5	13.3	13.8	6.3	12.4
Ratio V/I	1.46	1.73	1.22	1.17	1.85	0.86
All persons	17.2	7.4	12.2	13.4	5.2	12.2

Source: Judge and Benzeval (1993b): Based on data from the *General Household Surveys*, 1985-1989

children aged 0 to 15 years. Given considerable under-reporting, their true impact on children's health is difficult to assess (Hall, 1986).

Social class variations in child morbidity

The General Household Survey provides a fruitful source for investigating the class gradient in childhood morbidity, as indeed it has been used in the past for adult health (Black Report, 1980; Whitehead, 1987). Data on children's health, based on parental reports, for the period 1985-89 are shown in Table 3.8.

The class gradient is not as strong; it is consistent for boys but less so for girls. For boys, the ratio between social class V/I is quite strong for chronic (1.46) and limiting (1.73) illness, but less so for acute (1.22) illness. For girls, it is strong for limiting (1.85), but weak for chronic (1.17) illness; however, the correlation is reversed in the case of acute (0.86) illness.

Two points need to be borne in mind in interpreting this table. The exclusion of 'unoccupied' people means that this data set suffers from the same limitations discussed earlier in relation to social class differentials in infant mortality. There is also the problem here of the differential parental reporting of ill-health which itself has a class gradient – the tendency to under-represent morbidity among mothers in lower ranked social classes (Blaxter, 1990).

Since morbidity statistics reflect the extent, and a particular pattern, of use of services, which is influenced by a host of social and other factors, they 'offer a largely incomplete picture of health status and health problems in children and adolescents' (Kurtz, 1992); this is particularly the case about the health of deprived families and those who live in the inner city (Carstairs, 1981).

Disability and social class

While good data about the incidence of disability among children is available, reliable estimates about the relationship with social class are hard to find. A representative national survey by the OPCS in the mid-eighties estimated that there were 360,000 children with disabilities in Great Britain, of whom 5,600 were living in residential institutions. This constitutes 3.2 per cent of the under-16 population (Bone and Meltzer, 1989). However, given the research design of their survey, it was not possible to establish if there was any association between a parent's occupational status and the probability of having a child with a disability. However, other things being equal, given a rising trend in childhood disability, and the not inconsiderable cost of bringing up a child with a disability (frequently involving one of the parents – usually the mother – giving up work), such children are likely to be worse off materially in comparison with their peers (Baldwin, 1985). The OPCS survey found that adults with a disability tended to have lower standards of living (Martin and White, 1988), and this would affect their children.

Summary

In the last two sections, trends in mortality and morbidity were reviewed. A steady decline in infant mortality in the postwar period slowed down in the 1980s. There was a strong social class gradient in that babies from homes in social classes IV and V were twice as likely to die in the first year as those from professional homes.[6] Likewise, infant mortality rates were consistently and significantly higher among children from minority ethnic group backgrounds. Thus regional variations reflect in part these social class and ethnic variations in mortality.

Evidence suggests that social class differentials had widened especially in the second half of the eighties against the background of rising child poverty. Between 1978-79 and 1990, the ratio in infant mortality for births within marriage between social classes V and I had increased from 1.8 to 2.0. Except for mortality in the first week of life (when the social class differential decreased from 1.71 in 1978 to 1.45 in 1990), there was an increase in disparity between social classes for neonatal (from 1.49 in 1978 to 1.6 in 1990) and postneonatal mortality (from 1.8 in 1986 to 2.7 in 1990).

There is likewise a strong social class gradient in child mortality (one to 15), but the way official statistics are compiled at the moment, a misleading impression is created that these class inequalities are weakened as one moves from the one to five to 10-15 age-groups.

The disparity in mortality between social classes is likely to be even greater if **all** births are included in the analysis (that is, not just within marriage), including those in the 'unoccupied' component in the 'other' category, who are the most disadvantaged groups.

The improvement in life expectancy for children since 1979 has been gained at the cost of increased morbidity and disability, as there is a consistently rising trend in both these outcome measures. The class gradient is significant, but less strong: it is consistent for boys, but less so for girls. This data set also suffers from the same limitations discussed above in relation to inequality in child mortality. There is also a possibility that this data underrepresents mothers in lower social classes due to underreporting of their children's illness.

According to a representative national survey, there were 360,000 children with disabilities in Great Britain (GB) in 1985. In the context of a rising trend in disability, such children are likely to be worse off materially because of the additional cost of bringing up children with a disability.

Quality of children's health

Dental health among children

There was a distinct improvement in the dental health of children in the decade up to 1983, according to the two OPCS dental health surveys conducted in 1973 and 1983. The decrease in the proportion of children with dental caries was particularly marked for the five-year-olds, falling from 73 to 48 per cent. Improvements were found in all ages between five and 15 and in all regions in England and Wales. However, in 1983, about half of the children entering school still had some decayed teeth and both the proportion of **children** with dental caries, as well as the average number of decayed **teeth** per child, tended to rise quite sharply with age between 5 and 15 years. In both these respects, there were wide variations between the four countries of the UK, and between the different regions in England (OPCS, 1985).

Other surveys conducted by the British Association for the Study of Dentistry in the mid-1980s found no significant change nationally between 1983 and 1985-86 for the five-year-olds, but an accelerated decline in caries in the 14-year-olds in 1986-87 (DH, 1990). It appears that the decline in caries in young children is levelling out, judging by the fact that dental inspections of under fives for the last two years (1988-89 and 1989-90) revealed the same figure of 40 per cent as requiring treatment. The rate may actually be higher since the number of inspections carried out was down by 3.3 per cent over the last year (DH, 1991a).

Earlier research by Carmichael and others (1989) in Newcastle and Northumberland reported a relationship between social class and caries in five-year-olds – 'The percentage of subjects with caries experience was substantially higher in Social Classes IV and V than in social classes I and II'. Interestingly, the fluoridation of water supply helped reduce these differentials by benefiting children in social classes IV and V. However, a small increase in caries was found between 1981 and 1987 in all categories of the five-year-olds in the Newcastle study.

Persisting regional and social class variations are corroborated by the latest report of the Chief Medical Officer (CMO), *On the State of the Public Health for the Year 1990* (1991). Whereas seven RHAs in England showed an improvement in the dental caries experience of five-year-olds between 1987-88 and 1989-90, there was a deterioration in the remaining RHAs (all in the north of England), as well as in Wales and Scotland. For example, the mean number of decayed, missing and filled primary teeth in five-year-old children in the North Western Region (2.64) is more than twice that in South West Thames (1.14). The report also indicates a strong class gradient:

The statistics conceal some polarisation of the severity of disease, with those children from social classes III M*(manual), IV and V, and from deprived backgrounds, having appreciably higher levels of untreated caries. There is also evidence to show that there is a high level (up to 8 to 10 per cent) of rampant caries in pre-school children in some Districts (p.194).

It was reported by the CMO that the number of inspections carried out on children under five fell by 3.3 per cent in the previous year, and in children at school by 6.2 per cent.

Trends in growth and nutrition of children

National information on height is available mainly from two sources: the National Study of Health and Growth (NSHG) and from three national birth cohort studies (1946, 1958 and 1970). The NSHG survey of English and Scottish primary school children (4.5 to 11.5 years), which has been in operation since 1972, identified an underlying trend towards taller children between 1972 and 1979. However, estimates for the 1979-86 period showed that 'the trend towards increased height in five to 11 year-old children has now ceased' (Chinn, Rona and Price, 1989). This has apparently been confirmed by other evidence from the DES (Carr-Hill, 1986).

The 1946 and 1958 national birth cohort studies included measurements of height and weight at different ages during childhood, and showed consistent social class differences in height – children of fathers in manual occupations were generally shorter than those with fathers in non-manual occupations. A recent Department of Health survey of the *Diets of British School Children* (1989) found that children from families with an unemployed father, or drawing benefits, were significantly shorter. It has long been recognised that there is a social class gradient in adult height in this country. The British Regional Heart Study identified a class difference in mean height among men born between 1919 and 1939 (Walker and others, 1988); and, significantly, the analysis of the 1980 OPCS survey data (Knight, 1984) by Carr-Hill found 'no discernible narrowing either of the overall distribution or of the gap between social classes' in height at age 20 between 1940 and 1980 (1988).

The NSHG sample was enhanced in 1983 to include data on children from inner cities and minority ethnic groups. The findings indicate that African Caribbean children were on average taller than all other groups, while children from other minority ethnic groups and White inner city children were shorter as compared to the wider 1982 representative national sample (DH, 1990a). What is significant is that the social class differentials still remain in the 1980s, not only in height of adults but also in that of children, despite general improvement in living standards over the last half a century.

Obesity among children

Obesity is now a well recognised health hazard, linked to a number of diseases such as diabetes, high blood pressure, strokes and early death and aggravates many other health problems (Royal College of Physicians, 1983; Garrow, 1991). Professor Garrow, a specialist in nutrition and obesity, believes that the best time to prevent obesity is between the ages of seven and 12.

There is evidence to suggest that obesity in British children has increased in recent years (National Children's Bureau, 1987), and that it may be more prevalent among children in this country, as compared to some other European countries (Stark and others, 1986). Although social class differences are not obvious at younger ages (Rona and Chinn, 1982; Peckam and others, 1983), they become well established by middle age (Knight, 1984; Weatherall and Sharper, 1988).

Diet and children's health

Growth, under-nutrition, as well as obesity and other aspects of children's health are closely related to their diet:

The links between nutrition and health are many and varied, ranging from effects on growth to links with specific diseases like coronary heart disease and obesity, to general resistance to infections, most of which are also class-related (Whitehead, 1987, p.66).

There is growing evidence to justify the concern about children's diet in the eighties and nineties. The most important evidence comes from a national survey of diets of British school children sponsored by the Department of Health, in keeping with the Government's undertaking to Parliament in 1980 to monitor the effects of its new policy whereby the price controls and nutritional guidelines on school meals were abolished under the 1980 Education Act. The survey was conducted by the OPCS in 1983; the preliminary findings were reported in 1986 and the main ones in 1989.

The survey found that the main sources of dietary energy for British schoolchildren were bread, chips, milk, biscuits, meat products, cakes and puddings. Three-quarters of the child population's fat intake was higher than the officially recommended level, drawn mainly from chips and milk. The consumption of these two items was influenced most by social class and socio-economic variables: chips being consumed more by children from social classes IV and V, families with an unemployed father and those on Supplementary Benefit (now Income Support) and free school meals. On the other hand, the consumption of milk – an important source of calcium and other nutrients – was lower among most of these groups (DH, 1989). The survey also found that the intake of riboflavin, calcium and iron among girls was below the recommended level, and Scottish primary school children had lower average intakes of vitamin C, B-carotene and retinol (DH, 1989; White and others, 1992). A longitudinal study of 405 Northumberland children, average age 11.5 years, by Hackett and others, found that iron, calcium and protein intakes tended to be very low among children from economically deprived homes (1984).

In Leicester the diet of Asian children was found to be deficient in iron and vitamin D (Pearson and others, 1979). Surprisingly, however, the DH survey had nothing to say about the dietary patterns of children from minority ethnic groups, even though they were included in the survey '...in proportion to their numbers in each group in the schools' (p.8). The official explanation is somewhat ambiguous: 'Although there were local concentrations of children from different ethnic groups, the Group on School Meals (DH) advised that the total numbers...were too small for valid, separate analysis (1989, p8). If so, it is not clear why a larger weighted sample could not be obtained in the first place to permit such an analysis.

It was found that, in the absence of nutritional guidelines, school meals made a significant contribution to children's dietary pattern: 'Chips, buns and pastries dominated the weekday lunches of school children' (DH, 1989, p.28). If, as the recent research (Rona and Chinn, 1984; Gardner Merchant, 1991) has shown, many school children, especially the older ones, are still hungry after a school meal, they are more likely to be 'eating high fat, high sugar snacks and sugary drinks in the afternoon' (Holt, 1991). The '...change towards free-choice cafeterias and the need to generate income has resulted in increased provision of fast foods such as burgers, chips and fizzy drinks (White and others, 1992). In addition, the EC subsidy to schools giving discounts on full-fat milk and dairy products including cheese 'make lower fat alternatives prohibitively expensive' (White and others, 1992).

According to research done by Nelson and Paul, even before 1979 the school meals fell short of Government advice on nutritional standards, providing less than one-quarter of the Recommended Daily Amount (RDA) for energy, iron, riboflavin (as against one-third recommended by DES), and less than one-third of the RDA for protein, calcium, thiamin and Vitamin C (as against between one-half to one-third stipulated by DES) (1983). There is no evidence of general improvement in the diet of schoolchildren in the country as a whole, even though there are signs of improvement for children eating school meals in individual local education authorities, such as Northumberland, where these meals have been promoted. Recent studies confirm concerns about deficiencies in children's diets identified in the Government's 1983 survey (Nelson, 1991; Nelson and others, 1990; McNeil, 1991; White and others, 1992).

Importance of school meals

However, school meals '...provided on the whole higher levels of vitamins and minerals than either packed lunches or meals eaten from a cafe or take-away' (White and others, 1992). Other recent research reinforces the importance of a school meal for all children, recognised in 1982 in the seventh report of the Parliamentary Education, Science and Arts Committee. For instance, a survey in 1991 by Gardner Merchant, a catering company, in England and Wales found that about one in nine children go to school without any breakfast; ten years ago, in an earlier study by the National Dairy Council (1982), this figure was one in 20. More recent evidence from the Welsh Health Promotion Authority indicates irregular meal patterns among young people, including missed meals and regular snacking. For instance, more than half of 15 to 16-year-old girls do not eat breakfast every day (White and others, 1992).

School meals are particularly important for children from low-income families. For instance, the Gardner Merchant survey (1991) found that one in six children from low income families did not have an evening meal at home (see also Nelson and Paul, 1983). In addition, the DH (1989) study demonstrated that children from low income families were disproportionately represented among those having school meals, and also drew a larger percentage of their daily nutrients from these meals, as compared to children from higher income groups.

Summary

Despite some improvement in dental health of children in the decade preceding 1983, there were still almost half of five-year-olds entering school with some decayed teeth; and both the proportion as well as the average number of affected teeth per child tended to rise sharply with age between 5 and 15. This improvement appeared to level off by the late 1980s. Evidence suggests that the percentage of children with caries was substantially higher in social classes IV and V than in I and II. There was also considerable regional variation related to deprivation factors.

An underlying trend towards taller children detected in the 1970s had ceased by the mid-eighties; children of unemployed fathers were found to be significantly shorter, as were children from inner cities and minority ethnic groups, except for those of African Caribbean origin. Apparently, the large increase in unemployment and deprivation would appear to be related to this stoppage in growth of children which, in turn, is related to evidence about an unsatisfactory dietary pattern found among the British school children in the 1980s. It was observed that the school meal made a significant contribution to this dietary pattern, particularly among children from low income families following the abolition of the national guidelines on school meals. This dietary pattern also had a social class gradient.

Access to health services and equity

The NHS was founded on the principle that health care should be available to all according to need, irrespective of their income or social status. How has this principle worked out in practice in recent years in so far as children's health needs are concerned? The position will be reviewed briefly in relation to the take-up of immunisation, GP consultation and hospital admissions.

Deprivation and take-up of immunisation

Considerable progress was made in the UK in the 1980s in increasing the take-up of immunisation against major infectious diseases – diphtheria, polio and tetanus, measles, mumps and rubella, and whooping cough (*Social Trends*, 1992). Nevertheless, there were significant regional variations. For instance, Wales and Scotland had reached the WHO target of 90 per cent take up for diphtheria, polio and tetanus by 1988-89 – almost two years earlier than England – and three of the English Regional Health Authorities (RHAs) (East Anglia, Oxford and South Western) had even exceeded it (92 per cent); some RHAs were considerably behind (*Regional Trends*, 1991). According to the Chief Medical Officer's report '...the worst performances continue to come from the inner London area of the four Thames RHAs and the Birmingham District Health Authorities in the West Midlands' (DH, 1990b). DH research indicates that reasons for the variation include '...the mobility of young families, especially in socially disadvantaged localities, problems with the immunisation information systems and lack of conformity of schedules in different Health Authorities' (DH, 1990b).

Other research suggests that social factors play an important part in explaining the variations. Jarman and colleagues (1988) found that the low take up rates for diphtheria were closely related to overcrowding, lone parent families and population density. The Peckam Report (1989) found that social class, family size and the presence of a chronically ill child were significantly associated with vaccine uptake. It also identified two other factors: parental attitude, especially in disadvantaged families, and misconceptions among GPs about contra-indications for immunisation.

GP consultation and deprivation

The GHS data also suggests a general trend towards a higher incidence of GP consultation among under 16s – about 25 per cent increase over the last decade; the consultation for the under fives is two and a half times the rates for the five to 15 age-group (GHS, 1990). Analysis of GHS data for GP consultation in the two weeks before interview in GB, involving almost 130,000 individuals for the period 1983-87, indicates that there is a relationship between deprivation and GP consultation. Results show that consultations were higher among children whose head of household did not have access to a car (odds ratio 1:1.14), who lived in a council house (1:1.11), and who had lone mothers (1:1.11). Membership of a minority ethnic group did not make any difference to the frequency of GP consultation for children, but belonging to manual occupations marginally increased (1:1.04) the rate (Balarajan and colleagues, 1992). This is still the case for the under fives, but in the five to 15 age-group, there is a significant difference: children with professional heads of households are half as likely to consult their GP as those from semi- or unskilled heads (GHS, 1990; McCormick and others, 1990).

On the other hand, evidence available from another study indicates that people in social classes IV and V (and therefore presumably their children) are less likely than others to use ophthalmic and dental services (Ritchie and others, 1981). This may well account for, in part, the class gradient in dental health we had noted earlier. There is, however, a problem about interpreting this data in that one does not know whether and, if so to what extent, the greater frequency of consultation reflects an actual pattern of morbidity, or a greater propensity to consult.

Deprivation and hospital attendance and admissions

Attendance at an outpatient or casualty department of hospitals exhibits a stable long-term trend for children under 16. And unlike consultations with GPs, there is no significant difference between the under fives and the five to 15 age-group (GHS, 1990). However, statistics regarding attendance at hospital outpatient departments are influenced partly by the referral policies of GPs and partly by the consultation behaviour of people in the community, that is, whether and whom to consult. Although no social class breakdown is available for data on hospital attendance or admission, there is evidence to show that people who are highly mobile – travellers and homeless – and others who are very deprived tend to go more to the hospital casualty department rather than their GP (this is discussed further in chapter 4) (HVA and BMA, 1989; Conway, 1988).

Data on hospital admissions also displays a reasonably stable trend in the eighties. But here the age-gradient is strong, as with GP consultation: under fives are almost twice as likely to be admitted as the five to 15 age-band. Once again, there is a problem in the interpretation of data – to what extent any changes reflect shifting patterns in morbidity, or are they the result of changes in admission criteria and duration. The answer is that they probably reflect both. As we observed earlier (chapter 2), despite pressures on hospital budgets in the 1980s, more patients were actually admitted by reducing the duration of stay. There are additional problems, especially in early childhood, of disease definition, variation in coping skills and differential service provision and use (Rosenberg, 1984).

The link between deprivation and hospital admission is well known. For instance, in a study in Glasgow based on 1981 Census data, children from deprived districts (unemployment and overcrowding as indicators of deprivation) were nine times more likely to be admitted into hospital than children from non-deprived districts (Maclure and Stewart, 1984). However, the question arises whether socially deprived children are more ill more often or admitted to hospital more readily than their more privileged peers (Rosenberg, 1984).

Recent evidence based on a study in Sheffield has demonstrated a strong relationship between deprivation (living in deprived areas) and multiple admissions (three or more) for mainly, and exclusively, organic (medical) reasons in children under the age of two years; the association holds good for admission due to social factors as well (Spencer, 1993).

Repeated admissions, which constitute 30 per cent of all admissions under two years, adversely affect the child and the family (Spencer and Lewis, 1991). This burden, the study suggests, falls disproportionately on those living in deprived areas, young mothers and families with low birthweight infants.

Summary

Despite a rising trend, there were wide regional variations in the take up of immunisation, the low performing RHAs being in inner cities. Among the reasons involved, deprivation-related factors had an important part in explaining the variation.

GP consultation has also been on the increase, rising significantly if children's household head lived in LA housing, did not own a car or was a lone parent; the social class gradient was significant for the five to 15 age-group, but not for under fives. Use of dental and ophthalmic services tended to be lower, by contrast, for social classes IV and V.

The trend in hospital attendance (OPD and casualty) has been stable; no social class breakdown of data is available but there is evidence that travellers and other deprived groups like the homeless tend to use this service significantly more than others.

There is a close relationship between deprivation and hospital admission, including multiple admissions under two years of age.

However, there is a problem in the interpretation of data, since hospital attendance and admission rates are influenced by GPs' referral policies and hospital admission criteria, duration and so on. Even where the frequency of use is higher among the deprived groups, can one be sure that the difference accurately reflects their differential need?

Social inequalities in child health

Our review of evidence in this chapter has revealed a marked and consistent class gradient in all indicators of health outcome: child mortality and morbidity; as well as 'quality of health' indicators such as dental health, growth, nutrition and diet; together with access to services. At the same time we have charted a trend towards escalating child poverty since 1979. Are the two related? Or is it just a coincidence? The connection between poverty and death and morbidity among children is well recognised in the context of developing countries (Grant, 1991). It is also generally agreed that post-war improvements in health are largely due to a general rise in living standards, sanitation and an improved take up of immunisation (Rose, 1990). Consequently, the continuation of social class differentials in child health appears as anomalous.

How are such social inequalities generated and maintained? The Black Report (DHSS, 1980) considered four sets of explanations for this phenomenon. This section will review evidence in relation to these from the vantage point of children's health. As the Black Report made clear, these explanations are not necessarily mutually exclusive – each may be able to explain some of the variation between social classes, depending on particular circumstances.

The artefact explanation

The chief proponents of this idea, Illsley (1986) and Bloor and others (1987) argue that health differences between occupational classes are the product of the way they are measured – by the Registrar General's classification, which is unreliable and may artificially exaggerate these differences. The limitations of this classification were discussed in the introduction to Part II of this study when it was pointed out that these problems were not insuperable. Moreover, evidence from the OPCS longitudinal study shows that social class differences between groups 'are not... simply an artefact of comparing ever diminishing groups of individuals' (Goldblatt (ed), 1990); he maintains that these are real.

Social mobility as a factor in health

It has been argued that social inequalities in health are caused by social mobility: people in poor health tend to move down the occupational ladder, while those in good health tend to move up. According to this theory, the health selection effect occurs in two ways. First, using the height of women before marriage as an indicator of health, Illsey (1986) found that taller women tended to move up the social class gradient at marriage, while shorter women tended to move down. There was also some support for this observation in the 1980 OPCS survey of heights and weights in Great Britain (Knight, 1984). Analysis of recent data (1951-80) by Illsey (1986) on the outcome of pregnancies of first-time mothers in Aberdeen has confirmed his earlier studies, indicating a gradient in perinatal mortality, birthweight and height of mothers between different social classes. However, when the same data was analysed by Wilkinson (1986a), he found that social mobility due to height (and education data) was only around ten per cent of the observed social class difference in perinatal mortality rates – the remainder being accounted for by other factors.

Second, the health selection process also operates in another way: serious illness in childhood can also affect social mobility adversely in later life (Wadsworth, 1986). But, according to Wilkinson, this effect is small:

only about 1.5% of those seriously ill in adulthood had suffered downward mobility as a result of serious childhood illness (1986b).

Recent analysis of longitudinal data based on the 1958 birth cohort also came to a similar conclusion (Power and colleagues, 1992).

Structural and 'life style' factors

The other two models explaining health inequalities involve the materialist/ structuralist factors, and the 'life style'/behavioural factors. According to the Black Report, the former helps explain the greater part of the social class variance in health inequality, especially in childhood and adolescence. However, the two approaches are closely related and some people (such as Blaxter, Spencer) are questioning the validity of the distinction. For instance, as Spencer points out, 'Behaviour and "lifestyle" are inextricably bound up with social circumstances and are themselves part of the complex mechanism by which inequalities in health develop' (1991b, p.1256). This is well illustrated by the example of childhood mortality due to accidents, which are very much higher in social classes IV and V as compared to I and II. At one level, one could attribute this difference either to careless or irresponsible behaviour on the part of both children and parents of lower income groups; or one could explain it in terms of environmental hazards – unsafe play areas, the difficulty of supervising children's play from 'tower-blocks' and so on (Blaxter, 1983).

One could also argue that such class differences are partly due to differences in child-rearing patterns in different occupational groups.

But such "patterns" have to be seen in the light of the great differences in the material resources of parents...- income, property and territorial space...- which may place significant constraints on the routine level of care and protection that they are able to provide for their children (The Black Report, 1980, p.179).

Nor can one discount the importance of non-material factors - 'the higher incidence of stressful life events experienced by mothers' in working class homes – in explaining the greater prevalence of accidents in such homes (The Black Report, 1980, p.179).

However, even when particular aspects of 'lifestyle' are ostensibly implicated, such as smoking, diet, exercise and drinking, frequently some of these

behaviours may act as markers for the presence of distress or for particularly adverse socio-economic conditions rather than as major causative agents, and others are likely to be less significant than the structural factors which militate against the presence of good health in deprived and disadvantaged communities by creating a general susceptibility to disease. (Research Unit in Health and Behavioural Change, 1989, p.xx)

This is well illustrated by a study of smoking, low birthweight and perinatal mortality, which found that smoking during pregnancy was not directly implicated but was a proxy for a cluster of other variables – poor housing, inadequate diet, not enough sleep, and lack of social support (Rush and Cassano, 1983). In the same vein, findings from a recent study of working class mothers who smoke emphasise a clear link between women's smoking behaviour and low income. Their findings, which are in line with other studies, suggest that cigarette smoking 'is part of a complex array of coping strategies that women use when caring in low-income and disadvantaged households' (Blackburn and Graham, 1991).

As this discussion indicates, 'lifestyle' choices open to the poor are extremely limited in practice; and that 'The role played by material factors in the production and distribution of health and ill-health...is a complex one', because of the multifaceted nature of social class and'...the more diffuse consequences of the class structure: poverty, work conditions (...the social division of labour), and deprivation in its various forms' (DHSS, 1980, pp.162; 194).

Conclusions

Our review of evidence in this chapter indicates that the post-war trend of decline in the rate of infant mortality slowed down in the 1980s, and the social class differential widened, against a background of rapidly rising child poverty. There were also significant ethnic and regional variations in mortality, reflecting the operation of deprivation factors. Likewise, there was a significant class gradient in morbidity. Additional life expectancy (two years) for children came at a price – the steadily rising trend in morbidity and disability.

Improvement in dental health in the decade before 1983, and in growth (height) in the 1970s, had both levelled off in the 1980s, and reflected a strong class gradient. Steep rises in unemployment appear to have contributed to the stoppage of growth; as also the unbalanced diet in school children – which itself had a class gradient.

There were wide regional variations in the take-up of immunisation due in good measure to deprivation-related factors. The GP consultations also showed a significant, if small, class gradient. Hospital attendance, especially admissions, were very closely related to deprivation. Yet one cannot say on the basis of this data alone whether this pattern of usage reflected a good match between needs and service usage.

Finally, the reasons for the generation and maintenance of social class differentials in child health were discussed briefly, and the relationship between social class and deprivation considered. The next chapter will examine the relationship between health and discrete aspects of deprivation, such as income, diet, unemployment and housing.

Notes

1. There is a striking parallel here in the relationship between poverty, deprivation and inequality (see the Introduction).
2. For a detailed discussion of limitations of mortality data, see OPCS (1978).
3. Please note that data based on mother's country of birth is not the same as that on ethnic origin; it suffers from several limitations, the most important being the exclusion of mothers from minority ethnic groups born in this country.
4. It is reasonable to assume that the 'other' category used here is the same as the one containing disparate groups excluded by the OPCS when they produced their decennial supplement on Childhood Occupational Mortality (OPCS, 1988), and now identified by Judge and Benzeval (1993a): this point is discussed further under the heading 'social class variations in child mortality'.
5. Our figure for 1986 differs from that of Rodrigues and Botting (1989) – they show a ratio of 1.8 for 1989. We have not been able to reconcile the two figures, though our other figures tally with theirs.
6. The term 'professional home' or 'homes in social classes IV and V' is being used for convenience; strictly speaking, it should be children from households with the head belonging to social class I or whatever.

4. Poverty, deprivation and children's health

Introduction

...Poor health is often linked to the economic environmental and social problems ... (*Health of the Nation* Green Paper, 1991).

This chapter will explore the nature of the links between material and social aspects of deprivation and children's health. We shall do this in the light of our examination of social class variations in children's health in the last chapter in the period since 1979. Two main points stood out from this examination: a strong social class gradient in that the health of children in social classes IV and V is significantly worse than that of children in social classes I and II. Second, dramatic improvement in child health in the postwar period slowed down or stopped in the eighties: the rate of decline in infant mortality slowed down; improvement in dental health and growth in height slowed down or ceased, raising questions about children's diet; at the same time, disability and chronic sickness rose steadily. And, even more significantly, the social class differential in infant mortality (the ratio between social classes V and I) widened from 1.8 in 1978 to 2.0 in 1990.

The persistence, if not actual worsening, of social inequalities in child health, as well as a slowing down in improvements in health, have been accompanied by a steep rise in child and family poverty during this period. Is this merely a coincidence? Or are the two more directly related and, if so, in what way?

Deprivation and social class

Material and social deprivation has always underpinned conceptions of occupational or social class.
(Townsend, 1990a, p.6)

It is the lower ranked social classes (IV and V) which have the stronger links with various indices of material deprivation - poor housing, unemployment and low income (Platt and others, 1991). While the link between deprivation and ill health has been well established, it is necessary to disentangle the relative contributions to ill-health of the different components of material and social deprivation in order to better understand how social inequality in health is generated and maintained (Townsend, 1990a). This chapter will review briefly the links between health and income, diet, unemployment, housing and the environment. Finally, it will examine the relationship between multiple deprivation and health.

Income, diet and health

There have been very few studies in this country looking at the **direct** effect of income on health (Whitehead, 1987; Townsend, 1990a); and even fewer on children's health. The one exception looked at the effect of income on height of children in families of poor areas in London in the mid-seventies. A high correlation was found between a low amount of money spent on food per person per week and poor growth in children (Nelson and Naismith, 1979). Expenditure on food varies with household income and composition. A lower consumption of food in low income families with children means that 'there will be a corresponding lower dietary intake of essential nutrients' (Blackburn, 1991). A number of studies show that lack of money is the main reason restricting the choice and the quantity of food consumed by low income families with children (Burghes, 1980; Lang and others, 1984; Cole-Hamilton and Lang, 1986; and Graham, 1986). 'Healthy' food tends to be more expensive than 'unhealthy' food, calorie for calorie (Lobstein, 1988), and it is very difficult for low income families with children, particularly those living on social security benefits, to afford a healthy diet (Durward, 1984; Lobstein, 1988; Bradshaw and Morgan, 1987; Bradshaw and Holmes, 1989; Bradshaw and others, 1992).

Coping strategies for mothers faced with the stress of caring for the family on a low income include using sweets as convenient ways of keeping children quiet on shopping trips and on other stressful occasions; cigarette smoking as a way of easing tension and so on (Graham, 1991; 1986; and 1984).

Unemployment and health

It has been well established that ill-health has a strong link with unemployment as an indicator of deprivation. Reviewing recent research evidence, Whitehead found that, 'as in previous decades, the unemployed in the 1980s tend to have much poorer health than those in work, and areas of the country with high levels of unemployment have worse health records than areas with low levels of unemployment' (1987, p.19). While most of the research is concerned with the effects of unemployment on adult health, there is some evidence to indicate that the health of children of unemployed people is also adversely affected. For instance, research by Brenan and others in the 1970s and 1980s in the USA, Britain, France, Germany and Sweden, based on an analysis of aggregate national data, found a significant correlation between unemployment and elevated infant mortality (and other indicators), albeit with a time lag (DHSS, 1980). Despite limitations of this research,

...the broad global association between economic recession and worsening health still stands.
(Whiteside, 1988, pp.178-9)

Likewise, at the district level, a study by Maclure and Stewart (1984), based on 1981 Census data, used parental unemployment and overcrowding as indicators of deprivation. They revealed that hospital admission rates for children from the deprived districts of Glasgow were nine times higher than those from the non-deprived districts.

Another study in the Greater Dublin area reported a higher incidence of low birth weight in babies with unemployed fathers as compared to babies with employed fathers (Whitehead, 1987). Low birth weight, as we saw earlier, is associated with high rates of infant mortality and congenital abnormalities in childhood. We had also noted earlier that children of unemployed fathers tended to be shorter than those of employed fathers. In an in-depth case study of 22 unemployed families over a period of six months during 1979-80, Fagin, a practising psychiatrist, and Little (1984), found that some families had reported a deterioration of **their children's** health following unemployment. He thought that this was likely in the younger children. Some of the **children** in his study reported 'being afraid of the changes in their fathers especially when they lost their tempers' (p.202).

However, association between unemployment and ill-health does not necessarily imply causation. The relationship is inherently ambiguous for several reasons: states of health are not absolute, but relative; nor is the experience of unemployment uniform. Unemployment, moreover, is subject to the influence of structural factors such that during economic recession, sick or disabled people are more likely to lose their jobs than people who are in better health (Whiteside, 1988). Dormant symptoms of ill-health may reappear during unemployment or existing ones be aggravated, in addition to new ones appearing (Whiteside, 1988; Fagin and Little, 1984). Finally, other factors associated with unemployment such as low income, poor diet and bad housing may also be involved to varying degrees. It is therefore difficult to disentangle the effect of unemployment from that of other factors.

However, significant progress has been made in recent years in identifying the direction of change. The OPCS Longitudinal Study based on 1971 and 1981 Census data demonstrated not only higher mortality among men seeking work, but also their wives (as compared to employed men and their wives), and the difference could not be explained by the state of their health or social class before unemployment (Moser and others, 1984). Arber (1987) showed on the basis of GHS data for 1981 and 1982 on self-reported ill-health that both unemployment and low ranked social class had independent, if partly overlapping, adverse effects on health; and that the adverse effects of social class on the health of the jobless were greater than on that of the employed. In the same vein, Winter (1991) has demonstrated, contrary to previous research, on the basis of an analysis of GHS data over 11 years, an increase in (self-reported) chronic morbidity among the unemployed, but after a time lag of one year.

Evidence about the adverse effects of unemployment on mental health is strong. The stress effects of unemployment:

...may result in a variety of physical, emotional and behavioral changes including vulnerability to illness, impairment of performance and 'learned helplessness' which ensues upon attempting to get work and constantly failing.
(Martin and Hunt, 1989, p.106)

According to Fagin:

the consequences of prolonged unemployment are insidious... (adversely affecting a person's) identity, personal confidence and self-esteem.
(1984, pp.13-14)

Various studies have also confirmed an association between unemployment and suicide (Whitehead, 1987), although evidence of a causal link is less conclusive. A number of longitudinal studies, including one of school leavers in Leeds in the early eighties, have confirmed that psychological well-being declines during the transition into unemployment, and increases if the person moves back into work (Whitehead, 1987; Whiteside, 1988). A large scale, longitudinal survey of unemployed heads of families by the OPCS for the DHSS during 1983-84 confirmed earlier findings that unemployment leads to a substantial increase in feelings of anxiety and depression; and that the effect is almost as great in the wives of unemployed men (Heady and Smyth, 1989). The results also show that the psychological welfare of both husbands and wives is related to the family's financial situation and to their level of consumption. The survey provides strong evidence that some of the psychological impact of unemployment is due to material deprivation, and that the strongest correlation is for families in which the man has been registered unemployed for 15 months. This is consistent with an earlier finding that psychological stress was associated with debt among unemployed men receiving supplementary benefit (now Income Support) (White, 1985).

The social impact of unemployment goes beyond health and

...strikes at the very heart of family life' – it 'undermine(s) the structure and security of the family unit, the respect of children for their parents and of parents for each other.
(Fagin and Martin, 1984, pp.13-14)

Children may well be affected by the social stigma of unemployment, which in turn may affect their social relationships with their peers (Madge, 1983). Other studies of the impact of unemployment, especially when prolonged, reported increased marital conflict, increased likelihood of divorce, and greater relative deprivation of children in such families (Whiteside, 1988; Fagin and Little, 1984).

Poverty and housing deprivation

There have been significant changes in the Government's housing policy since 1979, as already observed in chapter 2. Expansion in owner-occupation and the alteration of LAs' role as the main providers of low cost social housing were two of its main prongs. The former was to be achieved, in part, at the expense of LAs by the sale of council houses, and severe restrictions on building new dwellings. The HAs did acquire a somewhat expanded role, but the increase in their budget for new dwellings was far below the scale of the cuts incurred by LAs on this account. Finally, the general subsidy for LA tenants was withdrawn in favour of a means tested HB, the level of which was subsequently considerably reduced. Coming on top of the increase in poverty in the eighties, this adversely affected the living standards of many families with dependent children.

The implications of some of these changes for families with dependent children will be considered in this section, in relation to housing as 'shelter' as well as its quality. This will be followed in the next section by a discussion of any repercussions on their children's health.

Increase in homelessness

The problem of homelessness has become acute over the last 15 years: contributory factors are the high level of house price inflation in the eighties, high interest rates, rising unemployment and breakdown in relationships leading to defaults in payment of rents and mortgage interest, and repossessions. At the same time, LAs' ability to rehouse homeless people has been sharply reduced by the sale of council housing and cutbacks in new building. Consequently, the number of households placed in **temporary** accommodation (such as Bed and Breakfast (B&B) hotels, hostels and other short-lease accommodation) between 1982 and 1991 jumped 11-fold in England (four-fold in Britain) from 5,000 to 55,000, of which over three-fifths were in London (Audit Commission, 1989; DoE, 1991b; Greve, 1991).

In addition, there are 60,000 people living in hostels and at least 2,700 people sleeping rough on the streets (1,275 in London). This figure is based on a count on census night, when poor weather affected the number of people sleeping rough (OPCS, 1991b). According to Shelter, the housing pressure group, this figure is a considerable understatement, and that there could be as many as 8,000 people in this category in England, including 3,000 in London (1991).

Homeless families in temporary accommodation

The costs of bed and breakfast hotels can be easily identified in pounds and pence but the costs of the physical and psychological damage suffered by the families who live in them cannot. Our children are our future and more than words are needed if we are not to condemn an increasing number to a cycle of deprivation which in the long term will have social and financial costs for us all.
(Councillor Simon Randall, Chairman, LBA Housing and Social Services Committee as quoted in Taylor and James, 1990, p.5)

Families with young children or pregnant mothers form the largest population of homeless households accepted by LAs[1] – constituting about four-fifths of the total. Their number increased by two-fifths (39 per cent) from 87,000 in 1986 to 121,000 in 1990, involving about half a million individuals, including some 50 per cent dependent children. Over the 1980-90 period, the numbers involved are three million and one and a half million respectively (Greve, 1992).

The number of homeless families in temporary accommodation has risen from 20 per cent in 1986 to 30 per cent in 1990 (NCH, 1992a). Of these a fifth were in B&B accommodation (Greve, 1992); the use of which increased six-fold between 1982 and 1989, but has now levelled off (NAO, 1990). Recent reports indicate that the use of B&B accommodation has declined since then, reflecting increased use by LAs of accommodation leased from the private sector (*The Times*, 11.9.92). According to the Conservative-controlled London Boroughs Association (LBA), there may be 9,000 or more children in B&B accommodation in London, and many more in other forms of temporary accommodation (1990).

Black families with dependent children are particularly vulnerable to homelessness (Howarth, 1987; Greve, 1992). An Association of Metropolitan Authorities (AMA) working party also observed that in London 'black households are some three or four times as likely to become statutorily homeless as white households' (1988, para. 1.7). It also noted that a high proportion of families in B&B hotels were Black, 80 per cent in Tower Hamlets, for instance (1988).

Likewise, one parent families with young children are of particularly high risk of becoming homeless – they are disproportionately represented among acceptances by LAs (Greve, 1992; Strathdee, 1989).

The average length of stay for families in temporary accommodation varies from 50 weeks for those with one child to 67 weeks for those with four children. However, for cost reasons, the length of stay in B&B hotels varies inversely with the size of the family: from 27 weeks for a family of four children to between 47 and 57 weeks for a family with one or two children (London Research Centre, 1991).

Information about ethnic origin of homeless families indicates that average length of stay of Black and Asian families was higher in three of the five Boroughs for which the information was available, and considerably higher for two Boroughs: in Tower Hamlets and Wandsworth it was 58 to 72 weeks respectively for Black and Asian families, as compared to 39 and 53 weeks respectively for White families. It is hard to say whether this differential is entirely explicable in terms of the larger size of Asian families or the concentration of Black and Asian families in these two Boroughs, as the LRC study suggests, or whether other factors such as discrimination are also involved.

A major problem is that statistics on the ethnic background of homeless families are patchy and less than reliable. However, an earlier survey by Howarth for the Thomas Coram Foundation found that Black families 'face direct and indirect discrimination in the homeless situation' (1987). And a review of evidence by Smith indicates that

...mainstream services discriminate on 'racial' grounds when catering to the general housing requirements of the public.
(1991, pp.18-19)

The Public Accounts Committee (PAC) expressed 'grave' concern over the scale and speed of increase of the problem of homelessness, and particularly over the extensive use of B&B hotels which '...is often very expensive and unsuitable for families' (Twenty-second Report, 1991, pp. v-vi). Earlier, the

National Audit Office (NAO) Report had criticised the use of B&B hotels, as had the Audit Commission, as being still 'unacceptably high' and usually offering '...the lowest standards at the highest cost (1990, p.7; Audit Commission, 1989). According to research commissioned by the DoE, about half of all temporary accommodation, 76 per cent of LA hostels and 91 per cent of B&B hotels were judged by surveyors to be below an acceptable standard, based on measures such as overcrowding, amenities (sharing cooking and toilet facilities with strangers and very limited privacy) and means of escape in case of fire (Niner and Thomas, 1989).

Homeless young persons (single)

Accurate figures about the numbers of single young persons (16 to 19) who are homeless are not available. They share accommodation with relatives and friends or stay in various kinds of temporary and often substandard accommodation, such as multiple-occupation houses, cheap B&B hotels, hostels and so on; while others squat in derelict buildings or simply sleep rough on the streets in 'cardboard cities', a phrase symbolic of the poverty and destitution experienced by increasing numbers in the eighties. In London alone, in 1989, the number of young homeless was estimated to vary between 64,500 to 78,000 (The Single Homeless in London Working Party, a Standing Group of London Boroughs of different political persuasions) (SHIL, 1989) and between 120,000 to 125,000 (National Federation of Housing Associations (NFHA), 1989). The corresponding national estimate in 1986 was around 180,000. A number of studies in major cities show a steep rise in homeless young people in their late teens and early twenties, with the fastest increase among 16 and 17-year-olds (Greve, 1991). Shelter estimates the number of single homeless among 16 to 19 to be around 150,000 a year with more than 50,000 of these in London (Pollitt, 1989).

It is estimated that 40 per cent of young London homeless people have been discharged or run away from care institutions, including children's homes, psychiatric hospitals, borstals and prisons (NCH, 1989; 1992b; Greve, 1991). Minority ethnic groups, especially Black and Asian, are disproportionately represented among the single homeless; their number increased considerably in the eighties as part of an accelerated longer-term trend which was first discernible in the late 1950s (Greve, 1991). Again, much of the homelessness among young Black people is hidden – largely for cultural reasons; they tend to stay in temporary arrangements with families, friends or in overcrowded conditions in privately rented substandard accommodation; a significant proportion are squatting but virtually none on the streets. They are also particularly prone to racial harassment and discrimination in the rented sector – public and private (Ferguson and O'Mahony, 1991).

The vast majority tend to live a precarious existence in extremely cramped and overcrowded conditions in older properties in run down inner-city areas. Consequently, failure of sharing arrangements or relationship breakdowns most often precede homelessness.

Causes of young homelessness

The causes of homelessness among the young are similar to those for adults but the situation is more acute: high unemployment, low pay, breakdown in relationships, and significant reduction in the availability of affordable accommodation, both in the public and private sectors. However, there are additional factors which make their situation a good deal worse. As already observed in chapter 2, debarring most of the 16 to 17-year-olds from claiming Income Support when unemployed or without training, and the difficulties of getting and keeping a YT place have contributed to a significant increase in homelessness (Greve, 1991; Thornton, 1989; Pollitt, 1989).

Moreover, the single homeless are not eligible under the law for rehousing by LAs unless they are deemed to be 'in priority need' by virtue of being 'vulnerable', that is, they have a mental or physical disability or made homeless because of fire or flood or 'other special reasons'. Because of pressures on accommodation, it seems that LAs tend to interpret these 'vulnerability' criteria quite narrowly (Shelter, 1991a). And those who are eligible have to spend increasingly longer periods in temporary accommodation because of the shortage of suitable 'move on' accommodation. 'Young single people are major losers in the rationing process inevitably undertaken by Housing Authorities in response to shrinking resources' (Oeil, 1989).

Most of the social services departments (SSDs), according to a report by CHAR, a housing charity, are failing in their obligation to house homeless 16 and 17-year-olds more than a year after the 1989 Children Act came into operation. Around three quarters of them had not even taken the initial step of discovering the extent of need in their areas, even though, the Act obliges LAs to provide accommodation for any 'child in need' whose welfare is 'seriously prejudiced'; almost two-thirds of LAs accept that 16 and 17-year-olds fall into this category (1992).

Trends in the quality of housing

So far we have largely considered housing in terms of 'shelter' and how Government policy and other factors have affected its differential availability among various population groups. In this section, we shall discuss the quality of housing directly in terms of presence or absence of some specific aspects of housing deprivation (lack of amenities, overcrowding, poor state of repairs, fuel poverty and poor environment) in relation to developments in policy since 1979.

However, data on children is generally not available, and one has to rely largely on the 1986 English House Conditions Survey (EHCS), published in 1988, since the one conducted in 1991 had not been published at the time of writing, nor was the data available from the 1991 general Census.

Lack of amenities

Lack of amenities, such as the sole use of wc and bath, has now ceased to be a significant problem except in the furnished private rented sector, where 29 per cent shared these amenities with others in 1989; ten per cent of small and three per cent of large families with dependent children were using this type of accommodation then (GHS, 1989: Tables 8.50 and 8.63). It is strongly associated with social classes IV and V, who are generally amongst the poorest in the population and living in some of the worst housing (Williams, 1991). Moreover, when sharing of amenities takes place in the context of overcrowding – that is 'hidden' homelessness, as so often happens among low income families with children, especially among minority ethnic groups – it can lead to friction and breakdown of the sharing arrangement, thus causing *visible* homelessness (Berthoud and others, 1981; Ferguson and O'Mahony, 1991).

Overcrowding – 'hidden' homelessness

Overall, the problem of overcrowding has become quite small, but still significant (even if less than before) for certain groups of people such as low income families with children, lone parents, and minority ethnic groups. As defined by the official 'Bedroom Standard' (1960), information about overcrowding is not available in the GHS, because such households form only a small proportion of the GHS sample (1989), nor is it available yet from the 1991 Census. However, using another somewhat tighter definition (one or more persons per room including kitchen but excluding bath/wc), Hills and Mullings (1991) have analysed the raw GHS data and found that, between 1979 and 1985, the ratio between individuals in the bottom and top quintiles increased sharply: the improvement in the former (from 24.7 to 22.3 per cent) was slower than for individuals as a whole (from 17.3 per cent to 13.3 per cent); likewise, children not only had higher densities, but the improvement in their position was also slower (from 32 per cent to 26.8 per cent). The rate of improvement had clearly slowed down for the bottom group as compared to the period 1974-79.

Density of occupation of heads of households born in New Commonwealth and Pakistan (NCWP) countries was two to four times greater than that of the UK-born (in GB) (lower even than that of the bottom quintile of income); by 1985, this differential had widened to 2.6 times the UK rate (Hills and Mullings, 1991).

There are reasons to believe that the problem of overcrowding is likely to have become worse for some groups adversely affected by the recession in the 1980s. First, only a small proportion of repossessions (one in eight) get reflected in official statistics of homeless. According to Shelter, there may be anything between 140,000 to 260,000 'hidden' homeless householders, that is people forced out of their homes either through repossession or high rents and short-term lease into sharing overcrowded, frequently substandard accommodation with their family and friends. Second, given the doubling of the number of **visible** homeless since 1978, the capacity of LAs (and HAs) to help relieve the problems of people on the waiting list, especially of families with dependent children, has been seriously eroded (Taylor and James, 1990; Greve, 1991; NAO, 1990).

Unsatisfactory housing conditions

According to the 1986 EHCS, the housing conditions of families with children (small families and lone parent families) deteriorated between 1981 and 1986 to the point that they were significantly worse off in 1986 as compared to households generally, whereas in 1981 they were better off than them. (DoE, 1988, Tables A9.3, 9.6 and 6.2) However, a very much higher proportion of households, whose head was born in New Commonwealth and Pakistan (NCWP) (mostly Black and Asian), lived in housing in poor conditions compared with all other households. In particular, the proportion living in unfit housing was two and a half times higher than that of other households (DoE, 1988, Table 6.2).

Housing and environment

Over ten per cent of all dwellings were in 'poor environment', that is, action was needed on four or more specific environmental improvement measures, according to the 1986 EHCS. However, the proportion affected was very much higher for LA flats (DoE, 1988; Hills and Mullings, 1991). There was a strong association in the survey between poor environment and dwellings in poor condition. For instance, the rate of poor repair was more than three times higher, and unfitness four times higher (DoE, 1988; Table A5.6). Research by Williams (1991) also shows that people lacking or sharing amenities are more likely to be living in neighbourhoods characterised by poor quality housing or with social disadvantage.

Poor environment is a common feature of housing in run-down inner-city areas with a mixture of either very old (pre-1919) multiple occupation housing, or high rise flats. It is the poor, the unemployed, the low paid families with children, lone parents and the minority ethnic groups who tend to be disproportionately represented in such housing (Martin and Hunt, 1989).

Problems in high rise flats

One feature of public housing which is of particular concern to families with dependent children is living in high rise flats. According to a DoE survey, over three-quarters of children living above the second floor, numbering 300,000 children (23 per cent of households with dependent children) were in the public sector (Littlewood and Tinker, 1981, p.6). High rise flats can be hard to heat, prone to damp and use asbestos; and they tend to lack space for children to play (Lowry, 1991). The practical problems faced by mothers with small children (frequent breakdowns of lifts, coping with children, shopping, prams and stairs) are '...compounded by the mothers' sense of isolation, the strain of keeping the children quiet, and anxieties about their children's safety', which were not unfounded (Littlewood and Tinker, 1981). A survey of mothers indicated that dissatisfaction with their accommodation tended to increase the higher up they lived, which in turn adversely affected their children's development (Littlewood and Tinker, 1981). Research by the National Children's Bureau on behalf of DoE confirmed that mothers' dissatisfaction with housing was a factor in their children's development (Sparrow and Ryan, 1983).

Damp, mould and cold housing

The 1986 EHCS revealed that over nine per cent of the housing stock had a problem of penetrating damp, over eight per cent rising damp, and six per cent some degree of mould growth. The private rented stock was much more likely to have penetrating or rising damp than the other tenures. Mould growth was more common in the rented sectors than in the owner occupied stock. There was a strong association between condensation and mould with the overall poor conditions characteristic of unfit houses (DoE, 1988). The most significant social factors associated with mould growth were low income and overcrowding – particularly vulnerable were families with an unemployed head, lone parent families and large families with dependent children (Moore, 1991).

According to the 1986 EHCS, in an English winter, up to four million homes (22 per cent of the stock) are liable to become particularly 'cold'[2], and a quarter of that are liable to become 'very cold'[2]. How many of these are cold at any one time depends on the range of outside temperatures reached (DoE, 1988).

Ability to keep a house warm depends on its age, condition, energy efficiency, particularly the availability of a comprehensive and efficient heating system and, above all, by the income of the household to pay for fuel consumption (Moore, 1991). Dwellings with central heating were substantially warmer than those lacking such a system. The GHS data indicates that possession of central heating, as already noted earlier, has been rising rapidly for all tenures over time; nevertheless, differences between tenures remain. In 1990, possession of central heating varied from 70 per cent for LA tenants to 87 per cent for owner occupiers; however, only 60 per cent of furnished and 42 per cent of unfurnished tenants had central heating (GHS, 1991, Table 8.59).

Nationally, cold homes were concentrated in the poorest housing stock (unfit for habitation), and frequently in the older properties, but the highest proportion was in purpose built flats. Two-thirds of cold flats were in LA ownership, virtually all of the remainder being privately rented (Moore, 1991). Scotland and the North held the highest proportion of cold homes (18 per cent), and the South East the least (8 per cent) (DoE, 1988).

House temperatures were strongly correlated with the joint incomes of household head and partner; cold homes progressively decreasing to below one per cent for those with annual income above £10,000 or more; and, likewise, increasing as income fell below this figure. The unemployed had the highest proportion of cold and very cold homes and the majority of these were LA rented. And, as the temperature dropped, the proportion of cold and very cold homes increased significantly for those with an annual income below £3,000. This indicates that people are constrained by their income from spending extra to keep themselves warm.

Fuel poverty

Fuel poverty may be defined as an inability to keep one's house warm in winter due to lack of adequate income. The number of households in fuel poverty in the UK has risen by over a quarter from 5.5 million in 1981 to 7 million in 1991 (Boardman, 1991a, p.8). This is due to '...the combined effect of greater poverty, increasing number of households and a low level of investment in energy efficiency improvements' (Boardman, 1991b). In addition, the number of gas and electricity users in severe difficulties due to fuel debt has risen by more than a half from 455,000 annually in 1981 to 692,000 in 1990 (Boardman, 1991a, p.9).

Households dependent on state benefits and living in the most expensive to heat housing lost over £100 million annually because of the abolition of the additional heating allowance and other changes introduced under the 1986 Social Security Act, which became operational in April 1988 (Crowe, 1991). This figure is based on a detailed comparison made by the author between the two systems. Some people (5.3 per cent) did gain, but the vast majority lost. The position of some of the gainers and losers relevant to this study is as follows: two parent families (tenants), who would not have qualified for any heating additions, have gained up to £3.54 per week; families eligible for either 'estate' rate or the higher rate heating addition lose between £2.56 per week and £6.10 per week. As for lone parent families, the large majority (71 per cent) stand to lose at least between £1.09 and £8.34 per week, more in some cases, depending on circumstances (Crowe, 1991). However, this loss has been mitigated to some extent for up to one out of the seven million households in fuel poverty, whose homes have been draught proofed, their loft insulated and the hot water tank and pipe provided with lagging with a grant from the Government under the Home Energy Efficiency Scheme since 1978 (Boardman, 1991b).

Poverty, housing deprivation and health

The foregoing review of evidence indicates that, while housing conditions have improved generally in the eighties, albeit at a slower rate, housing deprivation has increased for some groups adversely affected by the recession. There has been a dramatic increase in homelessness, particularly acute in inner city areas such as London, and affecting large number of families (lone parent and two parent) with dependent children, especially those belonging to minority ethnic groups, as well as many young people. Factors responsible for increased poverty since 1979 - unemployment, low pay and relationship breakdowns – have contributed largely, together with a sharp rise in housing costs in relation to income (both in the owner-occupied and privately rented sectors), to the rise in homelessness. The problem was aggravated by the Government's policy of selling council houses at heavy discounts, and major cutbacks in the construction of new LA dwellings, so that the ability of LAs to provide low cost social housing of reasonable quality, which they had done until the 1970s, was weakened in the eighties. Rapid expansion in owner-occupation in the 1980s had the effect of increasing social polarisation between tenures so that the rented sector (private and public) has now increasingly become the preserve of the poor. The upshot is that the traditional link between poverty and poor housing, weakened by the provision of low cost social housing in the postwar period (Berthoud and Brown, 1981) seems to have been reinforced in the 1980s.

Consequently, in addition to the homeless, the **quality** of housing accessible to low income families with dependent children has also for the most part declined in the eighties, with the exception of amenities and overcrowding, where there has been a distinct improvement generally. However, improvement in overcrowding had slowed down during 1979-85 for low income households; and the position may well have worsened since then for some groups worst hit by the recession. As low income families with dependent children tend to live in multiply-deprived areas with older multiple-occupied properties or high rise flats, such dwellings are more likely to be unfit or need considerable repairs or be lacking in amenities. They are also much more liable, as we saw, to be cold, damp and mouldy, and expensive to heat. As housing costs have risen in relation to income, there is correspondingly less money available to low income families with children to spend on other things such as fuel or food (CPAG, 1992; *The Guardian*, 26.9.92). Fuel poverty has therefore risen by a quarter, and fuel debts by a half in the 1980s.

As we can see from this brief resumè, the increase in housing deprivation is closely linked to the rapid rise in poverty since 1979. This is not surprising, since access to housing is a function of income, social class, race and gender (Murie, 1983; Morris and Winn, 1990). However, housing inequalities not only reflect these wider social inequalities, but also affect them in turn: depending on its location and quality, housing can enlarge or diminish opportunities for access to better health, education and employment (Murie, 1983).

The link between poor housing, environment and ill health has been well understood since at least the beginning of the nineteenth century, but for a variety of reasons it seems to have been obscured from public consciousness some time after World War II (Sir Donald Acheson, Chief Medical Officer of the Government in the eighties, 1991). Some of the difficulties in establishing a **causal** link between the two stem from the narrow definition of 'health as the absence of disease' and its disease-specific focus. These can be circumvented if one adopts a wider definition of health as suggested by the World Health Organisation (WHO) to include a person's physical, mental and social well-being (See chapter 3). In the light of this, this section will examine the relationship between the increase in housing deprivation since 1979 and the health of children.

Families in temporary accommodation – effects on health

A joint paper by the British Medical Association (BMA) and the Health Visitors Association (HVA), reviewing evidence of effects of living in B&B hotels, shows that it tends to damage the health of parents (physical, emotional and mental) as well as that of their children – physical, social and psycho-emotional (1989). There is also an association between the mother's poor health and her children's health problems (Furley, 1989; Storie, 1990). The following quotation sums up the kind of problems faced by such families:

Infectious diseases are common and easily spread. Diarrhoea and vomiting are common because of poor water supply and shared sanitation. Children often have upper respiratory tract infections because of overcrowding, dampness and the need to vacate the hotels by day. Other viral infections (such as the infectious diseases of children) spread rapidly, yet the uptake of immunisation is low. Infestation with scabies, lice, fleas, bedbugs and mice is common.

Both adults and children in bed and breakfast accommodation are malnourished. There is a high incidence of weight loss in adults and of low birth weight in babies. Most hotels lack adequate cooking facilities and some have none. Families often have to vacate the accommodation between 10 am and 4 pm. These factors add to the difficulty of maintaining proper nutrition.

Women living in bed and breakfast accommodation were more than twice as likely to have problems in pregnancy as women who became homeless after the birth of their baby.
(BMA and HVA, 1990)

Despite the fact that homeless families and their children are a high risk group, they find it difficult to get access to primary health care. Frequent moves disrupt the continuity of GP and child health services: one GP in Bayswater reckoned that 60 per cent of families he saw moved on every month. Not surprisingly, homeless families face difficulties in registering with GPs. Some GPs are reluctant to take on homeless families. Their children's take-up of immunisation and developmental health checks is also very low. Under the new system of GP contracts, there is no payment for immunising children who are temporary patients (Edwards, 1991b; Taylor and James, 1990; BMA/HVA, 1989; Conway, 1988).

Much of the evidence about the effect of B&B and other temporary accommodation on health is anecdotal but '... it points in one direction: that homelessness is likely to be associated with ill health' (BMA and HVA, 1989, p.13).

Single young homeless – effects on health

There is considerable evidence to show that ill health among the single homeless is quite high. A study of 50 young homeless people (16-25) on the streets of Nottingham provided

...a unique and devastating snapshot of life on the streets where ill health, poor diets and broken relations with families and friends are dogging more and more teenagers and young adults.
(*The Observer*, 20.10.81.)

Nearly half the group had physical and mental health problems. The average amount they spent on food each day varied between £1 and £2. Many had to go without food for several days at a time except for coffee. Not surprisingly, their daily diet was found to be deficient in essential nutrients (*The Observer*, 20.10.81).

Another study of single homeless in Manchester also found a significantly higher incidence of ill health, when compared to corresponding age and social class groups, particularly with regard to emotional reactions, social isolation and sleep, and especially in the younger age group (Pickin and others, 1991). Whether this was a consequence of homelessness was not clear; the relationship is complex. Homelessness can be both a precipitator of mental illness as well as its effect, as a report by the Royal College of Physicians points out (1991).

Even though single young homeless are at a higher risk of ill health, they tend to have only a limited access to primary health care (HVA and BMA, 1989;

Conway, 1988; Pickin and others, 1991). However, it was found in a recent London-wide study that homeless people tend to make what the professionals regard as an inappropriate use of acute hospital services, that is 2.5 times more than other people living in London (Scheuer and colleagues, 1991; Black and others, 1991). Whether this reflects increased morbidity on their part is not clear (Edwards, 1991b). However, a study of homeless people's attitudes by the Simon Community suggests that this is partly because the hospitals are more easily accessible, both physically in the areas where the homeless tend to hang around, and also that they do not have to make an appointment to attend the Accidents and Emergency Departments. However, there are feelings of ambivalence among the homeless about this: they complain of long delays in being attended to and also do not like what they see as hostility: 'sometimes it makes you frightened to go to hospital – they treat you like dirt'; or 'they wouldn't listen to me' (*Health Service Journal*, 7 November 1991).

There is also gross under-registration with GPs among the homeless (Pickin and others, 1991; *Health Service Journal*, 7 November 1991). This is partly because of difficulties in finding one who will accept, and partly their own choice, as they may not have confidence that the GP will take them seriously and be able to understand their problems. Instead, it is reported, they often prefer to see a doctor at the night shelter or the one at the day centre or mobile surgery, who, they think, may be more sympathetic to their predicament and understand what it is like to be homeless. 'In choosing to use services located within the world of homelessness, people are making a social decision: ...to minimise their psychological "risk" to themselves, not a medical decision about which services offer the best level of care' (*Health Service Journal*, 7 November 1991).

Adverse housing conditions and poor health

Association between poor health and adverse housing conditions such as overcrowding, poor repair, lack of adequate heating, lighting, ventilation, and lack of amenities (inside wc, bath and so on) has long been recognised (Schorr, 1964). In this section, we shall look at how specific aspects of housing deprivation - overcrowding, cold, damp and mould growth – affect the health of children in low income families who have to experience these conditions. We shall also look briefly at the area and environmental effects on children's health.

Effects of overcrowding on health

Overcrowding and lack of housing amenities and privacy can lead to marital conflict and maternal depression with indirect effects on the growth of children, accidents and acute infections such as gastroenteritis and respiratory disease (Rutter and Madge, 1976; Graham, 1989). The relationship between over-crowding and respiratory disease is well established. Earlier, concern about overcrowding was linked to the spread of TB (Martin and Hunt, 1989). This has since declined as a significant problem at the national level, but it does affect minority ethnic groups, especially Asians, to a significant degree (Black, 1985), who, as we noted earlier, are mostly trapped in some of the worst housing in overcrowded conditions.

Effects of cold, damp and mould on health

We have already seen that the incidence of these health hazards is strongly associated with older, poorer housing in the rented sector, involving single parent families and large families with children (overcrowding) and low pay. It is estimated that when winter is colder than average, each degree centigrade drop causes 8,000 extra deaths and this trend has been continuing since 1945 (Curwen and Davis, 1988). In fact, one study by Bentham (1990) has shown provisionally, on the basis of aggregate data for large areas, a link between fuel poverty and higher infant mortality in exceptionally cold weather: infant mortality tended to be higher in those areas with the largest concentration of poor people and a high level of dependence on electricity for domestic heating. Hyndman, in a recent study of Bengalis in East London, indicated that both measured and reported low temperatures in the home were closely associated with symptoms of 'hidden asthma' and that people in cold homes were twice as likely to suffer from poor chest health (1990). There is now considerable evidence to show a fairly conclusive relationship between the presence of chest conditions such as asthma, rhinitis and alreolitis to the presence of fungal spores in damp housing (Stracham and Elton, 1986). Research by Platt and colleagues carried out in Edinburgh, Glasgow and London has demonstrated that damp and mouldy living conditions have significant and severe effects on children, including symptoms of allergy and infection such as fever, sore throat, headache and respiratory complaints. And these effects were independent of the effect of low income and smoking in the house (1989).

Area and environmental deprivation and health

Design problems in buildings is another source of health concern. We have already seen that living in high rise flats can lead to a sense of isolation and depression in mothers, especially those of under fives, and serious accidents among children. A study by Fanning (1967) in Germany shows that morbidity (especially respiratory illness) was one and a half times more common in children living in flats as compared to those living in houses. He thought that this was due to children living in flats not being allowed to play outside as much as others. Another study by Coleman (1985) attributed a whole series of problems such as graffiti, vandalism, litter and even the number of children in the block in care to design problems. But its findings have been questioned; that '...she seems to have confused correlation between design and these problems with cause (Lowry, 1991).

There is considerable evidence depicting a strong association between areas with above average rates of material deprivation and areas experiencing above average rates of ill health and premature mortality (Townsend, 1990a). But there are not many studies which relate the area effect to the health of children. However, a recent study in Belfast by Blackman and colleagues looked at two council estates – one an inner- and the other an outer-working class estate – which were economically deprived, but one (Twin block) was thought by locals to have considerably better housing and facilities than the other (Divis). They found that the children and adults living on the Divis estate reported more psychological distress. These health differences, according to the authors, are an '...extreme manifestation of a wider problem of ill health in low income "mass housing" areas'; specifically they identified poor housing, especially bad design, structure, layout and heating determined by systems building technology, as the main explanatory variable (1989, pp. 22-23).

Housing conditions, housing type and residential area are obviously interrelated and can exert an independent influence on health. According to a study by Townsend and colleagues of 678 deprived Wards in the Northern region of England, 65 per cent of the variance in health, as measured by standard mortality ratios (SMRs), percentage disabled, and percentage of babies with low birth weight, was accounted for by four indicators of material deprivation: unemployment rate, percentage overcrowded, percentage with low income (as measured indirectly by lacking a car) and percentage with little wealth (denoted by non-ownership of a house). They found that the correlation between deprivation and ill health was not uniform: in particular, there was a marked discrepancy between Middlesborough and Sunderland in mortality, despite the fact that the socio-economic characteristics of these two towns were similar. A follow-up study by Phillimore confirmed the discrepancy, and identified pollution as '...the likely major missing factor in the explanation' (1989).

Multiple deprivation and health

So far we have looked at the relationship between health and individual indicators of deprivation – income, diet, unemployment and housing – which underpin social class. However, in real life clusters of disadvantage tend to be found together. Deprived individuals are '...exposed to several risk factors simultaneously, often for long periods of time, any one of which may make them more vulnerable to one or more of the others' (Martin and Hunt, 1989, p.106). Moreover, since deficits in child health in the most deprived groups 'may well persist through into adult life for a significant proportion' (Martin and Hunt, 1989, p.102), greater the number of indicators of deprivation, 'the more acute and intransigent are the problems' (Davie and others, 1972; Wedge and Prosser, 1973; Court Report, 1976). So the problem involved in disentangling the effects of deprivation is twofold; one, to identify the relative contribution of each of the indicators involved; second, to establish both the length and severity of exposure of individuals to its effects (Townsend, 1990a).

Deprivation and childhood mortality

Reverting back now to mortality as an indicator of health, in the last chapter, we had noted wide variations in infant mortality based on social class, region and ethnicity. Referring to these, the Report by the Comptroller and Auditor General (CAG) concluded that above average mortality rates in certain areas were likely to be associated with above average levels of social, economic and housing deprivation (1990). The Department of Health did not dissent from this view but told the Public Accounts Committee (PAC) that they '...needed better information about such a link', and expected the confidential infant mortality inquiry and the regional epidemiological surveys to throw light on this (PAC, 1990).

In fact, a significant and positive relationship has already been demonstrated between death in the 0 to 4 age group and low socio-economic status, high density housing, poor amenities and the rate of unemployment (Martin and Hunt, 1989). However, recent work by Judge and Benzeval (1993c) carried this investigation a stage further. Based on an analysis of mortality data from the Public Health Common Data Set (PHCDS) for 1989 and using Townsend's area deprivation index, they categorised all District Health Authorities (DHAs) into four groups according to their score on the deprivation index, and assigned to them average mortality rates for different ages calculated for each group.

Table 4.1   Deprivation and child mortality by age in England and Wales 1989

| Child health indicator | Average mortality rates for DHAs grouped by Townsend's Area Deprivation Index | | | | Ratio of most deprived DHA group to least deprived (4/1) |
| | 1 | 2 | 3 | 4 | |
	25 Percentile	25-50 Percentile	50-75 Percentile	over 75 Percentile	
Percentage of births under 2,500 grams*	5.96	6.25	6.96	7.57	1.27
Perinatal mortality**	7.36	7.91	8.72	9.30	1.26
Neonatal mortality**	4.20	4.52	4.92	5.23	1.25
Postneonatal mortality**	3.23	3.61	3.73	4.10	1.27
Infant mortality**	7.42	8.13	8.63	9.33	1.26
Child mortality rate Aged 1-4***	32.54	35.95	42.01	43.94	1.35
Aged 5-9***	14.49	17.02	18.63	25.24	1.74
Aged 10-14***	18.33	15.83	18.23	20.79	1.13

Source: (Courtesy) Judge and Benzeval (1993c): (Based on) *Public Health Common Data Set* (1989)

    * per 1,000 births
    ** per 1,000 live births
    ***per 100,000 resident children

NB The difference between the highest and the lowest group of DHAs is statistically significant for all rates, except child mortality aged 10-14.

As is clear from the data reproduced in Table 4.1, the average mortality rate is significantly higher in the most deprived 25 per cent of DHAs (Group 4) than in the least deprived (Group 1). This means, for example, that the infants in the most deprived group of DHAs have a 26 per cent greater chance of dying than those in the least deprived. These differences in mortality ratios between the most and the least deprived group of DHAs are statistically significant for children of all age groups except for 10 to 14. The latter may be due to the small numbers of deaths that occur in this age group in a single year (Judge and Benzeval 1993c). Except for the 10 to 14 age-group, these results illustrate, that deprivation is related to infant and childhood mortality.

Deprivation and childhood morbidity

Mortality data only gives a small part of the picture of child health. However, if the former is related to deprivation, might not the latter as well? To test this proposition, Benzeval and colleagues (1993d) did a secondary analysis of data obtained in the *Survey of Londoners' Living Standards*, conducted by Townsend during 1985-86, using his deprivation index, covering both material and social deprivation components in accordance with his broad definition of deprivation (see chapter 1). The survey was based on a representative sample of 1,716 households containing 2,703 adult respondents in Greater London; health information was gathered for 930 children in 524 families – it consists of parental perceptions of children's health status. Parents were asked to categorise the health of all children in the household as 'good' or 'fair/poor' over the last 12 months.

Table 4.2   Deprivation and child health in London 1985-86

| | Deprivation categories | | | | |
Individual children	1 (Least deprived)	2	3	4 (most deprived)	N=
	%	%	%	%	
Good	95.9	92.4	81.9	64.9	782
Fair/Poor	4.1	7.6	18.1	35.1	148
N=	147	330	248	205	930

Source: (Courtesy) Judge and Benzeval (1993d). (Based on an analysis of data from *The Survey of Londoners' Living Standards* by Townsend (1986))

Having compiled a four-category index of deprivation, Benzeval and colleagues show that '...there is a clear and consistent increase in the proportion of children whose health is reported as fair/poor as the level of deprivation increases' (Table 4.2).

Using multivariate statistical techniques, they go on to investigate the relative importance of different components of deprivation in child health.

Their results are reproduced in Table 4.3. The principal conclusion from their analysis is that:

Table 4.3   Probability of child having poor or fair health in London 1985-86

Indices Type of disadvantage	Half score on components	Probability	Max score on components	Probability
No deprivation	0	0.05	0	0.05
Housing deprivation only	5	0.12	10	0.27
Dietary deprivation only	2	0.07	5	0.10
Clothing deprivation only	3	0.07	6	0.12
All material deprivation	*10*	*0.25*	*21*	*0.71*
Difficulty managing on income	1	0.09	1	0.09
Lack of integration into the community	2	0.10	4	0.19
All adverse circumstances	*13*	*0.62*	*26*	*0.96*

Source: (Courtesy) Judge and Benzeval (1993) (Based on data from *The Survey of Londoners' Living Standards* by Townsend (1986))

both the material and social circumstances of parents are closely associated with child health...it is the most basic material conditions of living, closely associated with a broad definition of poverty, together with some form of social deprivation for parents, which have the most impact on children's health. When parents find it difficult to manage on their income, consumables such as food, fuel and clothing are squeezed. Low income, poor housing and lack of social integration are all associated with poor child health. (Judge and Benzeval, 1993d)

The above analysis indicates that child health, whether measured in terms of mortality or morbidity, is closely related to deprivation – material and social. From this it follows that, as child poverty and deprivation have risen rapidly in the UK since 1979, any deterioration in child health that we noted earlier (chapter 3) is also likely to be associated with this trend.

Conclusions

Unemployment, low pay and child health

Our review of evidence suggests a close link between different aspects of deprivation and children's health – both individually and severally. A significant correlation was found between unemployment and higher infant mortality, as well as a higher incidence of low birth weight in babies; children of unemployed fathers also tended to be shorter than those of employed fathers. A high correlation was, likewise, found between a low amount of money spent on food per person per week and poor growth in children. This is not surprising, since research evidence indicates that families with low incomes (whether due to unemployment or low paid employment or because they are lone parent families) cannot afford to spend enough on food for their children. This restricts their choice in terms of both quality and quantity, and adversely affects the growth of their children. Prolonged unemployment was also shown to increase the risk of family breakdown with adverse consequences for the psychological welfare of children. A longitudinal study of school leavers in Leeds indicated a decline in psychological welfare during the transition into unemployment, but an improvement when the person got a job.

It follows that, as the level of unemployment and low pay has increased sharply since 1979 (as have the number of lone parent families), with an attendant increase in the number of children living in low income families, this will tend to have an adverse effect on the health of those children – in terms of their physical growth and psychological welfare, if not also higher mortality and morbidity in some cases. The children may be cushioned from these adverse effects up to a point, and for a while. There may be a time lag before these effects manifest themselves; and there may also be a greater time lag before official statistics or research begin to reflect them.

Housing deprivation and child health

Our discussion of the relationship between housing and health revealed two main conclusions: one, there was a general improvement in housing conditions in the eighties, particularly a rapid increase in owner-occupation, and an improvement in amenities, and in overcrowding. However, this improvement was either much less for, or bypassed altogether, certain sections of the population adversely affected by the rising poverty during this period; for some of them, conditions had deteriorated, in fact. Two, there was a strong relationship between poor housing, environment and ill health.

There was a sharp increase in homelessness affecting many families (two parent and lone parent) and young people, especially those belonging to minority ethnic groups. Many of these families had to spend a considerable amount of time in temporary, mostly B&B, accommodation with adverse effects on their children's health. These included a higher incidence of low birth weight babies, malnourishment, infectious diseases, as well as viral infections connected with living in crowded and damp conditions. A significantly higher incidence of ill health – physical and psychological – was also found among young single homeless, especially those sleeping rough. Despite having a higher risk of illness, both these groups had only a limited access to health services.

Low income families with dependent children tend to live mostly in older properties in multiple occupation or high rise flats often in a poor state of repair, and generally in run-down inner-city areas which are frequently cold, damp, and mouldy. Despite a degree of improvement for some, lack of amenities and overcrowding are still significant problems for these families. Because of their generally low incomes, fuel poverty increased by a quarter, and fuel debts by a half in the 1980s. As the number of low income families with dependent children has increased substantially since 1979, as a direct result of rapidly escalating poverty, the number of families living in housing conditions described above is likely to have increased too, particularly in the private sector where such conditions tend to be more prevalent. This is not yet reflected in official statistics, since the results from the 1991 Census and the 1991 English House Conditions Survey are not yet available; and the GHS does not contain an analysis of overcrowding based on the official standard, because of under-representation of such households in their sample.

The adverse effects of living in such conditions on children's health have long been recognised and well documented. These, according to our evidence, include more frequent accidents, acute infections such as gastroenteritis and respiratory disease, slower growth, loss in psychological well-being, and possibly higher infant mortality.

Multiple deprivation and child health

Since low income families tend to be multiply deprived, and often for long periods, the cumulative effect on their children's health is likely to be greater than that of any one indicator of deprivation. Our examination of the limited evidence that was available on two indicators of health – childhood mortality and morbidity – indicates that there is a close but inverse relationship between deprivation – material and social – and child health; in other words, if the former increases, the latter is likely to worsen. From this it follows that, as child poverty has increased sharply since 1979, any deterioration in child health observed in this study is likely to be linked with this trend.

Notes

1. LA acceptances are a flow, not a stock; they indicate the kind of pressure on LA resources.
2. The 1986 EHCS defined a house as 'warm' if its warmest room and the main dwelling temperature was at or above 18°C, and very warm, if the temperature of the warmest room was at or above 21°C. Conversely, a house was 'cold' if the warmest room temperature was below 16°C and the mean temperature was below 12°C; and it was 'very cold' if the warmest room temperature fell below 12°C.

5. Poverty, deprivation and education

Introduction

In the last two chapters, we reviewed recent trends in children's health and established that a noticeable decline in their health in the eighties and early nineties was closely associated with the rise in child poverty in the UK since 1979. We shall now explore the relationship between the rising child poverty and children's education in several ways.

First, we shall briefly look at how discrete aspects of parental poverty and deprivation impinge directly or indirectly on a child's educational progress. Second, we shall examine the relationship of social class in general, and deprivation in particular, with educational performance – first at the primary, and later on at the secondary school levels. Other things being equal, one might expect the performance of children of social classes and groups who have experienced a significant deterioration in their socio-economic position since 1979 to be adversely affected, albeit with a time-lag. In this connection, we shall also look at the evidence linking educational performance with factors such as ethnicity and the school. Among other things, the former merits attention because of the known higher prevalence of poverty and deprivation among minority ethnic groups, as compared to the rest of the UK population; the latter, because of evidence that it (the school) exerts an independent influence over pupils' performance over and above that of other factors. Third, we shall examine the problems of truancy in the context of its relationship with deprivation and other factors, including the role of the school. Fourth, we look at how trends in educational expenditure and changes in policy affect schools' ability to perform. Fifth, we look at how far opportunities for access to further and higher education (FHE) are differentially distributed according to social class, gender and race; and whether it is possible to relate these differences to deprivation.

Finally, we conclude this chapter by assessing the relative contribution of deprivation and other factors in explaining the variations in educational performance, and in access to FHE; and, if possible, how changes in the level of deprivation over time affect this relationship. However, this is not going to be a straightforward process, not least because socio-economic causes of poverty and deprivation, such as unemployment, tend to affect various households with dependent children differentially, and generally with a time-lag. Moreover, the data about educational outcomes of their children may not be available at a level or in a form to allow one to make the necessary links.

The situation has also been complicated by the sweeping legislative changes affecting the whole field of education in recent years. These include the introduction of the national curriculum and new modes of assessment, involving regular tests at ages 7, 11, 14 and 16; and the replacement of the dual system of examination, (General Certificate of Education (GCE 'O' level) for pupils in the top 20 per cent of the ability range, and the Certificate of Secondary Education (CSE) for the remainder) with a single examination (General Certificate of Secondary Education (GCSE)) for all 16-year-olds. Other changes affect the management and organisation of schools and their relationship with parents, the Governing Bodies and, above all, the local education authorities (LEAs). Whilst the repercussions of some of these changes are already being felt in schools, it will be a while before the effects of others work themselves through. However, it is very difficult to know how these changes will impact on the educational performance of children, and all but impossible to disentangle their effect from the 'normal' school effects, let alone from that of deprivation.

Parental poverty and deprivation – effect on a child's education

We noted earlier that it is the lower ranked social classes (generally IV and V) which bear the brunt of deprivation underpinning social class. We shall now review some evidence as to how discrete aspects of parental deprivation such as low income, unemployment, poor housing and environment affect a child's educational attainment either directly or indirectly through his or her health.

Low income and education

As we saw in chapter 1, two in five children in 1991 were living in or on the margin of poverty. Low income means parents have less money to spend on books, educational toys, extra-curricular activities (such as music, sport), or outings to museums, art galleries, cinema or theatre or a concert, whether organised by the school or at home. And some parents are too poor even to be able to afford essentials such as extra clothes and shoes required for sporting activities, let alone to go on holidays (Mack and Lansley, 1985).

Typically, parents with low income jobs tend to work long, unsocial hours, frequently doing shift duty or heavy work in unpleasant conditions – especially people in unskilled and semi-skilled jobs, as are so many minority ethnic group people (Amin with Oppenheim, 1992). They may also have to spend more time on household chores, thus leaving little time (or energy) to spend with their children. Thus low income and poor working conditions of parents indirectly affect the educational experience of their children, for their ability to take an active interest in their children's education – identified by research as an important factor in attainment (Blatchford and colleagues, 1985) – is severely constrained. Moreover, the ability of low income groups in manual occupations to support their children's education is also limited by their relative lack of knowledge of the education system and the skills to influence it (Bernstein,

1971). This is even more true of parents from minority ethnic groups, especially those such as Bangladeshis, who are often not very fluent in English (Hutchinson and Varlaam, 1985; Tomlinson and Hutchison, 1991). It has also been argued that a sense of powerlessness experienced by many people in lower status occupations may spill over into other aspects of life and induce passive acquiescence of low standards of educational provision or decisions made about their children at school, about which they are unhappy (Mortimore and Blackstone, 1982).

Unemployment and education

Unemployment, especially long-term, as we saw in chapter 2, was the biggest single cause of poverty. However, in addition to the material consequences of poverty (low income) already discussed above, unemployment in the family can indirectly affect adversely the well-being and education of children, because of its stressful effects on the physical and mental health of parents, and the significantly greater potential for marital discord (see chapter 4). It may also exert pressure on children to take up odd jobs, thereby reducing the time and energy available for studies, thus adversely affecting performance. It may also pressurise some children into leaving school early to take up employment, because their parents can no longer afford to look after them. This, as we noted in the last chapter, was a significant factor in teenage homelessness.

Poor health and education

According to the Court Report (DHSS, 1976), 'there is now extensive evidence that an adverse family and social environment can retard physical, emotional and intellectual growth, lead to more serious illness and adversely affect educational achievement and personal behaviour'. We saw in chapter 3 that children from low income families tended to have an inadequate diet – some went to school without any breakfast – and slower growth, and the greater incidence of morbidity. As another DHSS report points out, 'a hungry child is unlikely to be alert during lessons' (1978, p.43).

We also observed in the last chapter that deprived children tended to have a higher incidence of dental decay. Other evidence suggests that there is also a higher level of *undiagnosed* hearing and visual impairment among deprived children (Black Report, 1980; Wedge and Prosser, 1973). Considering that the use of health services among families with deprived children is proportionately less, these conditions are likely to affect attainment (for instance, because of inability to hear the teacher or to concentrate because of toothache). Likewise, absence (authorised) from school due to their generally higher level of other kinds of illness is also likely to leave them behind their peers in their studies.

Poor housing, environment and education

Housing disadvantage in terms of overcrowding and sharing (or lack of) amenities (a hot water supply, a bathroom and an indoor lavatory) are significantly associated with lower social class (as we saw in chapter 4), on the one hand, and to lower educational attainment on the other. Analysis of

National Child Development Study (NCDS) data showed significant correlations between housing disadvantage and attainments in reading and arithmetic at age seven (Davie and colleagues, 1972), as well as at age 11 (Wedge and Prosser, 1973). Poor facilities for homework (lack of a quiet room) or disturbed sleep were also implicated with lower attainment in another study (Dale and Griffiths, 1965). Tibbenham (1982) also noted an association between poor housing and truancy. But, as Rutter and Madge point out, for the most part, 'the associations are indirect and the mechanisms ill-understood' (1976, p.79). It is generally the case that people who are experiencing one kind of deprivation such as housing, are also liable to be suffering from one or more of other kinds such as low income or ill-health. The problem is how to disentangle the effects of housing deprivation from others, especially when they interact with the area effects, as in inner cities. As is well known, the cumulative effects of poverty, low pay, unemployment, poor housing and environmental pollution are felt in the inner cities in an acute form. That this pattern of multiple deprivation is long established and deep-seated has been well documented since the publication in the mid-seventies of the DoE-sponsored inner-area studies (1977).

It may be the case, as the Plowden Committee suggested, that the link between poor housing and educational disadvantage was due to the prevalence of poor schools in inner city areas with concentration of poor housing (1967). This is supported by the recent HMI comment that the quality of teaching in inner city schools tends to be less good (DES, 1992). Among other things, this may be due to inadequate resources, higher turnover of staff and the employment of inexperienced teachers (Mortimore and Blackstone, 1982). However, it is more likely that educational failure in this situation is the result of an interaction between the disadvantages experienced by the child at home, in the school, and the area (environment) in which they live (Essen, Fogelman and Head, 1978).

Homelessness and educational attainment

As we saw in the last chapter, homelessness among families with dependent children increased substantially in the eighties, when around half a million children were affected. A survey by the HMI in 1989 revealed that living in temporary accommodation (mostly B & B hotels) disrupts their schooling and adversely affects their performance (DES, 1990a). The survey of 28 schools (23 primary and five secondary) was carried out in London, Manchester, Blackpool and Greater Yarmouth. In London, all the surveyed families were in B & B hotels – many were from ethnic minorities: Bangladeshi, Kurdish and Somali children formed the largest groups; some were refugee children.

Many of the problems stemmed from their transient nature: discontinuities in school arising from frequent and sudden moves, irregular attendance with 'substantial numbers' not even enrolling at any school; others having to wait for a place at a school; or being offered restricted, often inappropriate, choice in options in secondary schools.

Moreover, as we noted in the last chapter, children living in temporary accommodation had to cope with the problems of poor housing and overcrowding typical of B & B hotels, with all their implications for inadequate diet and ill-health. The HMI survey reveals that all the effects of living in such conditions on educational attainment, already discussed in this section, were present in the case of these children – only in a more acute form.

Schools' response to homeless children

From the point of view of the schools, they had to cope with precipitate arrivals and departures, sketchy records with little information about children's previous achievements or progress, and inadequate communication between schools, LEAs and housing authorities, with no additional resources for most schools to meet the increased pressures arising from a sudden influx of large numbers of transient pupils. The lack of additional resources 'to help provide for the needs of homeless pupils undermined the schools' ability to cope...'(DES, 1990, p7).

The schools' response to the needs of homeless children was quite variable. Some were able to make allowances for their particular needs and provide educational support as, for instance, English as a Second Language (ESL) support for bilingual children. But their learning difficulties as well as social or emotional needs were either not recognised, or neglected; schools were 'rarely able to compensate for gaps in pupils' knowledge and understanding'. The lack of self-esteem of transient pupils, together with 'under-expectation by teachers, served to compound pupils' difficulties' (p.5).

Social class, deprivation and education

We have already seen that social class is a multi-faceted concept – a proxy for a range of material and social disadvantages which impinge directly or indirectly on a child's educational progress. Although some attempts have been made to develop indices of deprivation and relate these to educational attainment (these will be discussed below), much of the research evidence is concerned with social class differences in attainment, and these tend to be discussed alongside the difficulties experienced by children coming from materially deprived homes without distinguishing clearly between the two. As Mortimore and Blackstone (1982) point out, this is because of the difficulty of operationalising the concept of disadvantage (or deprivation).

Primary education

Declining standards?

Government policy has been characterised by greater emphasis on the achievement of basic standards in education (Glennerster and Low, 1991). However, until recently, it has been difficult to know what was happening to standards in primary schools – whether they were rising, falling or staying the same. In the case of literacy standards, for instance, this was due to a lack of good quality comparative data over time, based on a standardised reading test given to a nationally representative sample of children. Related to it was the lack of consensus on '...a particular definition or view of the reading process' (Gorman and Fernandes, 1992, p.3) involved in a reading test, and changes in its definition over time. Consequently, the debate on reading standards has tended to be highly sensitive, contentious and inconclusive, which is not surprising, given the multiplicity of vested interests – political and professional. This situation is likely to improve now with the introduction of national testing at ages 7 and 11.

In the meantime, recent evidence from a variety of sources indicates that the average standard of literacy, for example, has not only **not** risen, but actually fallen in the eighties. The National Foundation for Educational Research (NFER) has made an important contribution to this debate by confirming earlier, more tentative, evidence of a decline in reading standards in the primary school in the eighties. Their study was based on two independent, nationally representative, samples of schools, one of which also participated in a similar survey in 1987. Using a standardised reading test, reflecting current conceptions of the purpose of reading, they found that there had been a decline in the reading performance of Year 3 pupils (aged between seven and eight) of 2.5 points between 1987 and 1991, which was statistically significant. Although the achieved sample was relatively small (37 and 24 schools), and the response rate was low (52 and 69 per cent respectively), the authors claim that the results are convincing because the evidence of a drop in standards in the sample which participated in the 1987 survey is corroborated by results from the other sample: the two sets of results are in the same direction and of comparable magnitude (2.5 and 2.6) (Gorman and Fernandes, 1991).

According to Gorman, an average decrease of 2.5 points of standardised score suggests a decline in the reading age of at least three months (Gorman, *The Times*, 14.2.92.). This estimate is likely to be even higher if one takes into account other evidence of a fall in reading standards since 1985. Indeed, Turner, an educational psychologist, released in 1990 hitherto unpublished reading test scores showing that there had been a three-point decline in standards between 1985 and 1989 (1990). In the same year, NFER researchers, Cato and Whetton, also collected evidence from 26 LEAs which tested reading performance, using norm-referenced reading tests. They found that there was some decline in reading performance in 19 LEAs, roughly estimated to average one point of standardised score in the mid-1980s, and another one point between 1988-1990. However, they had reservations about the generalisability of these findings across England and Wales, and also about the contemporary relevance of the reading tests used by LEAs (1991). Nevertheless, when seen alongside the 1991 NFER study, it does lend support to the view that reading standards in primary schools began to decline in the mid-eighties.

Is the decline in standards confined only to reading? Or does it extend more widely to other subjects such as mathematics? According to the views of head teachers in the 1991 NFER reading survey, 80 per cent of those who had detected a downward trend in reading attainment were also aware of a similar trend in other subject areas, for example, in mathematics (Gorman and

Fernandes, 1991). Other research by NFER also provides some evidence in corroboration of this. In Croydon, the performance in mathematics 'had shown the same pattern of decline as performance in reading in the period 1986/87 to 1989/90 (London Borough of Croydon, 1992). Intuitively also this makes sense, since factors which tend to affect pupils' performance adversely in one subject are also likely to do so in others.

Reasons for falling standards in primary education

As there is a debate even as to whether the standards are falling, there is even less consensus on the reasons. In principle, the educational performance of a child depends on the interaction between the child, the home and the school. In practice, there is very little hard evidence about the relative contributions of each: the number of factors involved are many, and the processes are very complex and poorly understood. The reasons for a rise or fall in performance can lie in any one or more of these three settings in different permutations. Add to this the professional and political interests involved, it is not too difficult to understand why there is so little consensus on this issue.

In discussing the reasons for falling reading standards, the NFER study discounts the effect of changes in teaching methods on standards (1991), since only a tiny minority (five per cent) of teachers rely exclusively on 'Real Books' approach to reading, which had come in for considerable criticism (Education, Science and Arts Committee, 1991; DES, 1990b). They suggest, among other things, that the fall may be related to the rise in (child) poverty in the eighties. There is some support for this proposition from their research, for it indicates that the fall is not uniform across the country. In fact, nine out of 24 schools showed an improvement, on average. None of these was an inner city school, or had other indications of disadvantage – they were all located in shire counties, rural areas or affluent middle class suburbs. On the other hand, seven of the 15 schools showing a decline were in large urban or industrial areas of the country (Gorman and Fernandes, 1992). This does suggest a tentative link between disadvantage and reading performance, even though the sample is relatively small.

Deprivation and low attainment in the primary school

Other research also indicates that there is a close relationship between socio-economic deprivation and poor attainment. In a study of London Educational Priority Area (EPA) schools, Barnes and Lucas (1975) found that:

as children's objective circumstances become more disadvantaged, so their reading performance tends to be lower.

Having controlled for all the indicators of deprivation in the home backgrounds of children, they found that there was a gap of more than two years in reading age (26 points of reading score) between the children of professional, middle class, White parents and those of unskilled workers of West Indian origin. This conclusion is strengthened by a study of social mobility by Fogelman and Goldstein (1976) when they analysed the data derived from the National Child Development Study (NCDS), based on a cohort of all children born in one week in 1958 (3-9 March) in Great Britain. They found that children from 'upwardly mobile' families had improved their attainment scores as compared to static families, who, in turn, had improved their scores in comparison with 'downwardly mobile' families.

Both these findings have a particular relevance to the situation in the eighties when the rising child poverty impacted differentially on children's lives. As we saw earlier (chapter 1), not only has child poverty tripled since 1979, but that income inequality has increased too – involving a net transfer of tax income from the poor to the rich, and effective cuts in welfare spending with concomitant movement of people up and down the social scale. In this situation, the NFER study finding that reading standards are rising in affluent areas but falling in deprived areas begins to ring true.

It is pertinent to point out here that in a wide-ranging review of research by Mortimore and Blackstone, they concluded that:

there is a strong and persistent relationship between social class and attainment in primary school, and, in particular, between socio-economic disadvantage and low attainment (1982,p12).

This is also supported by the latest HMI report which observes that 'standards of work in schools serving areas of marked social and economic disadvantage were commonly much less satisfactory than elsewhere'. For instance, they found that at Key Stage 1 (age five to seven), the standard of work was poor in 36 per cent of classes in inner city schools, as compared to 28 per cent in other schools. The difference was even more marked at Key Stage 2 (age eight to 11), where the corresponding figures were 45 and 32 per cent respectively (DES, 1992). Significantly, a number of HMI reports in the 1980s and 1990s have expressed concern about the persistent under-achievement of pupils in schools in deprived inner city areas (see, in particular, DES, 1990b; 1990c; 1991a; 1992b). This suggests in general that standards in schools in such areas are not only lower than in affluent areas, but that they are not improving; they may even be falling, in contrast to schools in affluent areas where they appear to be rising, as the NFER study suggests.

Gap in social class attainment widens in the primary school

In principle, the school can mitigate the disadvantaged circumstances of its pupils. However, measures by successive governments over the last two decades to compensate for the child's disadvantaged circumstances, such as the establishment of educational priority areas or the provision of grants under section 11 of the 1966 Local Government Act, have met with only limited success (Mortimore and Blackstone, 1982). And there is considerable evidence to show that the initial gap between the children of different social classes, and different ethnic groups, tends to widen as the children progress through the primary school. In their analysis of NCDS data, it was estimated by Fogelman and Goldstein (1976) that, at age seven, children of social class I, II and III non-manual were 0.9 years ahead of social class III manual and IV in reading; and 1.6 years ahead of social class V. However, by the time those children were 11-years-old, the gap in reading had widened to 1.9 and 3.0 years respectively. The results of the mathematics tests also showed similar differences. Likewise, in a study of another cohort of children born in one week in March 1948, Douglas (1964) had found that the difference of 7.6 points in non-verbal intelligence tests at eight between non-manual and manual class children had widened to 9.4 (an increase of 12 per cent) by the time they were 11, but the divergence in the reading and vocabulary tests was less marked.

Gap in achievement between ethnic groups widens in the primary school

Two research studies in the late 1970s and early 1980s suggest that, even when minority ethnic group children start on a par with their White peers at age five, they tend to fall behind by the time they are seven. According to a study by Scarr and colleagues (1983) in the Midlands, at age five, there were no differences between the reading scores of Asian, West Indian and White children in the same school. When they were six-years-old, the middle class White children were ahead of the rest; by the time they were seven, both groups of White children had a higher reading score than both West Indian and Asian children.

These results were confirmed for children of Afro-Caribbean origin in a longitudinal study in inner London by the Thomas Coram Research Unit in early 1980s (Blatchford and others, 1985). Classroom observation revealed that White boys had more contact with teachers about school work and received more positive feedback than other children. Black boys had least contact with teachers about work; the latter were also more critical of them (Tizard and colleagues, 1988).

The study by Scarr also shows that the gap between the children of West Indian and White origin continued to widen between the ages of seven and ten; the gap between Asians and Whites, having opened up at the age of five, continued up to the age of 12. These results have since been confirmed by a much wider study of junior schools in inner London in the mid-eighties by Mortimore and colleagues (1988). Children of Afro-Caribbean origin obtained lower scores in reading and mathematics at ages seven, nine and ten; and these differences remained even after allowing for the effect of factors such as socio-economic group. The sample of Asian children was not large enough to allow for a detailed analysis, but it was clear that the results differed widely, depending on the language group of the children, and their fluency in English. Those who were not fluent in English got considerably poorer scores for reading and mathematics.

It is clear from this brief review of evidence that children of working class, and of Asian and Afro-Caribbean origins, tend to make significantly slower progress in the primary school when compared to middle class White children; and consequently, the gap between them becomes even wider than it was initially at age five.

Interaction between the home and the school

Close as the relationship between deprivation and attainment is, it is not without complexity. Examination of NCDS data by Wedge and Prosser (1973) shows that, whereas on average deprived children were three and a half years behind other children in their reading scores, one in seven deprived children did better in the reading (and mathematics tests) than half the non-deprived children. This suggests that poor educational attainment of children cannot be explained entirely by their disadvantaged circumstances. Reasons why a proportion of children from deprived homes can do well at school, while the majority tend not to, are not clear in the literature.

Factors contributing to school effectiveness

It appears that not all schools in deprived areas have lower standards. As the 1990 HMI Reading Survey (DES, 1990b) showed, good standards of work were achieved in **some** schools in **all** areas, whether advantaged or disadvantaged. Why is it that **some** schools in inner city areas are able to achieve good results, while the majority are not?

According to the HMI, 'such schools were characterised by effective leadership; teaching of a consistently high quality; carefully planned well-managed classwork; a low turnover of staff; and good teaching resources' (DES, 1992). The report added that such characteristics occurred less frequently in schools located in deprived areas, and that this was a longstanding concern.

The above statement of HMI goes some way towards explaining the recent decline in education standards in the primary school, but it needs to be amplified. Some of the factors mentioned above would appear to be within the control of the school, such as leadership and the planning and organisation of classwork. However, others such as a stable and high calibre staff and good teaching resources depend among other things, on the overall availability of resources. This issue will be discussed later on in this chapter.

Summary

In this section, we have discussed some discrete aspects of deprivation and found that these can adversely affect a child's educational progress in primary school in three main ways. One, the actual experience of living in conditions of poverty – such as poor housing, inadequate diet and frequent ill-health – tends to have a direct adverse effect on a child's education, even though it is difficult to quantify it. Second, children from poor families tend to be relatively deprived of the wider cultural and educational experiences and participation in extra-curricular activities which other children take for granted. Third, poverty tends to restrict the ability of such parents to take an active interest in their children's education and to support them in other ways.

We have explored the relationship between education and deprivation, social class and race in the context of the primary school. We have found that the gap between children from different social class and ethnic backgrounds tends to widen as they progress through the primary school, even when initially they are on a par with each other. Moreover, there is considerable evidence to support the view that children from deprived homes tend to do less well at school, and that their performance tends to fluctuate in line with their parental economic fortunes.

This is relevant to the debate on educational standards, in the context of rising child poverty. There is tentative evidence to suggest that standards in primary schools have tended to improve in schools in relatively affluent areas, but generally not in deprived inner city areas, where they may, in fact, be falling.

Finally, we have posed the question as to how some schools in deprived areas can do well despite the odds, but not the majority. In this connection, we have touched on the factors which, in professional judgment, can make a school effective. In the next section, we shall consider some research evidence bearing on the effectiveness of schools, in addition to further exploring the relationship of social class, race and deprivation with educational outcomes – albeit at the **secondary** level.

Secondary education

Trends in examination performance

Table 5.1 gives details of educational attainments of school leavers in England between 1979-80 and 1990-91.

It depicts a general pattern of improvement in that a significantly higher proportion of young people now get some passes than was the case in 1979: the proportion of those attempting an examination but getting no graded result has dropped from 12 per cent in 1979 to 8 per cent in 1990-91. Other improvements include the following: the percentage of those getting five or more passes at grade 'G' or better has gone up (from nearly 70 to 81) in this period; and so has the percentage of those getting five or more passes at grades A-C (from 24 to 38).

The results also indicate that girls have made an all round improvement in their relative position *vis-a-vis* boys. Whilst both sexes have secured higher passes at different grades, the gap between the two has widened in favour of girls. Girls in 1979 already had a lead over boys in both the categories of five A-C grade passes, and five passes at G grade or better. Given the dramatic improvement in the proportion of A-C grade passes obtained by girls (from 24 per cent in 1979 to 41 per cent in 1990-91), as compared with boys (from 24 to 35 per cent), the lead has been considerably widened. It has also been widened, but less dramatically, in the case of five passes at grade G or better; and maintained in the category of pupils getting no graded result (7 per cent of girls as against 9 per cent of boys) (DFE, 1991b, 1992b).

Girls have also improved considerably their relative position when one looks at A-C grade passes in GCSE in selected subjects. For example, girls have maintained their lead in English, but have narrowed the gap significantly in sciences, and dramatically in mathematics. Whereas in 1979 the gender gap in mathematics was six points in favour of boys (29 per cent A-C grade passes for boys, against 23 per cent for girls), it was reduced to two points by 1990-91 (40 per cent A-C grade passes for boys as against 38 per cent for girls) (DFE, 1991b, Table 10; DFE, 1992b, Table 10).

Table 5.1 School leavers in England – Achievement at GCSE/'O' Level/CSE examinations 1979/80–1990/91

	1979-80	1984-85	1986-87	1987-88	1988-89	1989-90	1990-91
Pupils (000s)	750.7	736.2	716.0	656.0	617.7	578.1	541.9
5 or more grades A-G passes (%)	69.9	74.3	73.5	74.7	76.9	78.1	81.0
5 or more grades A-C passes (%)	24.0	26.8	26.4	29.9	31.9	35.2	37.8
No graded results[1] (%)	12.3	9.7	9.8	10.1	9.1	8.5	8.2

Source: DFE (1991a, 1992) Statistical Bulletin, 22/91, 15/92.

Notes: 1. Includes a small percentage of leavers with 'A' level results, but not 'O' level, CSE or GCSE qualifications.

However, most of the improvement in examination results occurred following the introduction of the new GCSE examination, taken by the first cohort in the summer of 1988 (see Table 5.1). There was a 7.5 per cent improvement in the A-G grades passes in the four-year period 1987-88 to 1990-91, as against 4 per cent in the seven years prior to the start of the GCSE; the difference was even more striking in the case of A-C grades passes – 11 per cent in the post-GCSE period, as against 2 per cent in the earlier period.

There are considerable problems in comparing examination results over time, particularly while 'O' level/CSE were in operation (Glennerster and Low, 1991). Nor are these two examinations (GCSE and 'O' level), strictly speaking, comparable. Apart from other things, the 'O' level was based on a 'norm-referencing' system which compared a pupil's performance against others in the cohort; the GCSE, on the other hand, has moved towards a criterion-referencing system, that is where performance is assessed on the basis of what a candidate knows, understands and can do. Moreover, some of this improvement reflects, firstly, the policy goals and expenditures of previous decades; and, secondly, is due to the cumulative effect of progressive extension of the comprehensive school movement since the mid-sixties (Glennerster and Low, 1991).

Deprivation and educational attainment

We shall now discuss the relationship between educational performance and deprivation. Table 5.2, reproduced here from *Urban Trends 1* (1992), displays school leaving examination data for the ten-year period 1979-80 to 1989-90, aggregated in groups of three years, for the 14 most deprived LEAs in the country, together with corresponding regional and national averages. Originally, the authors (Willmott and Hutchinson, 1992) had intended to present the data for the 30 most deprived LEAs based on the DoE deprivation(Z)scores for the Urban Programme Authorities. However, seven of these 30 turned out to be 'Shire' districts; and of the remaining 23 LEAs, they decided to treat the inner London LEAs, for the purpose of this analysis, as if they were still part of the Inner London Education Authority (ILEA) (which they were until March 1990), thus reducing the number to 14.

As Table 5.2 indicates, the improvement has not been registered evenly across the country. In fact, there is a definite relationship here between deprivation and low attainment. In 1979, the proportion of school leavers with five or more passes with A-C grades in all the deprived-area LEAs was **below** the national, and the corresponding regional, averages. This has remained so throughout the eighties; if anything, the gap has widened. Even among these highly deprived LEAs, the gap between those with a relatively low deprivation score (Rochdale and Salford) and those with a high deprivation score (Newham) has also widened in this period. In fact, the position of some other LEAs has also deteriorated: for instance, Knowsley and Coventry made little or no progress, and Bradford's results were poorer in 1989-90 than in 1979. Whilst the decline in the case of Bradford's results may be explicable, in part, in terms of their low level of net institutional expenditure on education per secondary

Table 5.2 Those leaving secondary school with five or more CSE grade 1, and/or 'O' level grades A-C, and/or GCSE grades A-C[1] in England 1979/80 — 1989/90

England

Percentages of all school leavers

	Rank order of deprivation (Z) Scores	1979/80 80/1, 81/2	1982/3 83/4, 84/5	1985/6 86/7, 87/8	1987/8 88/9, 89/90
Brent	(8)	17.5	19.4	19.1	23.3
Haringey	(6)	15.0	15.5	17.3	19.8
Newham	(2)	12.8	10.4	14.3	14.3
Inner London Education Authority[4]		14.0	15.2	16.1	17.4[2]
Greater London		20.2	21.5	21.9	24.6
Birmingham	(14)	18.5	18.6	18.3	22.7
Coventry	(18)	19.8	20.2	20.7	21.3
Sandwell	(19)	12.6	13.1	14.6	17.4
Wolverhampton	(13)	14.9	16.9	17.8	21.2
West Midlands		20.2	21.7	22.7	26.6
Knowsley	(22)	11.4	13.1	10.0	11.6
Liverpool	(14)	16.5	18.5	17.9	20.7
Manchester	(11)	15.7	17.8	15.9	20.2
Rochdale	(29)	16.5	21.1	18.7	24.5
Salford	(30)	14.5	18.0	21.8	24.9
North West		20.7	23.3	24.1	28.4
Bradford	(26)	18.9	18.0	16.0	16.9
Yorkshire & Humberside		20.4	21.5	21.7	26.0
England		21.9	23.6	24.4	28.6

Source: DES Statistics of Education: School Leavers CSE and GCSE, annual publications until 1988; DES Statistics of Education: School Examinations GCSE and GCE, annual publications 1989 and 1990. *Reproduced from Urban Trends 1 (1992)

Notes:
1. Aggregations of school leavers in groups of three academic years.
2. Data for inner London boroughs used for 1989/90.
3. Based on DoE deprivation (Z) scores for the 57 Urban Programme Authorities.
4. Includes 7 of the 10 most deprived LEAs in England; and 10 out of its 12 boroughs (except Camden, Westminster and the City of London) are among the 30 most deprived LEAs in England; 85 per cent of the population of these inner London boroughs live in the 30 most deprived areas in England.

pupil (third lowest of all 91 LEAs in 1989-90), this is not the most likely explanation for the slower progress in the case of other deprived area LEAs, since nine of these 13 LEAs were in the top 13 LEAs in terms of their net institutional expenditure per secondary pupil (*Hansard*, 3.2.92, cols 42-44). It is fair to point out here that, since this table is based on DES data on 'School Leavers' covering the 16 to 18 age-group, this comparison is also likely to be influenced by differences in post-16 participation rates between these LEAs.

The link between deprivation and low attainment is reinforced when we look at Table 5.3, which gives details of school leavers who were unable to obtain any graded results, again for the same set of 14 deprived-area LEAs for the 1979-80 to 1989-90 period, comparing them with their corresponding regional and national figures.

As this table shows, the percentage of those leaving school with no graded results in these deprived-area LEAs was above the national average – in most cases, more than 50 per cent above. This applied to all these LEAs all through the eighties, except for Coventry which in the last three years of the decade was just able to exceed the national average. However, in the case of Knowsley, Liverpool and Manchester, the proportion of pupils leaving with no graded results actually **increased** in the eighties, while it more or less stayed put in the case of Birmingham and the Inner London Education Authority (ILEA), against the national trend of a **decline**.

A survey by Jesson and Gray (1991) of Nottinghamshire's secondary schools in 1989-90, based on a 20 per cent random sample of Year 11 pupils (2,106) in 71 secondary schools, provides more direct evidence of a close association between deprivation (as measured by the take-up of free school meals (FSM)) and low attainment. It shows, that half of those in receipt of FSM had an examination (GCSE) score below 15 points[1], as compared to one sixth of pupils not in receipt of FSM. If anything, FSM **understates** the true extent of poverty. As Grimshaw and Pratt (1986) have pointed out, according to one official estimate, now perhaps somewhat out of date owing to adverse economic trends, 40 per cent of those eligible do not claim FSM (*TES*, 6.11.81). When schools were allocated according to their degree of social disadvantage (measured by three indicators: FSM, family size and ethnic origin), it was found that there was a consistent and strong relationship with examination entry and performance: the number of GCSE subjects for which pupils were entered declined from eight in the least disadvantaged cluster to just over five in the most disadvantaged cluster; similarly, the median score (in the GCSE examination) for the least disadvantaged cluster was 35, as against only about 10 for the most disadvantaged cluster. This is not to say that disadvantage invariably signified poor performance. As Jesson and Gray point out, some of those in receipt of FSM did manage to achieve relatively high examination scores. All one can say is that '... as a group those in receipt of FSM perform on average very much less well than their not so disadvantaged peers' (Jesson and Gray, 1991, p.12). Findings from Scottish research also indicate that educational performance tends to be lower in schools in deprived areas after pupil ability and family background have been taken into account (Cuttance, 1988; Garner, 1989).

Table 5.3 Those leaving secondary school with no graded results[1] in England 1979/80 — 1989/90

England	Rank order of deprivation (Z) scores[3]	Percentages of all school leavers			
		1979/80 80/1, 81/2	1982/3 83/4, 84/5	1985/6 86/7, 87/8	1987/8 88/9, 89/90
Brent	(8)	16.2	12.4	11.5	10.4
Haringey	(6)	20.8	20.1	15.6	15.6
Newham	(2)	25.2	22.6	21.7	22.2
Inner London Education Authority[4]		21.5	21.2	21.3	21.1[2]
Greater London		15.7	14.1	14.5	13.5
Birmingham	(14)	14.4	14.8	14.6	14.3
Coventry	(18)	12.7	12.2	10.4	8.9
Sandwell	(19)	19.6	15.9	15.3	12.9
Wolverhampton	(13)	16.0	17.3	13.9	11.9
West Midlands		14.1	11.7	10.9	9.5
Knowsley	(22)	21.1	21.9	25.2	24.5
Liverpool	(14)	19.2	19.0	23.3	21.5
Manchester	(11)	21.7	20.1	21.2	22.8
Rochdale	(29)	17.0	16.5	16.5	15.9
Salford	(30)	16.7	15.2	13.4	11.0
North West		14.2	12.0	12.2	11.1
Bradford	(26)	18.8	16.5	17.8	15.0
Yorkshire & Humberside		13.0	10.9	11.6	10.4
England		12.0	10.0	10.0	9.0

* Source: *DES Statistics of Education: School Leavers CSE and GCSE*, annual publications until 1988; *DES Statistics of Education: School Examinations GCSE and GCE*, annual publications 1989 and 1990. * Reproduced from *Urban Trends 1* (1992).

Notes:
1. Aggregations of school leavers in groups of three academic years.
2. Data for inner London boroughs used for 1989/90.
3. Based on DoE deprivation (Z) scores for the 57 Urban Programme Authorities.
4. Includes 7 of the 10 most deprived LEAs in England; and 10 out of its 12 boroughs (except Camden, Westminster and the City of London) are among the 30 most deprived LEAs in England; 85 per cent of the population of these inner London boroughs live in the 30 most deprived areas in England.

Reasons why a proportion of deprived children tend to achieve better than non-deprived at school, while the majority do not, are not well understood (as we noted in the last section). At a general level, research indicates that the relatively greater progress of children who do well at school, despite their deprivation, is related to ability, will-power, achievement-oriented attitudes and values; and circumstances such as emotional support and security at home, other favourable life experiences of various kinds and, above all, the availability of opportunities (Brown and Madge, 1982; Pilling, 1990). Moreover, variations in the effectiveness of schools either in general, or in relation to groups from particular backgrounds, may also account for this phenomenon. In other words, the school can compensate for the disadvantage of a child, as well as aggravate it. We shall discuss this issue in the next section.

Deprivation and equality of opportunity in education

How disadvantage affects school performance is at the heart of the debate on equality of opportunity in education and was thrown into sharp relief in the context of the *Swann Committee of Inquiry into the Education of Children from Ethnic Minority Groups*. The Committee was handicapped by a lack of adequate official data, comparing the educational performance of different ethnic groups. However, it went on to summarise existing research, and commissioned the DES to fill some of the gaps.

It was very concerned to find that pupils belonging to minority ethnic groups, especially those of Caribbean origin, were doing less well at school, and in public examinations, as compared to their White peers. When discussing the reasons for this, the Swann Committee, after a thorough investigation, rejected low IQ as '...a significant factor in under achievement', which it attributed mainly to social class, relying on the long known correlation between it and school performance. Research by Rutter and others (1979) had shown a strong correlation between social class and examination performance, with children from social classes I and II achieving on average twice as many high grade passes at 'O' levels as those from social classes IV and V. Likewise, ILEA examination data, using an indirect measure of social class from their work on Educational Priority Areas (EPA), indicated a strong relationship between schools with a higher proportion of pupils from families in social classes IV and V and a lower performance in the public examinations (ILEA, 1981).

The Swann Committee was aware, as we have noted previously, that the level of deprivation was considerably higher among the minority ethnic groups, as compared to the rest of the population, as a result of their disproportionate representation among the unemployed, the low-paid, and among those in poor housing and ill-health. It recognised that:

the ethnic minorities...are particularly disadvantaged...and there can no longer be any doubt that this extra deprivation is the result of racial prejudice and discrimination especially in the areas of employment and housing (Swann, 1985, p.89).

According to Swann, this extra deprivation over and above that of disadvantaged Whites substantially explained ethnic under-achievement; the rest of under achievement, it believed:

is due in large measure to prejudice and discrimination bearing *directly* on children, within the education system, as well as outside it (emphasis in the original) (pp.89-90).

It also felt that the issues were complex and the research evidence on teacher expectations and stereotyping was inconclusive, and called for more research to illuminate this whole area of how the school affects the performance of different groups of pupils.

Deprivation and ethnic differences in attainment

A review of research over the last 20 years by Drew and Gray confirms that there is a significant Black and White gap in examination results of secondary school pupils. Their own research, based on a large nationally representative sample (14,429) indicates that the average gap between the White group and African-Caribbeans was of five examination points (1990). Subsequent research has confirmed the gap (though of differing magnitude) not only in relation to African-Caribbeans, but also Bangladeshis (Jesson and Gray, 1991; Jesson, Gray and Tranmer, 1992; Nuttal, 1992). With a few exceptions, most of these studies seek to explain ethnic group differences in terms of social class. It is worth reminding ourselves here that social class is only a proxy for a range of other factors – by itself it can explain nothing, otherwise we run the risk of fostering, what Mortimore and Coulter (in a similar context) call '...a deterministic view of a socially disadvantaged child' as a poor attender or a poor student (1982, p.8). And by disregarding the possible impact of the school on performance, these studies come close to 'blaming the victim' (Jesson and Gray, 1991), and fall prey to what Parekh has called the 'fallacy of the single factor' explanation (1983).

Interaction between race and social class

We noted in the previous section that, in the primary school, the gap between White and minority ethnic group children tends to widen as they progress through the school, even when they are at par at the beginning. Research by Maughan and Rutter (1986) on secondary school pupils concludes that, whatever the initial gap between the ethnic groups, it remains unaffected by subsequent progress made during the five years of the secondary school. However, studies based on ILEA data claim that minority ethnic group pupils are making the same or greater progress than White pupils. 'Progress' is judged by comparing actual examination performance at age 16 with the performance predicted on the basis of ability at age 11. Each pupil is allocated to one of three verbal reasoning (VR) bands on the basis of **assessment** of the primary school head at age 11.

However, measuring 'progress' in this way is problematic: its reliability depends on the accuracy as well as the predictability of the concept of ability used. For instance, in the study by Kysel (1987), it was claimed that the results achieved by Caribbean pupils '...were not significantly different from the results predicted on the basis of sex and VR band' (p13). It was observed, though, that there was considerable over-representation of Caribbean, as well as of Asian, pupils in VR bands 2 and 3, and their under-representation in VR band 1. Kysel conceded that there may be '...some bias in the assessment of pupils from different ethnic groups', that primary heads tended to under-estimate the ability of minority ethnic group pupils, and over-estimate that of White pupils (p16). Further investigation (in the Junior School Project) revealed that, in 79 per cent of cases, there was agreement between the primary heads' assessment of Caribbean pupils' ability and VR test results, as against 86 per cent of cases for English, Scottish, Welsh and Irish (ESWI) pupils. 'However, where there was a mismatch, Caribbean pupils were more likely to be assigned to a lower band (that is, band 2 or 3) by the head than their VR test results would indicate, while the reverse was true for ESWI pupils' (Kysel, 1987, p16).

The author goes on to observe that:

...under-estimation of the VR banding of Caribbean pupils by primary heads (compared to VR test results) was of sufficient magnitude to alter...(her original) conclusion that Caribbean pupils were not under-achieving in examinations (p16).

In other words, their performance at 16 was not only worse than that of White pupils in absolute terms, but was also significantly below that predictable from their **actual** VR test results. This means, in effect, that on the basis of this evidence, the initial gap between the Caribbean and White pupils, which had opened up in the primary school, has not only not been narrowed in the secondary school; it may even have been widened, if the 'progress' made by the Caribbean pupils were to be proportionately less than that made by ESWI pupils.

As for Kysel's other main conclusion, that Asian pupils (of Indian, Pakistani and SE Asian origin) tend to achieve results which are significantly better than predicted on the basis of their sex and VR band, she admits that this cannot be explained by ethnic differences in VR banding at age 11. However, as Kysel points out, unlike the Caribbean pupils, the effect of likely bias in the under-estimation of Asian pupils' ability by the primary heads cannot be quantified, due to the small size of the sample of Asian pupils in the Junior School Project.

Kysel also offers another explanation which questions the **predictability** of VR band assessment for some groups who are not very fluent in English at age 11, but become fluent by the time they are 16. Pupils lacking in fluency in English only constitute a proportion of the aforementioned Asian groups. It is unlikely, therefore, that this factor alone can account for the apparently greater 'progress' of these Asian groups. For this to happen, they will in any case have to catch up **over and above** ESWI pupils in the secondary school – there is no evidence that this is happening.

In our view, what is questionable is not just the predictability, but also the accuracy, of verbal reasoning as a relatively crude tool with three insufficiently differentiated bands to assess the **general** ability of pupils (Drew and Gray, 1991). Its use for pupils lacking fluency in English at 11 is even more questionable even as a measure of their 'general ability', let alone their mathematical ability. These shortcomings in the concept of verbal reasoning, reinforced by a high probability of bias in the primary heads' assessment of minority ethnic pupils' ability at age 11, tend to undermine, in our view,

Kysel's main conclusion that Caribbean and certain Asian pupils were making the same or greater 'progress' than White pupils.

The above mentioned comment has implications also for subsequent research based on this measure, such as that by Nuttal (1990), and Nuttal and Goldstein (1992).

Differential school effectiveness

Recently a number of studies have directly looked at school effectiveness. Rutter and others (1979) in a study of 12 inner London comprehensives found that schools with similar intakes, similar level of resources and catchment areas vary in their effectiveness. A longitudinal study by Smith and Tomlinson (1989) in the first half of the eighties, based on a sample of 18 inner city schools in four LEAs, also found wide differences in average effectiveness between schools when controlled for intake and other background factors. For instance, a pupil in the top quartile of effectiveness obtained on average two more 'high grade' 'O' level passes than one in the bottom quartile. They also found that Black pupils made greater progress in some schools than others, but claimed that these differences (never quantified) were eclipsed by the much larger differences in the average effectiveness of schools in general. Their main conclusion was that the schools that were '...good for White pupils tended to be about equally good for Black pupils' also (p.305). This seems to be somewhat inconsistent with their other conclusion that **some** schools were more effective in relation to Black pupils. Their tentativeness on this question is due, according to Drew and Gray (1991), to the sampling strategy of their study and, in particular, to its relatively small sample size.

However, their key finding about the general effectiveness of schools has been directly challenged by Nuttal and Goldstein (1989), whose own study is based on a large sample (31,623) of pupils in three cohorts of about 140 ILEA schools during 1985-87. They question the notion of a single dimension of school effectiveness. For they found that schools were differentially effective across the ability range: some schools were more effective in relation to high ability intake than those of low ability; while others showed the reverse effect. Rarely was a school equally effective in relation to pupils of all three ability bands. In the same way, they found that:

some schools are more effective in raising the achievements of one or more ethnic minority groups in comparison with those of ESWs, and others where ESWs do relatively better than minority students (p.21).

They contend that 'ethnic' differences, though smaller than school differences, were substantial; moreover, part of the school differences were attributed to differential effectiveness with different ethnic groups...(p.21).

For example, in the case of pupils of African-Caribbean origin of similar prior attainment, difference in examination success between two schools could be one 'high grade' 'O'level pass; while the difference in the case of Pakistani pupils could be as much as two 'O' level passes. In view of these findings, they concluded that it did not make sense to talk about school effectiveness in unidimensional terms. Besides, some of the difference in effectiveness **between** schools also reflected differences in effectiveness **with** different ethnic groups.

However, as Drew and Gray (1990) point out, Nuttal and Goldstein's study, relying as it does on ILEA data, suffers from the same problems discussed above in relation to Kysel (1988): that is '...the rather crude (three category) nature' of the prior attainment variable (VR Band scores) which '...makes it less adequate than might at first appear' (p.170); and the possibility of teachers making 'inappropriate assignments' of pupils from minority ethnic backgrounds to the three VR Bands. They suggest that the study's conclusions could have been strengthened considerably if information about the social class backgrounds of pupils were available for use alongside verbal reasoning bands.

The overall conclusion drawn by Nuttal (and Goldstein) from their own and previous research in this field is that:

it is by no means clear whether social class factors or ethnic factors are more important in explaining differences in the performance of different ethnic groups; in the present research, they are largely confounded, but it is safe to conclude that both kinds are involved in some measure (p.23).

However, as Drew and Gray (1991) point out, it is also unclear whether schools are *the* major contributing factor in explaining the Black-White gap in educational attainment. Nevertheless, they conclude that, on both the question of school effects and the question of differential effectiveness, these studies 'provide support for the view that schools make some difference' (p.170). In other words, they can compensate as well as aggravate the educational disadvantage of deprived pupils in general, and those from minority ethnic groups in particular.

Interaction between the pupil and the school

School effectiveness studies, using advanced statistical techniques such as multi-level modelling, are useful in indicating differences in effectiveness, but cannot generally tell us about the underlying causes. They generate more questions than answers (Nuttal, 1990). Why are some schools more effective for some groups of pupils than others? How do practices like streaming, setting and banding, and associated teacher expectations of pupils, affect the progress of different groups of children? What role do teachers play in pupils' choice of subjects for, and level of, public examinations? How do quality and turnover of teachers affect children's education? Finally, what impact does the (varying) quality of interaction between the school and different groups of pupils have on the latter's progress? In short, does the school encourage or inhibit different groups of pupils, irrespective of their gender, race or disability, and especially those who are already deprived, from achieving their full potential? These are large and complex questions to answer. One cannot even begin to tackle them except through carefully planned, good quality ethnographic research (Gillborn and Drew, 1992). We shall briefly review what evidence is available on some of these questions from the viewpoint of deprived children in general, and minority ethnic group pupils in particular (since they are disproportionately represented among the deprived, as noted earlier), bearing in mind the scarcity of evidence about the direct influence of the variables involved on educational outcomes (Mortimore and Blackstone, 1982).

Review of research evidence by Mortimore and Blackstone (1982) indicates that streaming may contribute to educational disadvantage in a number of ways. Pupils from deprived homes tend to be over-represented in the lower streams, as we saw in relation to ILEA pupils in the eighties (Kysel, 1987). For such pupils, the chances of upward mobility tend to be low; they are likely to be taught by inexperienced teachers, and perform according to low expectations of them. This may lead to low self-esteem, low attainment, boredom and lack of motivation, probably hostility among some towards the school and what it represents (Mortimore and Blackstone, 1982).

In addition, the process of streaming may not be entirely free from bias: a study by Middleton (1983) found that African-Caribbean boys in the schools in his study tended to be allocated to lower bands and be less likely to be placed in 'O' level classes, even when measured ability did not justify a lower placement.

A case study recently published by the Commission for Racial Equality (CRE) shows how setting and banding arrangements in a North of England comprehensive school 'effectively disadvantaged and potentially discriminated against ethnic minority pupils' (1992a, p.12). It reveals that Asian pupils were under-represented on English and Mathematics GCSE courses in Year 10 and 11. This was due, firstly, to the fact that Asian pupils were more likely than White pupils to be placed in sets below their ability levels as assessed by their primary schools. Secondly, Asian pupils:

deemed to require ESL (English as a second language) support were placed in the lower ability Maths and English sets and generally remained there throughout their period at (the) secondary school (CRE, 1992a, p.13).

Apparently, the school confused children requiring ESL support with those having learning difficulties, thus resulting in their misallocation to lower ability sets; this could not be corrected because of the rigidity of the setting system (CRE, 1992a; 1992b).

Choice of subjects and allocation to examination levels

In the early 1980s, analysis of official data indicated that West Indian pupils were over-represented in CSE streams – 46 per cent as against 33 per cent of pupils nationally. This finding comes from a school leavers' survey in six LEAs accounting for roughly half of ethnic minority pupils in England and Wales, which was conducted by the DES for the Swann Committee (Swann, 1985, Annex B). Since then a major new study of 18 multi-ethnic comprehensives carried out by Tomlinson during 1983-84 for the DES has become available. According to this study,

evidence does seem to be accumulating that normal school processes, not designed to be 'racist' and often operated by liberal and well-intentioned teachers, can have the effect of disadvantaging pupils from particular ethnic groups, in addition to those from lower socio-economic groups and some girls. Curriculum option choice at 13 plus is one such process and the process can be regarded as a structural inequality. (Tomlinson, 1987, pp.105-6)

This is also supported by an intensive ethnographical study during 1982-84 of two multiracial comprehensives by Wright (1987).

Ostensibly, Tomlinson argues, the allocation of pupils to subjects and examination levels is based on ability, but this is an ambiguous concept. Factors related to class, gender, race, and behaviour 'can be shown to affect the placement of pupils at option time, even those of similar ability' (p.106). Likewise, similar considerations influenced entry to particular examination levels. She observed that, depending on the school:

the composite effect of socio-economic group and ethnic origin would result in some pupils with equal attainment scores, but with differing physical and social characteristics, being entered for examinations at different levels (p.101).

In her study, Wright (1987) found that a higher proportion of African-Caribbean students was allocated to examination sets below their ability, suggesting that '...within this school overt discriminating practices were operating against the Afro-Caribbean students' (pp.123-24).

Both Tomlinson and Wright point out that, given the powerful role of teachers in the option choice process, if they hold stereotyped views or 'low' expectations about people from a particular socio-economic, gender or ethnic group, their decisions are likely to disadvantage (and discriminate against) such pupils; firstly in the level of education and qualifications they obtain and, subsequently, in the job market (1987). Not surprisingly, in two schools with a high proportion of minority ethnic group students, the latter were less likely to accept teachers' judgement of their ability (Tomlinson, 1987).

Summary

In this section, we looked at trends in examination results at 16 plus and found a significant improvement in performance since 1979. This was particularly so in the case of girls, who had widened their gap with boys in general as well as in English, while closing it in Mathematics and Science. However, most of the improvement had occurred in the period after 1988 when the first cohort of 16-year-olds sat the new GCSE examination. It was markedly less in deprived-area LEAs. There was also research evidence indicating a close link between deprivation and examination performance.

We also reviewed research on the interaction between race and social class. The gap in performance between White and Black pupils is well documented in the literature, but there is divergence of views as to the relative importance of social class and race in explaining the gap. We critically examined the claim that pupils from minority ethnic backgrounds were making the same, if not greater, progress, than the White pupils, and concluded that this notion of 'progress' was based on an unreliable, if not also a biased, assessment of pupils from minority ethnic groups. On the question of school effectiveness, there is conflicting evidence as to whether schools are generally effective, or differentially so in relation to particular groups whether defined by ability or ethnicity. Evidence is unclear whether schools are the major contributor to the White-Black gap in performance, but they evidently make some difference. However, qualitative research by Tomlinson (1987) and Wright (1987) demonstrates that the way the normal school processes of setting, banding, selection for option choices and examination level operate, tend to be inherently disadvantageous and frequently discriminatory against pupils belonging to lower-ranked social classes in general, and minority ethnic groups in particular.

Truancy and deprivation

In this section, we shall look briefly at the nature and scale of the problem of truancy, its general pattern, its relationship with poverty and deprivation and other factors, including the role of the school. It has been a longstanding problem of public concern, for it detracts from the basic principle underlying the 1944 Education Act, of education for **all**, and adversely affects the life chances of a significant minority of young people who are excluded from the full benefits of education.

The nature and scale of truancy

Truancy is a particular form of non-attendance and defining it is problematic (Gray, 1990). Since non-attendance includes several different forms of absence, including genuine illness and truancy, it is not easy to separate the two (Mortimore, 1982). As statistics are collected from a variety of sources, employing different definitions, and at different times and places, reliable information on the scale of the problem is hard to find, especially in the absence of nationally representative studies, as the DES (now DFE) is well aware (DES, 1989). There are basically three main sources of information: the school's attendance register; teachers' estimates; or pupils' self-reports. Whilst none of these is altogether free from bias, the techniques of relying on asking pupils appears to have been developed to the point that the data yielded by it has a high correlation with data from other sources (Mortimore, 1982); and reflects, according to Gray and Jesson (1990), a shared 'common view (among young people) of what constituted truancy...'. The added advantage of this method is that it can also provide information on post-registration truancy, that is pupils who leave the school after registration, or simply 'bunk off' particular lessons which they do not like, while still being on the premises. This is an under-researched area – the problem was highlighted in a recent small scale study (Stoll and O'Keefe, 1989).

Information on the size of the truancy problem has become available only recently with the publication of a large-scale study by Sheffield University, based on data derived from the Youth Cohort Study of England and Wales (Gray and Jesson, 1990). This is a major national survey of young people in their fifth form at school during 1984, 1985, 1986 and 1988 respectively. It records their experiences of school work, post-compulsory education and training. It is based on pupils drawn from nationally representative samples of secondary schools, with response rates averaging upwards of 70 per cent. In compiling their estimates, the authors have combined the responses of over 40,000 young people, and taken into account the known differences in non-response.

Inexplicably though, there is no data on ethnicity in this otherwise comprehensive study. Or is it the case that the ethnic dimension has been neglected in the publication?

The evidence of 'serious' truanting (defined as absence for several days or weeks at a time) is not high – just over one in 20 pupils (six per cent) reported it. 'Selective' truanting (missing school for particular days or lessons) was higher – one in ten reported this. Just over a third (36 per cent) reported truanting occasionally ('a lesson here and there'), while just under a half (48 per cent) claimed they had 'never' truanted. The levels of truancy reported by boys and girls were very similar, contrary to the popular impression that truancy was more of a male problem. It can also vary with the time of day (being higher in the morning than in the afternoon), and between terms – it tends to be higher in the autumn and spring terms than in the summer term (Mortimore, 1982). Recent research from Wales indicates that summer-born children are more likely to miss school (Carroll, 1992). Other research indicates that truancy is closely related to the school level. It is a minor problem at the primary level, and in the first two years of the secondary school; it begins to rise in the third year till it reaches a peak in the fifth year (Mortimore, 1982; DES, 1989). There is considerable stability in the general pattern of truancy, over time. The study by Gray and Jesson found no evidence that it was getting worse during the 1984-88 period; this was also confirmed in a survey of school attendance by the *Times Educational Supplement* in 1989 (3.11.89).

However, for a small minority of pupils, absenteeism levels reach over 50 per cent. Although, there are no figures at the national level about the scale of this problem, two studies in Sheffield, in 1976 and 1982, suggest that it affects around two per cent of pupils (Galloway, 1979; Grimshaw and Pratt, 1986). There is a high correlation between persistent absenteeism and overall attendance rates (Galloway, 1985). About three-quarters of persistent absenteeism in 1976 was regarded as unjustified and therefore termed truancy[2]. On this basis, 1.5 per cent of pupils in 1976 were deemed to be persistently truant. There was a small increase in persistent absenteeism between 1976 and 1982 (from 2.0 to 2.2 per cent) which was statistically significant. Otherwise, the pattern was very similar to that noted above (Grimshaw and Pratt, 1986).

Variations in truancy between schools

In line with previous research (Gray and others, 1983), Gray and Jesson found considerable variation in truancy between schools: in the great majority (over 70 per cent), the proportions of 'serious' truants were low. However, in one in five schools it was over ten per cent; and in about one in 12 schools it was over 20 per cent.

Truancy and disadvantage

There is a strong association between truancy and disadvantage. Gray and Jesson's study found that truancy was a serious problem in 'inner city' areas, that is 'areas experiencing severe economic, environmental and social disadvantage in major population centres' (1990, p.4). About one in seven young people attend schools located in such 'inner city' areas: ten per cent of them reported 'serious' truancy, as against six per cent overall; and 13 per cent reported 'selective' truancy, as against ten per cent overall. At the school level too, the incidence of 'serious' truancy reported by fifth year pupils in inner city secondary school was higher than in other schools. 'Serious' truancy of over ten per cent was reported by one in four of inner city secondary schools, as against one in five generally; likewise 'serious' truancy of over 20 per cent was reported by one in eight of inner-city secondary schools, as against one in 12 by other schools. There is also strong evidence of regional variation in attendance, reflecting not only differences in socio-economic factors, but also '...differences in tradition, attitudes to education and the influence of employment and the local economy' (DES, 1989, p.44).

Factors associated with truancy

Some people have sought to explain truancy in terms of personality traits or psychological well-being of individual pupils, but the evidence appears to be contradictory (Mortimore, 1982). Both Davies and Woods found a close relationship between socio-economic status and absence – the lower the parental occupational status, the lower the attendance (Davies, 1980; Woods, 1980). In the early 1980s, in a survey of all 35 secondary schools in Sheffield, Grimshaw and Pratt (1986) showed a strong association between absenteeism and poverty (as measured by eligibility for and take up of free school meals); as well as by an index of cumulative disadvantage based on census returns. The main exception to this trend was pupils of West Indian origin, who had higher attendance rates, whatever their socio-economic status (Davies, 1980; Woods, 1980). It is also pertinent to mention here that only a minority of children from disadvantaged backgrounds are implicated in 'serious' truancy and even fewer in persistent absenteeism (Galloway, 1985).

Poor school attendance is also linked to certain family circumstances. Both Woods (1980) and Fogelman (1976) found an association between the size of family (more than four siblings) or an unemployed father and truancy. Parents' attitude to their children's schooling was strongly linked to truancy (Davies 1980). There is considerable evidence to suggest that schools also exert an independent influence on pupil attendance after differences in catchment areas, ability and parental occupation are taken into account. Rutter and others (1979) found that differences between secondary schools in London were most marked in the fifth year, but were also noticeable in the younger age-group, even after they had controlled for the above-mentioned factors; somewhat similar results were obtained earlier in South Wales by Reynolds and others (1980). The findings of these and earlier studies (Davies, 1980; Woods, 1980) are applicable to urban as well as rural areas. One can infer from this accumulating evidence that what the schools do and the quality of education they offer does make a difference (DES,1989; TES, 3.11.89).

As Galloway (1985) points out:

...poor attendance can only be understood in terms of an interaction between these factors (individual, family and community) and the school (p.39) [that is] ...factors within the school which may encourage, or inhibit regular attendance.

He adds that, just as schools vary in effectiveness, so do individual teachers within a school. This may help explain the widespread phenomenon of selective 'bunking' from particular lessons – deemed a rational choice by some researchers (Stoll and O'Keefe, 1989; Gray and Jesson, 1990).

Woods' (1980) study had shown a close relationship between disruptive behaviour (as seen by teachers) and low attendance. It also found a high correlation between low attainment and poor attendance, though it was not clear which came first. Davies (1980) had similarly found a correlation between ability (as measured by transfer tests taken at age 11) and attendance. A 'pilot' study by Bird (1987) of fifth form boys of an inner city comprehensive school developed an explanatory model based on data on attitudes to school life, along with socio-economic and school factors. It found that the causes of non-attendance were social and institutional rather than psychological. Low attendance was attributed to non-entry examinations and alienation from school life; that is, pupils:

who found neither intrinsic interest in study nor extrinsic pleasure in their contacts with teachers and other pupils. Their only enjoyment in school was in misbehaving...The picture was one of a small, but not insignificant, minority disaffected with school...and, perhaps, disregarded at home, by the exigences of families living in difficult social and economic circumstances (Bird, 1987, p.7).

There is corroborating evidence from the Gray and Jesson (1990) study, which found that seven out of ten 'serious' truants from inner city areas obtained no qualifications on leaving school, as against 28 per cent of non-truants, and one in five of all pupils nationally. Not surprisingly, the same proportion felt that the 'school had done little to prepare them for life when they left school'. Likewise 'serious' truants were most unlikely to stay in full-time education: only one out of ten, as against almost five out of ten of non- or occasional truants. And they were nearly three times more likely to be out of work as compared with non-truants. The post-school experiences of 'selective' truants were also quite similar to those of 'serious' truants (1990).

Summary

It is argued in this section that the problem of truancy affects a significant minority nationally, but a sizeable one in the multiply-deprived inner city areas, thereby signifying that there is a close link between deprivation and absentee-ism. The causal factors seem to be essentially socio-economic and institutional (family and school) rather than psychological. The problem of truancy, which greatly diminishes the educational experiences and life chances of a significant proportion of young people, is best understood, we feel, in the context of an interaction between the individual, the family and its socio-economic circum-stances, and the school. The school can exert an important influence on the levels of attendance by the kind of ethos and policy it adopts, since there are significant variations between schools in the extent of truancy which are independent of differences in catchment areas, socio-economic status and ability of their intake of pupils.

Education policy and expenditure – implications for provision

So far we have considered how some of the factors in the child's home/social background interact with the school and affect his or her educational performance. But this discussion has been in isolation from the institutional and financial contexts in which the school operates. In this section, we shall try to fill this gap by considering how trends in expenditure on education have impinged on schools' ability to perform. In this connection, we shall also briefly consider the resource implications of some recent changes in the Government's education policy, which were mentioned at the beginning of this chapter. At best this will be a tentative exercise, giving a general picture, not least because of changes in the format, style and coverage of issues and the extent of detail in the annual HMI reports, which is the principal source of evidence on this question.

We should like to endorse at the outset two points made by the HMI to provide a framework for the ensuing discussion. One, they were concerned not simply to answer the question whether the educational provision, and the quality of education itself, had declined as a result of Government's financial policies; but also whether 'the education now provided is good enough'. That is whether the level of resources was adequate to meet not just current commitments, but also to make improvements in accordance with changing needs in order to achieve the Government's goal of achieving basic standards in education. To this end, they clarified that their description of a service as 'satisfactory' merely meant that it was 'at least acceptable' by the prevailing standards, but that it did not:

...imply those improvements dependent on resources which were identified...(by them) as desirable or necessary to meet changing expectations (DES, 1981, para 6).

They also made it clear that it was:

...not possible to disentangle in the returns (made by their District Inspectors on the schools) the results of financial policies and inflation from the effects of falling rolls (1981, para 6).

They believed that the latter, in addition to the need for overall reductions, would involve diseconomies of scale, and problems of meeting commitments to pupils in secondary schools who had already started courses varying from two to seven years' duration (DES, 1981).

Second, HMI point out in their 1985 Report that, whereas the level of resources is only one of several factors influencing the quality of work, and that their relative importance varies between primary, secondary and special schools, there is nevertheless:

...a statistically significant association between satisfactory or better level of resources and work of sound quality... (DES, 1986, para 30).

Adequacy of expenditure to needs?

As we saw in chapter 2 (Table 2.9), there was a significant reduction in current education expenditure in primary schools, and a modest one in secondary schools, in the first half of the eighties. Admittedly, this was before taking into account the effects of falling rolls – which, as the HMI found, is problematic – but affects LEAs differently in terms of the amount of savings they have to make. Thus, whereas in 1980 15 per cent of LEAs had less than satisfactory provision in a majority of aspects in schools, by 1985 this number had more than doubled. And even with reference to the majority of LEAs which appeared to have maintained their overall levels of provision for schools, the HMI did not consider their baselines for some of that provision to be sufficient for them and their schools to meet demands for improvement (DES, 1981; 1986). In fact, they were regarded by the HMI to be:

getting by... by robbing Peter to pay Paul; doing less; or with the help of sizeable contributions from parents (DES, 1986).

Wide variations between LEA expenditure

In their 1985 report, the HMI observed that there was sharp polarisation in provision between schools in different parts of the country both within and between LEAs, and that these variations were increasing. Independent research by Glennerster and Low has also confirmed that the range of spending between local authorities had widened in the 1980s (1991). This reflects the fact that, whereas the central Government can, and did, impose an upper ceiling on educational expenditure as part of its general restrictions on public expenditure in the 1980s, the LEAs were free to make their own decisions on the level of education spending consistent with their statutory obligations. Among the other contributory factors mentioned were variations in pupil-teacher ratios, capitation, parental contributions and so on. Moreover, at the school level:

it is the least able in all types of school... who bear the brunt of reduced or inappropriate provision (DES, 1986).

The situation has apparently not changed much since then, as the HMI, referring to variations in standards in the system, reported in 1991:

There are worryingly poor standards among particular groups and in particular parts of the education service. They are serious, and almost all, regrettably, are of long standing. They include the children caught up in that stubborn statistic of around 30 per cent poorly provided for in the compulsory years of primary and secondary schooling; the less academically able who continue to suffer disproportionately from whatever chronic or acute problems affect the education service; those primary pupils learning to read in one of the 20 per cent of schools in which the teaching of reading is poor, and pupils in some inner-city schools where teacher turnover is such that continuity in learning and high standards of achievement are virtually impossible (DES, 1991a, p2).

Capital funding – impact of cuts

As we saw earlier (Table 2.9), there was a 7.5 per cent fall in **current** provision for premises at the primary level, and a ten per cent fall at the secondary level, in the period 1979-80 to 1988-89. These decreases were accompanied by dramatic cuts of 43 per cent and 56 per cent in **capital** spending for schools at the primary and secondary levels respectively. These cuts in capital expenditure put paid to the school renewal programme of mid-1970s, which therefore only reached a quarter of its target for 1987-88, with consequent build up of a backlog of obsolete buildings (Glennerster and Low, 1991).

Adequacy of provision for maintenance?

That the level of provision for the maintenance of school buildings was inadequate in the eighties and would have been even if the reductions had not been made – is clear from the following comments of HMI in their 1984 and 1992 reports. In 1984, the programme of maintenance was regarded as less than satisfactory or poor in 65 LEAs, almost the same as in the previous year. Poor or unsuitable accommodation was adversely affecting the quality of work in over one-fifth of all the lessons observed in the primary, secondary and special schools. 'All in all, much of the country's school building stock is in a sorry state of repair and getting worse' (DES, 1985b). A DES survey in 1986 showed that just under two-fifths (38 per cent) of primary, and a quarter of secondary, schools needed work on roofs, or heating systems, or walls and windows (*Education*, 16.8.91). Six years later, the situation was, if anything, worse. The HMI reported that accommodation in primary schools was less than satisfactory in two-fifths of schools. Even in the remainder where it was generally satisfactory or better, there were:

many instances in which lack of space... affected the quality of work. In secondary schools, there were accommodation deficiencies in 30 per cent of schools inspected, where problems included split sites, insufficient specialist accommodation and maintenance arrears (DES, 1992a).

The physical condition of school buildings continues to cause concern, according to a report by the NAO (1991). With the backlog of repairs and maintenance building up, the NAO report is concerned that insufficient money is being spent to offset the damage to education standards caused by badly designed buildings, vandalism and arson (NAO, 1991).

Shortfall in teaching resources or poor management?

The aggregate local authority expenditure shown in Table 2.9 showing a modest increase in the 1980s, is a poor guide to what individual schools get. For, as HMI explain, there are considerable variations between LEAs, both about the scope, as well as the rate, of capital allowances for different age-groups (DES, 1985b).

The situation also varies considerably over time. In 1980-81, the HMI reported that the provision of books was unsatisfactory in just under half the LEAs, and in half the secondary schools; but in primary schools, in only one-sixth was the provision not satisfactory. The decline in rolls had eased the situation somewhat, especially in primary schools. However, shortages in secondary schools had led to sharing of text books in class and the curtailment of homework. Inadequate library book stock was also reported as a problem (DES, 1981).

By 1985, the situation had improved somewhat in that the provision for books, materials and equipment was regarded as satisfactory in just under two-thirds of LEAs – the provision being less satisfactory for the secondary than for the primary level. Despite this improvement, work was reported by HMI as being less than satisfactory in a substantial number of lessons and the provision of teaching resources as inadequate.

By 1992, the HMI reported the overall level and quality of resources in secondary schools as generally adequate. However, it noted that the standards of provision and use of libraries were satisfactory or better in just over half the schools. At the primary level, it reported that the library provision 'varied' widely but was rarely very good. In many schools a considerable proportion of the non-fiction and reference books was seriously out of date and poorly matched to National Curriculum requirements, particularly in history and geography' (DES, 1992a). Overall, it reported that about a third of the schools did not have sufficient resources to meet National Curriculum requirements in the core subjects where '...shortage of practical equipment for mathematics, science and physical education and tools for art and technology restricted the quality of the work' (DES, 1992a).

It is fair to add, as the HMI have frequently pointed out, that the reasons for inadequate provision are not related exclusively to the **level** of expenditure. Other factors implicated include schools' buying policies, teachers' inadequate identification of pupils' educational needs, and poor school or departmental management.

Role of parental contributions

In a Gallop survey of 892 parents for BBC television, 60 per cent cited shortages of books as the greatest obstacle to raising standards (*The Guardian*, 31.1.92). Parents clearly feel strongly about the shortages in teaching resources; this is therefore an area where their monetary contribution is the most significant, in addition to help in kind. Both have become increasingly important in the eighties, as successive reports from the HMI have testified.

Recently, a survey of over 1,000 primary and middle schools by the National Association of Schoolmasters/Union of Women Teachers (NAS/UWT) found that nearly a third of schools had an inadequate supply of books; and that parents and other adults at seven out of ten (67 per cent) urban schools, and at over eight out of ten (84 per cent) rural schools, had helped to buy school books (*The Times*, 8.8.92). A Department for Education (DFE) spokeswoman responding to the survey characterised the parental contribution to the schools' running costs as marginal (*The Times*, 8.8.92). It is true that, overall, it ranges from 0.1 to 1.2 per cent of budgets (DFE, 1993). However, HMI reports suggest that, in the area of teaching resources, the parental contribution can be quite significant, especially in primary schools. For instance, in 1984 the HMI reported that in half the schools (over 300) on which they had information about parental contributions, these had exceeded a third of the school's capitation allowance provided by the LEA. The corresponding figure for 1985 was that two-fifths of 777 schools had received parental contributions on this scale (DES, 1985b; 1986).

Policy changes and resource implications

Of the principal changes in policy initiated by the Government in recent years, the GCSE examination is well established by now, and has led to improved results, as we noted earlier. The introduction of the National Curriculum (NC), with broad party political and public support, has made significant progress but, according to the latest HMI Report, has not so far led, except in primary science and some aspects of primary English, to any discernible general rise in standards, though many specific benefits have accrued (DES, 1993). Together with the introduction of assessment and national testing and the Local Management of Schools (LMS), these changes imposed a wide variety of new demands on staff time and skills. As the 1992 HMI report points out, primary class teachers, particularly in the late stages of Key Stage 2:

may fast be reaching the limits of their expertise and may be unable to teach the full nine-subject National Curriculum... (DES, 1992a, pp.13-14).

Other areas of concern mentioned in the HMI report include:

- difficulties experienced by teachers in the NC assessment, recording and reporting arrangements and practice;
- difficulties teachers face in all subjects and Key Stages in matching tasks to the ability of individual pupils (DES, 1992a; 1993);
- the need to increase the non-contact time of primary Heads/and class teachers to enable them to cope more effectively with increasing demands on their time and skills.

These difficulties are essentially 'teething troubles' to be expected in the implementation of a major reform, but do have training and resource implications. The latest HMI report says the restrictions on local authority budgets have made it harder to train teachers for the NC.

On the implementation of the LMS, the HMI report warns that experienced teachers face an increasing threat of redundancy, as schools with delegated budgets, based on average teacher salaries, come under increasing pressure to economise. Consequently, some schools are hiring large number of probationers, while others are using more part-time or short-time contracts or delaying promotions. While the LMS does give schools a measure of flexibility, if the trend to economise at the expense of experience gains momentum, it does have implications for educational standards (DFE, 1992j).

Summary

In this section, we have considered the implications of the Government's education expenditure for educational provision, in the light of its concern for achieving good basic standards. According to HMI reports, the level of expenditure since 1979 has been enough, in the light of falling rolls, to maintain basic provision in the majority of schools – in about a third of schools even this is not enough. However, this level of expenditure is insufficient to sustain improvements required to cope with the changing needs and new demands emanating from the major policy and legislative changes introduced by the Government in this period. The shortfalls have been substantial in capital expenditure affecting the school renewal programme, and significant in the maintenance of premises and in the provision of books, materials and equipment, with adverse effects on the quality of teaching and learning. However, inadequacies in the provision of teaching resources is due not just to Government restrictions on expenditure, but also to the stance of individual LEAs and the buying policies, management and planning skills of individual schools.

The second major concern aired by the HMI is that there are wide variations in expenditure both between as well as within LEAs, and that these have been increasing over the years. Even more worrying, they point out, is the fact that it is the least able pupils in some of the most deprived inner city schools who tend to suffer most from inadequate and inappropriate provision. Finally, while the recent policy and legislative changes are broadly welcomed, despite some anxieties in their implementation, these do place considerable new demands on the time and skills of teachers, with implications for additional resources.

Access to further and higher education

In this section, we shall chart trends in access to further and higher education (FHE), giving social class and ethnic breakdowns where available, and making links with deprivation if possible.

Participation of 16 to 18-year-olds in education

Table 5.4 and Figure 5.1 show separate trends for the participation of young people aged 16, 17 and 18 years in education. In all three age-groups, there have been impressive increases in participation rates for full-time education – about three-fifths for 16-year-olds; four-fifths for 17-year-olds; and almost doubled for 18-year-olds. The increase was small in the first eight years (1979-80 to 1987-88), but was quite rapid in the next four years – of the order of two-fifths for 16-year-olds; and a half for 17 and 18-year-olds. The overall participation rate in full-time education for the 16 to 18 age-group went up by about a third from 28 per cent in 1979-80 to 37 per cent in 1989-90. The staying on rate at school increased from 16 to 20 per cent in this period, while participation in FHE increased from 12 to 17 per cent (DES, 1991, *Statistical Bulletin* 13/91, Table 2).

The increase was due in part to a reduction in the proportion of pupils in part-time education (especially for those aged 16 years), but mainly it was attributable to a reduction in the proportion of those who previously were having no education in this age-group. In terms of educational qualifications,

Figure 5.1   Participation of 16 to 18-year-olds in education 1979/80 – 1991/92

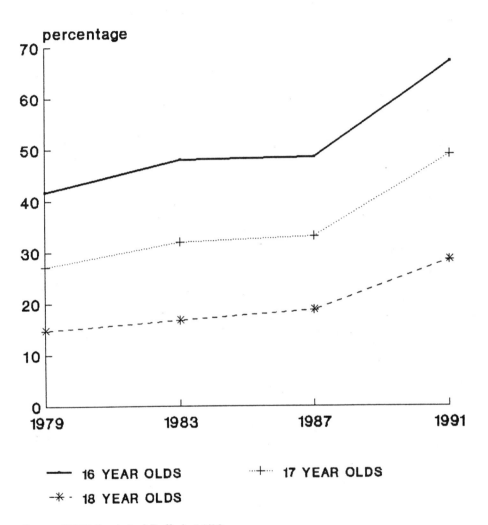

Source: DFE *Statistical Bulletin* 14/92

Table 5.4   Participation of 16 to 18-year-olds in education in England 1979/80-1991/92

England	1979/80	1983/84	1987/88	1991/92
	Percentage of estimated population			
16-year-olds				
Full-time education	41.7	47.9	48.4	67.1
Part-time education	14.0	16.6	17.1	9.7
Not in education	44.3	35.5	34.5	23.2
17-year-olds				
Full-time education	27.1	31.9	33.1	49.0
Part-time education	17.5	14.3	18.2	14.0
Not in education	55.4	53.8	48.7	37.0
18-year-olds				
Full-time education	14.7	16.7	18.7	28.5
Part-time education	15.6	13.5	13.8	13.1
Not in education	69.7	69.8	67.5	58.4

Source: Department for Education (1992) *Statistical Bulletin* 14/92.

most of the increase was accounted for by increased numbers in 'A' level courses for the 16 to 17 year group. For 18-year-olds, it was partly due to increase in 'A' level enrolment, but mainly to increased take-up of places in higher education. It is pertinent to point out here that there was a significant increase in the percentage of students obtaining one or more 'A' level passes in the eighties – it increased by just under five points (DES, 1992d). Since most of the increase in participation at FHE level took place after 1987-88 and in 'A' level courses for 16 to 17-year-olds, it may well be linked in part to the introduction of the GCSE from the summer of 1988, which led to significantly higher passes in that examination in the period 1988-92, as we saw in the previous section. The other reason may well be the high level of unemployment throughout this period.

Deprivation and access to further education

The link between deprivation and low participation is evident from Table 5.5, which shows that increased participation of 17-year-olds in full-time education is unevenly shared across the country. In all but three of the 14 most deprived area LEAs, the participation rate was well below the national average for England throughout the eighties. And in half of these authorities, the percentage **increase** in participation during this period was **below** the national rate. In other words, the gap in participation between these seven authorities and England was even wider at the end of the decade than at the beginning.

Of the three exceptions, Brent and Haringey already had participation rates substantially above the national level in 1980-1981, and maintained their lead all through this period; the rate for the ILEA (the third exception) was at par with the national level in 1980-81 and this position was more or less maintained during this period. It is no coincidence that these three were among the top 13 LEAs with the highest per capital net institutional expenditure on education.

Table 5.5 Participation in full-time education by young people aged 17[1] in England 1980/81-1989/90

Percentages

England	Rank Order of Deprivation (Z) scores[2]	1980/1	1983/4	1986/7	1989/90
Brent	(8)	38	43	43	60
Haringey	(6)	33	35	34	43
Newham	(2)	23	26	29	30
Inner London Education Authority[3]		26	29	31	38
Greater London		NA	NA	33	41
Birmingham	(14)	23	26	30	36
Coventry	(18)	25	28	27	30
Sandwell	(19)	18	22	22	26
Wolverhampton	(13)	24	28	27	29
West Midlands		NA	NA	31	35
Knowsley	(22)	15	18	20	22
Liverpool	(14)	21	27	25	34
Manchester	(11)	24	28	30	35
Rochdale	(29)	23	27	26	29
Salford	(30)	21	26	26	29
North West		NA	NA	31	36
Bradford	(26)	22	27	24	30
Yorkshire & Humberside		NA	NA	27	33
England		26	31	31	37

Source: Department of Education and Science *Statistical Bulletins* 9/86; 14/91. ★ Reproduced from *Urban Trends 1* (1992).

Notes:
1. Figures for the maintained sector only.
2. Based on DoE deprivation (Z) scores for the 57 Urban Programme Authorities.
3. Includes 7 of the 10 most deprived LEAs in England; and 10 out of its 12 boroughs (except Camden, Westminster and the City of London) are among the 30 most deprived LEAs in England; 85 per cent of the population of these inner London boroughs live in the 30 most deprived areas in England.

NA = Not available.

Participation rates in education at 16 plus tend to be closely related to qualification levels at 16 plus. However, research in Sheffield indicates that schools serving similar populations of young people can 'boost', or reduce, recruitment to 16 plus education by as much as ten per cent, depending on how they interact with their local communities (Jesson, 1992).

Access to further education – the ethnic dimension

Data on ethnic breakdown of access to FE is extremely limited, patchy and not very reliable. In 1990-91, for the first time, DFE collected ethnic data on FE enrolments in England, but the information was missing or refused in between 15 and 20 per cent of cases. Moreover, since **minority** ethnic group participation rates cannot be worked out until data from the 1991 Census is available about their age profile, one cannot compare these with **majority** ethnic group participation rates in FE.

However, some data on ethnic participation in further education is available for ILEA for the year 1986-87, but with a high proportion of information about ethnic origin missing. This shows that whereas the Black participation rate in full-time courses was higher than that for White students (34.4 per cent against 27.2 per cent), the rate for Black students on day-release or block-release courses was less than half that for White students (11.5 per cent as against 24.8 per cent) (Sammons and Newbury, 1989). Research indicates that Black school leavers experience greater difficulties in obtaining employment involving further education or training sponsored by employers than White school leavers (Eggleston and others, 1986).

Participation of 16 to 18-year-olds in education – international comparison

Table 5.6 and Figure 5.2 compare the level of participation in further education in the UK for the 16 to 18 age-group for 1987 with 12 other advanced industrialised countries. Looking first at full-time education, one finds that the UK rate (50 per cent) for the 16-year-olds was the lowest, below Italy (whose rate of 54 per cent was for 1982) and Spain (65 per cent), and almost half that of the USA (95 per cent). Likewise, for the 16 to 18 age-group, the UK rate (35 per cent) was once again the lowest, below Italy (47 per cent, for 1982), Germany (Federal Republic (49 per cent)), and Australia and Spain (50 per cent each); moreover, it was less than half of Denmark (73 per cent) Canada (75 per cent), Sweden (76 per cent), Netherlands and Japan (77 per cent each), USA (80 per cent) and Belgium (82 per cent). However, if we look at participation in part-time education, the UK rate for 16-year-olds (41 per cent) was the highest; and second-highest (34 per cent) for the 16 to 18 age-group, with Germany (43 per cent) being the highest.

Access to higher education – social class, gender and race

There has been a significant expansion in higher education in the eighties, when enrolment for home students for the first year of full-time degree courses in universities and polytechnics expanded by 44 per cent; the bulk of this

Table 5.6 Participation of 16 to 18-year-olds in education and training[1] by age and type of study; international comparison, 1987[2]

Years and percentages

	Minimum leaving age (years)	16 years			16 to 18 years		
		Full-time	Part-time	All	Full-time	Part-time	All[3]
United Kingdom[4] 1987	16	50	41	91	35	34	69
1989	16	53	40	93	37	33	70
Belgium	14	92	4	96	82	4	87
Denmark	16	89	2	91	73	6	79
France	16	80	8	88	69	8	77
Germany (Fed. Rep.)[5]	15	71	29	100	49	43	92
Italy[2]	14	54	15	69	47	18	65
Netherlands[2,5]	16	92	6	98	77	9	86
Spain[6]	16[11]	65	-	65	50	-	50
Australia[2]	15[12]	71	11	82	50	16	66
Canada[7]	16/17	92	-	92	75	-	75
Japan[8,9]	15	92	3	96	77	3	79
Sweden[10]	16	91	1	92	76	2	78
USA[8]	16-18[13]	95	-	95	80	1	81

*Source: Department of Education and Science. * Reproduced from Social Trends (1992).

Notes:
1. Includes apprenticeships, YTS and similar schemes.
2. 1985 for Sweden; 1982 for Italy; 1986 for Netherlands and Australia.
3. Includes higher education for some 18-year-olds.
4. Includes estimates for those studying only in the evening: also includes estimates of private sector further and higher education.
5. Includes compulsory part-time education for 16 and 17-year-olds.
6. Excludes 18-year-olds in universities.
7. Excludes certain part-time students. 10% at 16-18.
8. Includes private sector higher education.
9. Estimated for special training and miscellaneous schools providing vocational training.
10. Includes estimates for part-time.
11. By 1988-89: formerly 14.
12. 16 in Tasmania.
13. Varies between states.

**Figure 5.2   16 to 18-year-olds in full-time education and training
– International Comparison, 1987**

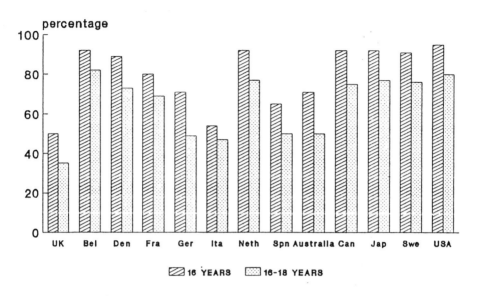

Source: *Social Trends*, 1992

expansion occurred in polytechnics and colleges rather than in universities. In the same period, the proportion of under 21s in the first year of a degree course increased from 12.6 per cent in 1980 to 19.3 per cent in 1990 (DES, 1992e). In the Government's White Paper on higher education, this is forecast to increase to 28 per cent by 1995, and to 32 per cent by the year 2000 (1991d).

Previous research evidence indicates that opportunities for access to higher education are differentially available according to social class, gender and race (Mortimore and Blackstone, 1992; DES, 1985). By 1990, women had more or less caught up with men – numerically at least. The take-up of places by women in full-time degree courses increased almost twice as much as by men (61 per cent against 31 per cent) to reach almost half (48 per cent). Overall, women's advance has been disproportionately in part-time education (DES, 1992e).

But as regards the distribution of opportunities between social classes, there has been very little change in the eighties: students from professional and managerial homes still achieved the same proportion (about two-thirds) of acceptances for university places in 1990 as they did in 1980; the proportion of students from the manual classes stayed at under one-fifth (18 per cent) during this period (UCCA, 1991). However, Glennerster and Low (1991) have argued, on the basis of analysis of General Household Survey data, that in view of reductions in the proportion of people in manual, especially semi- and unskilled, occupations, they have improved their position somewhat. There is also a significant disparity in the **rate** of acceptance: two-thirds for students from a professional background, as against about a half for those from unskilled or semi-skilled backgrounds. This disparity persists, albeit in a weaker form, even when their educational qualifications are similar (UCCA, 1980; 1991). According to Halsey, the general tendency towards inequality of educational attainment is likely to be strengthened in the future with the movement from grants towards loans started in 1989 (1992).

Ethnic breakdown of data on participation in higher education has begun to be collected on a regular basis only in the last couple of years. The Universities Central Council on Admissions (UCCA) has published these statistics for 1989-90 and 1990-1991. These indicate that minority ethnic group students constitute about six per cent of all students admitted to full-time first degree courses in the conventional universities in the UK. Further breakdown suggests that about five per cent are of Asian origin, and about one per cent of Black (African-Caribbean) origin (UCCA, 1991). Their representation in Polytechnics is significantly higher by comparison: 3.3 per cent for Black and 8.7 per cent for Asian students in full-time first degree courses (PCAS, 1991). It is not possible to work out the comparative participation rate for minority ethnic group students until the relevant data is available from the 1991 Census. There were significant variations between the different ethnic groups in their rates of **acceptance** (as a proportion of applications), around 30 per cent for Black students, 40 per cent for Asian students and 50 per cent for White students. The average acceptance rates for Black students were significantly lower than for White students even when allowance was made for differences in 'A' level grades – suggesting a consistent bias in the selection process. This was less of a problem for Asian students, whose average acceptance rates were below the national average only towards the lower bands of 'A' level examination scores (UCCA, 1991). Interestingly, no such disparity in average acceptance rates was found for minority ethnic group candidates in admission to polytechnics.

Recent research by Taylor, commissioned by the Committee of Vice Chancellors and Principals (CVCP), confirms the existence of an 'apparent bias' in acceptance rates, which differ significantly between ethnic groups, even when various factors such as qualifications and social class are taken into account. This is a matter of concern since other research indicates that people of minority ethnic origin, especially those of African-Caribbean, Pakistani and Bangladeshi origins, are under-represented in higher education (Smith and Tomlinson, 1989). Significantly, among his recommendations to the CVCP, Taylor has called for a critical reappraisal of acceptance criteria '...to ensure universities are not indirectly discriminating' (1992).

Summary

There has been a significant increase in the rate of participation of the 16 to 18-age-group in education in the eighties, even though it is not shared evenly across the country – young people in deprived-area LEAs having benefited the least. Likewise, there has been a considerable expansion in numbers in higher education, and women have now more or less caught up with men in their rate of participation. The improvement for students from manual occupations has been modest, so that the social class gap in access to higher education remains substantially the same.

As for the participation of students from minority ethnic groups, in FE, the picture is unclear as there are no reliable statistics. Available figures for HE suggest that their representation is better in the 'poly-universities' than in the conventional ones. UCCA statistics show that this may be due to a much lower rate of acceptance, especially for African-Caribbean students. Recent research by Taylor (1992) indicates that the lower rate of acceptance persists even for those Black students whose entry qualifications are similar to those of their White peers, thereby suggesting the existence of a bias in the selection process.

Conclusions

A review of evidence in this chapter indicates that there is a close, if complex, relationship between deprivation and education. We saw how discrete aspects of parents' deprivation adversely affect the education of their children both directly and indirectly in a variety of ways. These include the experience of living in actual conditions of poverty – poor housing, inadequate diet, frequent ill-health – and of being relatively deprived of wider cultural and educational experiences, which other children enjoy as a matter of course. These children also suffer because of the reduced ability of their parents to take an active interest in their education. We also found that the relationship between deprivation and education was consistent across its various stages. In the primary sector, reading standards tended to improve in schools located in relatively prosperous areas, but stay put, if not decline in deprived urban areas. There were also similar links at the secondary level. Improvement in the proportion of school leavers with GCSE passes occurred mostly in relatively prosperous areas; in deprived areas, the progress was either very much slower or none at all – there was even some deterioration in a few areas. Likewise, participation in further education (at 17) was significantly lower in deprived-area LEAs. Again, the incidence of truancy was far higher in inner city schools than generally in the country. This was explicable not only in terms of direct evidence linking low attainment with disadvantage, but also between social mobility and attainment. As poverty has increased since 1979, so has income inequality, so that children of families whose economic position has improved relative to others may be expected to do better at school; and vice versa for children whose families' economic position has worsened during this period.

This is corroborated, as we noted, by evidence from HMI reports – symbolised by 'the stubborn 30 per cent statistic syndrome' - referring to the phenomenon of persistent under achievement of around a third of pupils in schools in deprived inner city areas. In addition to the deprived material and social backgrounds of these pupils, there were three other reasons mentioned by the HMI for the perpetuation of this situation. One, whereas the level of Government expenditure on education for the basic provision has been adequate for the majority of schools, this has not been the case for about a third of the schools, especially in deprived inner-city areas. Moreover, the provision for new or changing needs, which are arguably far greater in schools in deprived areas than in others was found to be inadequate for most schools. Second, the widening disparities in provision between schools in different parts of the country both *within* and *between* LEAs were bearing down particularly hard on the lower ability pupils in deprived inner city schools in often very old and dilapidated buildings. A third, and related, reason was that schools in such areas tended to be much less effective than those in relatively affluent areas because of the lower calibre and higher turnover of staff, and the availability of inadequate and inappropriate teaching resources.

The level of resources, like deprivation, is closely but not exclusively related to the quality of education, as we saw earlier. HMI had found, for instance, that some schools in deprived inner city areas manage to achieve good results despite the odds stacked against them – also confirmed in Rutter's (1979) research – just as a proportion of pupils from deprived homes did particularly well at school. So what role does the school play in affecting educational outcomes of pupils? Does it compensate for pupils' disadvantage and thereby help to narrow the gap in performance due to gender, social class and race? Our evidence suggests that, in the primary school, the gap between children from different social class and ethnic backgrounds had actually widened at the end, even when they were level pegging at the beginning. Whether the Black-White gap is also widening at the secondary level is an open question, for we found the claim by Kysel (1987) and Nuttal (1990; 1992), that it was narrowing, not very convincing. There was evidence, however, of a substantial narrowing of the gender gap both at the secondary school level (16 plus examination), and in access to higher education. Despite some improvement, the social class gap in access to higher education remains substantially unaltered. There are no statistics on the participation **rates** of minority ethnic group students in higher education. There is evidence, however, of a significantly lower acceptance rate at universities for African-Caribbean students even when their qualifications are similar to those of White students.

While the existence of the Black-White gap in school performance has been well documented, there is no agreement as to the relative contributions of social class and race in explaining the gap; nor whether schools are the major contributor to the existence of this gap, though it is accepted that they do make some difference. The argument turns on whether schools are thought to be **generally** effective (or not) in relation to all pupils (Smith and Tomlinson 1989); or whether they are **differentially** effective in relation to particular groups of pupils defined by ability, gender or race (Nuttal, 1990).

However, as we have seen, qualitative research by Tomlinson (1987), Wright (1987) and the CRE (1992) provides classical examples of how schools can exacerbate, instead of compensating for, the initial disadvantage of pupils. This research provides evidence as to how the operation of normal school processes, such as setting, banding, option choice at age 13 plus and selection for different examination levels, can unwittingly discriminate against pupils on the basis of their social class, gender or race. They also illustrated, in addition to instances of overt racism against African-Caribbean pupils, how social class interacts with race to discriminate against minority ethnic groups pupils. These processes are apparently so pervasive and deep-seated that both Tomlinson and Wright consider these as exemplifying structural inequalities. This phenomenon was powerfully demonstrated earlier by Halsey (1975). As Troyna (1987) has argued, gender, race and social class inequalities not only reflect the wider structural inequalities in society, but also help to sustain them.

Notes

1. To enable comparison of examination performance of pupils from different backgrounds, Jesson and Gray (1991) allocated points for each GCSE grade on the following basis:
   GCSE Grade A B C D E F G H
   Points   7 6 5 4 3 2 1 0
2. Apparently, judgements differ considerably as to the true extent of unjustifed absenteeism – see, for instance, Grimshaw and Pratt (1986).

6. Conclusion

Rise in child poverty

Our review of evidence, based on a variety of measures of poverty, indicates the continuation of an unmistakable trend towards sharply rising child poverty since 1979. The number of children living in poverty increased threefold in the period 1979-90/91, from ten per cent to over thirty per cent of the population; with another ten per cent living on the margin of poverty. By comparison, the number of adults living in poverty was proportionately less – just under a quarter of the population. This has been accompanied by a widening of the gap between the rich and the poor – because of increasing divergence in their shares of both incomes and wealth – thereby reversing the post-war trend towards stability in income distribution. There is no evidence that low income families with children have benefited from any 'trickle down' effect of improvements in the living standards of the better off.

In fact, the living standards of low income families with children – increasingly dependent on social benefits because of rising poverty – have on the whole been adversely affected by changes in benefits since 1979. On the other hand, higher income groups have largely benefited from the tax cuts and other changes in taxation, thereby contributing to the widening of the gap between the rich and the poor.

Underlying factors

Factors related to the increase in child poverty since 1979 were:

- relatively high levels of unemployment through most of the 'eighties, and again since March 1990;
- increase in the incidence of low pay by a quarter since 1979, affecting the income of ten million workers in 1991 -nearly half the workforce: 36 per cent of full-time workers, and 70 per cent of part-time workers were low paid; four-fifths of the latter were women;
- increase in the number of lone parent families by two-fifths to over one million in the 1980s or one in six of all families with dependent children – the latter rose to 1.9 million. This increase in the number of lone parent families, combined with a relatively low level of economic activity in this group, and

heavy dependence on social security benefits, was a significant factor in the increase in child poverty.

The risk of living in poverty was found to be the highest among children living in families with one or more adults unemployed, followed by those living in lone parent families, and lastly those in families with low-paid workers. Since minority ethnic groups were over-represented in at least the first and the third of these groups, their children stood a significantly higher risk of living in poverty. This in turn reflected minority ethnic groups' unequal position in the labour market, due partly to their geographical and economic segregation in traditionally low paid industries, and semi- or unskilled jobs; and partly to their experience of racial discrimination and disadvantage. On the other hand, the risk of living in poverty is far less for children in two parent, two earner families.

Limitations of the study

How have the lives of children in the UK been affected by the escalating child poverty in the period of this study? In answering this question one has had to rely on a variety of evidence drawn from a wide range of sources of varying quality; there were also occasional gaps in the availability of evidence. The principal limitations of different kinds are outlined here to enable the reader to appreciate that some of the conclusions of this study are inevitably more tentative than others.

A key difficulty has been that, while there is a good data base in the UK on family and household living standards and social conditions, this is not **child-centred** in the main. For instance, reliable data on the number of children living in homeless families is hard to come by, as is data on morbidity among children. Frequent changes in definition and format, such as in unemployment statistics, make consistent comparison over time difficult. Sometimes, the available information is dated – as in the case of the relationship between income and children's diet; or produced late – Government statistics on Households Below Average Income for 1988-89 were published only in July 1992. But there has been some improvement here in that HBAI statistics for the years 1990/91 were published in June 1993. The ready availability of Government statistics also varies: some are available for the UK as a whole, others for Great Britain, and others still for England and Wales only.

A major gap in the availability of data relates to minority ethnic groups: income data is not broken down according to ethnic origins, so the level of poverty among them has to be inferred indirectly from unemployment data; the latter is based on the Labour Force Surveys, so it suffers from all the limitations inherent in sample surveys. Likewise, there are large gaps in information on the effects of poverty on minority ethnic groups: it is patchy and unreliable on access to educational opportunities and outcomes.

Even in large social surveys by the Government or academic institutions, the ethnic dimension in research is frequently overlooked; and when it is included, more often than not it is not built into the research design from the start so as to generate a large enough data set to allow a proper analysis. A classical example of this, as we saw in chapter 3, was the national survey of the diets of British schoolchildren, which was carried out by the OPCS in 1983 on behalf of the Department of Health and Social Security.

The data on child poverty and deprivation, health and well-being is often not population-based, is cross-sectional and does not allow for the analysis of change over time. Almost all the major longitudinal data sets on children are now very old. Moreover, the impact of some of the changes is difficult to identify because of the multiplicity of factors involved, as in education where a child's achievement may depend on a complex interaction between his or her ability, socio-economic and cultural factors in the home background, and the school effects; the position is often complicated still further when the effects of one change (that of deprivation on educational outcome) is probably neutralised by others (apparently beneficial effects of the introduction of GCSE on examination results). Moreover, the impact of certain changes (the National Curriculum) may be felt with a considerable time-lag.

Finally, it was found that there was not much quantifiable evidence directly linking children's experience of deprivation with outcomes in housing, health and education. For the most part, therefore, one had to be content with using social class as in health, or its proxies (free school meals) in education. As we saw in chapters 3 and 4, the relationship between social class and deprivation is not exact; it also suffers from some other limitations. However, the overall effect of these limitations is to suggest caution in the interpretation of findings, and to qualify, rather than to nullify, the conclusions reached in this study.

Deprivation and ill-health

Rapid increase in child and family poverty since 1979 has led to an increase in deprivation – material and social. In addition to unemployment and low income (already mentioned), homelessness increased sharply, especially in inner city areas, affecting many lone parent and two parent families with dependent children, and young people. Consequently, these people had to spend a considerable amount of time in temporary, mostly Bed and Breakfast, accommodation with adverse effects on their health - physical and psychological – and education.

Expansion in owner-occupation and general improvement in housing conditions in the 1980s benefited much less, or bypassed altogether, many low income families with dependent children, who tend to live mostly in older properties in multiple occupation or high rise flats. These are often in a poor state of repair and generally in rundown inner city areas; they are frequently cold, damp and mouldy, and expensive to heat. The number of families living in such conditions is likely to have increased significantly as a result of the sharp rise in child and family poverty since 1979 in general, and the rise in the cost of housing in relation to income in particular. However, this would not be reflected in official statistics until the results of the 1991 Census and the 1991 English House Conditions Survey have been analysed. Fuel poverty was also found to have increased by over a quarter, and fuel debt by a half, in the eighties. The adverse effects of living in such conditions on children's health have long been recognised and well documented.

Other aspects of deprivation also contributed to ill-health among children. There was a significant correlation between unemployment and infant mortality, as well as ill-health - physical and mental. Prolonged unemployment was shown to increase the risk of family breakdown with adverse consequences for the psychological welfare of children. Likewise, growth in children was found to vary with the amount of money spent on food per person per week. Since expenditure on food varies with household income and composition, and since the number of families with low income has risen substantially since 1979, their spending on food for their children is likely to have gone down, thereby restricting their choice in terms of both the quality and the quantity of food, and adversely affecting the growth of their children. This may explain in part why improvement in growth (height) and dental health of children, observed in the 1970s and early 1980s had levelled off by mid- to late 1980s; it may also explain in part the existence of a strong class gradient in growth and dental health, and also the fact that children of unemployed fathers tended to be shorter than those of employed fathers.

Social class, deprivation and ill-health

Since low income families tend to be multiply-deprived, and often for long periods, the cumulative effect on their children's health is likely to be greater than that of any single indicator of deprivation. Our evidence suggests a direct and close relationship between deprivation – material and social – and child health, as measured by mortality and morbidity: both tend to increase with deprivation. This explains why, with a rapid rise in child poverty and deprivation since 1979, the steady decline in infant mortality in the post-war period slowed down in the 1980s; and a steadily rising trend in morbidity, and GP consultation, was observed. The latter varied significantly with deprivation, as did hospital admissions. Improvement in the take-up of immunisation was also lower in the deprived inner-city areas, and among children of deprived families, as was the use of dental and ophthalmic services.

Most of the data on health (and education) outcomes are broken down according to social class rather than deprivation *per se*. Our review of evidence revealed a marked and consistent class gradient in all indicators of health: infant and child mortality, and morbidity; as well as the quality of health indicators, such as growth and dental health. It is significant to note here that a widening of income inequality in the 1980s was accompanied by a widening of the social class differential in infant mortality: the ratio between social classes V and I increased from 1.8 in 1978 to 2.0 in 1990.

It has been argued in this study that the widening or the persistence of social class differentials in child health are related to the increase in the level of deprivation consequent upon the rise in child poverty. As noted earlier, social class variations reflect differences in access to income and other resources and lifestyles; and that it is the lower-ranked social classes (IV and V) with limited income who tend to bear the brunt of the deprivation underpinning the concept of social class. Given the close relationship between deprivation and ill-health, it follows that the increase in deprivation since 1979 among social classes IV and V would be related to the widening (or persistence) of social class differentials in child health.

Deprivation and education

There was a close and consistent relationship between deprivation and education across its various stages. Reading standards in primary schools tended to improve in schools located in relatively prosperous areas, but declined in deprived urban areas. At the secondary level too, improvement in the proportion of school leavers gaining GCSE passes occurred mostly in relatively affluent areas; in deprived areas the progress was very much slower or none at all.

Participation in further education at 17 was significantly lower in deprived-area LEAs, against an increasing trend nationally.

Truancy was a serious problem in deprived inner city schools affecting ten per cent of schools, as against six per cent nationally.

The relationship between deprivation and educational outcome was explicable not only in terms of direct evidence linking the two, but also between social mobility and attainment. As the increase in child poverty in the period 1979-90/91 was accompanied by greater income inequality, children in families whose economic position had improved relatively to others were likely to do better at school; and vice versa for children in families whose economic position had deteriorated in this period.

In addition to the deprived material and social conditions of pupils, there were three main reasons according to the HMI, for the persistent under-achievement of nearly a third of pupils in deprived inner city schools: inadequacy of resources to meet the needs of even the basic educational provision, let alone to pay for the new and changing changing needs; the widening of disparities in provision between schools in different parts of the country both **within** and **between** local education authorities; and the considerably lower effectiveness of schools in such areas due to the lower calibre and higher turnover of staff.

This emphasises the importance of resources and the role of the school in affecting educational outcomes, in addition, that is, to that of deprivation. Our discussion of the school effect suggests that, at the primary level, the gap between children from different social class and ethnic backgrounds had actually widened at the end of their primary schooling, even when they were level-pegging at the beginning.

Whether the Black and White gap in performance is also widening at the secondary level is an open question. Evidence about its narrowing is less than convincing. Nor is there any agreement as to the relative contributions of social class, race and the school in explaining the existence of this gap.

However, qualitative research shows how the operation of normal school processes such as setting, banding, option choice at 13 plus and selection for different examination levels can unwittingly discriminate against pupils on the basis of their social class, gender and race. The processes are so pervasive and deep-seated as to constitute structural inequalities.

There was evidence, however, of a substantial narrowing of the gender gap both at the secondary school level (16 plus examination), and in access to higher education. The social class gap in access to higher education was still substantial, even if slightly narrowed in recent years. Evidence indicates significantly lower acceptance rate at universities for students of African-Caribbean origin, even when their qualifications are similar to those of White students.

Government response to rising poverty

In sum, the lives of children have been profoundly affected by the sharp rise in child poverty since 1979: poor housing, ill-health and educational disadvantage have diminished the life chances of nearly one in three UK children. Arguably, this situation could have been substantially mitigated, if not prevented, if the loss in income suffered by these children's parents, whether due to unemployment or low wages or lone parent status, had been properly compensated. For, as this study has shown, there are serious questions as to the adequacy of social benefits. However, the difficulty remains the absence of an official definition of poverty, and the refusal of governments to acknowledge the existence of poverty. An example of this is the statement made by the former Prime Minister, Margaret Thatcher, in the House of Commons in reply to a question by David Owen on the level of poverty in Britain:

There is no official definition of poverty. There are some 7 million people who live in families that are supported by Supplementary Benefit. There are many other different definitions of poverty...Many of the low-paid on Supplementary Benefit have incomes about 40 per cent above that level. They are wholly artificial definitions. **The fact remains that people who are living in need are fully and properly provided for**. (emphasis added) (*Hansard*, 22.12.83, col. 561)

Government reluctance to be drawn in on the question of defining poverty has a long pedigree and includes Labour as well as Conservative Ministers. Thus Margaret Herbison, a Minister in the Wilson Government, in her Foreward to the 1967 *Circumstances of Families* report stated that it was not '...the purpose of this report to propound a theoretical definition of poverty...' (p.iii), even while she recognised the difficulty of using the Supplementary Benefit (SB) as a yardstick for measuring poverty. Since then successive government ministers and officials have been generally content with disavowing, often in almost identical language, attempts by others to use the Supplementary Benefit and Income Support, and its various multiples, to infer the magnitude of poverty, without proferring one of their own (DHSS, 1988; *Hansard*, col 518, 23.1.92).

Evasiveness on the question of defining poverty seems to have served successive governments well, for they thereby retain the freedom to decide whether and, if so, by how much, to uprate the various social security benefits. As we have seen (chapter 1), the approach of the Conservative Government on this question since 1979 has been characterised by attempts to redefine 'need' in ever narrower terms, given their commitment to reducing public expenditure. This has been so, notwithstanding the fact that there is a growing and widespread belief among the general public that the poor should also have a fair share in the prosperity resulting from an enormous expansion in living standards for the majority of British people in the postwar period (Mack and Lansley, 1985; Frayman, 1990).

It is true that any definition of poverty which has considerable resource implications is likely to generate controversy (Gans, 1970), especially when as in the eighties the political climate was already polarised, and poverty was, and also widely seen to be, actually rising. The case in point is the statement by John Moore, the former Secretary of State for Social Security, in which he declared 'the end of the line for poverty' and claimed that it was no longer meaningful to talk about poverty in view of the 'dramatic' improvement in living standards in this century, and accused those, advocating a concept of 'relative poverty' of '...pursuing the political goal of equality' (1989)[1]. He was apparently using the term 'poverty' in an 'absolute', if not in its Dickensian sense, to mean destitution. Nor has he been alone to attack the concept of 'relative' poverty; other senior ministers have done the same, if in less vociferous terms, and extolled the virtues of 'absolute' poverty. For instance, Sir Keith Joseph as Secretary of State for Education argued:

An absolute standard means one defined by reference to the actual needs of the poor and not by reference to the expenditure of those who are not poor. A family is poor if it cannot afford to eat (Joseph and Sumption, 1979, pp.27-28).

He added that by any absolute standards there was very little poverty in Britain today.

As Mack and Lansley have observed, whereas in the nineteenth century the concept of 'absolute' poverty was used to draw attention to the plight of the poor, now it is '...associated with attempts to limit the needs of the poor...' (1984, p.17).

'Dependency culture' or blaming the victims?

At the same time an attempt is made by the 'New Right' to blame the victims of poverty by reviving the distinction common in Victorian times between the 'deserving' and the 'undeserving' poor: the latter are thought to be feckless and improvident, and responsible for their own condition (Walker, 1990). Despite the fact that this view had already been questioned by Tawney (Titmuss, 1958), it has now found expression in the contemporary usage of the term 'dependency culture' – ostensibly fostered by an easy availability of social security benefits in the 'Nanny' state in postwar Britain. Thus in a reference to parents of children on Income Support, John Moore spoke of '...the sullen apathy of dependence...' (1987)[2], and Margaret Thatcher, when Prime Minister, expressed herself against '...encouraging dependence on the state' (1989)[3]. In the same vein, justifying the introduction of loans to Income Support claimants under the Social Fund, Nicholas Scott, the then Minister of State for Social Security, expressed the Government's aim as '... reducing their dependence on the "benefit culture"...' (1987)[4].

The 'underclass' and rising child poverty?

The idea of 'dependency culture' has been reinforced by the 'New Right' thinking emanating from the United States where Charles Murray (among others) was propounding his concept of the 'underclass' – a sub-category of the poor characterised by their 'deviant' behaviour: illegitimacy, the dropping-out of the young from the labour market while feeding off the State, and violent crime. His contention that the 'underclass' in the UK was likely to grow to US proportions in ten years time was based on statistics showing an increasing trend in crime rates and in births to single mothers, and an assumed increase among the young drop-outs from the labour market (1990).

It is not proposed to discuss here the concept of 'underclass' per se, which is imprecise and inevitably contentious[5]. Murray's analysis is disputed, for instance, by Field (1990). Our purpose is simply to question its value in explaining the growth of child poverty in the UK since 1979. As Piachaud (nd) has argued, certain individuals and groups in society have always tended to 'opt out' of the mainstream of life and its values, but there is no clear evidence that their number has expanded significantly in recent times. Likewise, a certain amount of abuse of the social security system has been going on for a long time, just as white-collar crime on a much larger scale has been evident, perpetrated also by people at the higher end of the income distribution. Despite the tightening of the 'availability for work' test in recent years, there is no evidence to indicate that abuse of the social security system by the young unemployed has increased, whereas youth unemployment has been rising since March 1990.

It is true that the increase in births outside marriage in the 1980s (to single as well as to divorcing mothers) is certainly related to the increase in child poverty in this period. As was noted earlier (chapter 2), whereas births to single mothers increased significantly in this period, these were increasingly registered jointly, mostly from the same address suggesting an actual or intended cohabitation. Murray (1990) rightly argues that this does not imply that cohabitational relationships are as stable as marriage. But neither does it mean the opposite – reliable information on this is lacking. Significantly, however, analysis by Ermisch (1986) suggests that a high proportion of single mothers end-up marrying, 60 per cent by the time the child is five-years-old, and 70 per cent by the time he or she is seven-years-old. Moreover, the median duration of lone parenthood of single mothers tends to be considerably shorter (35 months) when compared to divorced mothers (59 months). This may account for the fact, as analysis by Brown (1990) has shown, that single mothers as a group tended to spend significantly less time on benefits than divorced or widowed mothers. Moreover, despite a rapid growth in their number in the 1980s, single mothers formed a significantly smaller proportion of the total number of lone parents in 1990 than did divorced or separated parents.

As for the lower economic activity rate among lone mothers, as compared to married mothers, it was primarily found to be due to their unequal economic position in the labour market combined with the shortage of affordable good quality childcare; and society's ambiguous attitude to mothers – especially single mothers – with young children going out to work.

It follows from this discussion that, on the face of it, an increase in the size of lone parents (primarily divorced/separated and single mothers) has contributed to the increase in child poverty since 1979. However, as we have shown in this study (chapter 2), a closer examination suggests that it is the result of a complex interaction between two separate but interrelated sets of phenomena; one, the wider demographic and social changes in society affecting attitudes to marriage, divorce, family and children; two, the socio-economic and political factors impinging on the management of the economy, the level of unemployment, and the availability of childcare. Consequently, evidence suggests that the increased dependence on benefits of people – owing to an increase in unemployment, incidence of low pay or lone parenthood – stems essentially from a lack of choice rather than the development and spread of 'dependency culture', as the Government maintained, let alone 'deviant behaviour', as Murray and others have sought to argue. As a recent study of families with children living on benefits concludes:

...at a time when British poverty is again being discussed in terms of an underclass, it is of crucial importance to recognise that these families, and probably millions more like them living on social security benefits, are in no sense a detached and isolated group cut off from the rest of society. They are just the same people as the rest of our population, with the same culture and aspirations but with simply too little money to be able to share in the activities and possessions of everyday life with the rest of the population. (Bradshaw and Holmes, 1989, p.138)

This study confirms the findings of earlier research in the United States in the 1960s when the idea of 'underclass' found expression under the label of 'culture of poverty'. It was found that only a small minority of the poor was completely detached from the values and aspirations of the broader society. Where attitudes and behaviour differed, say, among some of the urban poor, this was partly in response to the current economic situation, and partly an internalised response to the past. Rejecting the notion of a 'culture of poverty', it has been argued by Gans (1970) that if one applies it only to the poor, the onus for change falls too much on them.

...In reality, the prime obstacles to the elimination of poverty lie in an economic system that is dedicated to the maintenance and increase of wealth among the already affluent (1970, p.156).

Social class, ethnicity and cycles of disadvantage
In the UK, a variation on the theme of the 'culture of poverty' was taken up by Sir Keith Joseph, the then Secretary of State for Social Services, who posed the question in 1972: 'Why is it that...deprivation and problems of maladjustment so conspicuously persist?' (Rutter and Madge, 1976, p.3).

His view that this may be due to the 'cycle of transmitted deprivation' led to a major research programme stretching over a decade. The first study by Rutter and Madge (1976) concluded that familial cycles played an important part in the perpetuation of disadvantage, but they accounted for only a part of the overall picture. They found that the continuities were much weaker over three generations than over two. The extent of continuity varied considerably both according to the **type** as well as the **level** of disadvantage. In addition to familial continuity, there were other important continuities accounting for the perpetuation of disadvantage over time, such as those in particular regions, social classes or ethnic groups. Finally, **discontinuities** were also very striking. At least half the children born into a disadvantaged home did not repeat it in the next generation; while over half of all forms of disadvantage tended to arise afresh in each generation.

The final study in the series by Brown and Madge (1982), summarising the findings of the entire research programme, concluded that there are many cycles of disadvantage with a range of interlocking social problems that affect not just a 'deviant' minority but also large social groups, involving complex processes of '...interaction of individual characteristics with socio-economic forces', implicating '...the whole structure and fabric of society' (p.350). More specifically, they found that multiple deprivation and interlocking networks of disadvantage 'are a feature of certain ethnically and occupationally defined social groups' (p.350).

This is remarkably similar to the conclusion of our own study about the close relationship between (child) poverty, deprivation, ethnicity and social class (inequality), whether one is looking at housing, health or education. Attempts to individualise poverty tend to divert attention from the wider social-structural explanations of the phenomenon; and blaming its victims is tantamount to adding insult to injury. After all, poverty and squalor blight the lives of children and are an affront to human dignity.

Policy implications

The ultimate justification for a study of this kind derives from a belief in the possibility of change aimed specifically at a significant reduction in child poverty. Even if there were an agreement in principle, given the wide sweep of the subject, there is bound to be fierce controversy as to the desirability and scope for social action, the role of the State, the forms of State intervention, and so on. In the following pages, therefore, an attempt will be made to identify areas where certain polices have a particular bearing on child poverty, while recognising that there are a wide variety of ways of implementing these and other policies. The purpose of this study will have been served if it contributes to a more informed debate on the issues surrounding child poverty and their implications for policy.

Poverty, inequality and social policy

As was stated at the outset, poverty presupposes an unacceptable degree of inequality. One cannot understand the former, let alone tackle it effectively, except in the wider context of class-related patterns of deprivation. But as Brown and Madge point out, the latter,

...is **not** inevitable: occupational differences need not involve whole networks of socio-economic differences, trapping the most vulnerable and encouraging the strong to fight their way to the top;...it is necessary to reassert the potential for a different and better

society, along with the reality of deprivation in the present one, before one can make sense of the implications for change.
(Brown and Madge, 1982, p.351)

Indeed the present Prime Minister, John Major, has expressed his vision of a classless society and, in one of his first speeches on taking office, said that he wanted the country to 'make the changes necessary to provide a better quality of life for **all** our citizens' (emphasis added) (28.11.1990).

Children's rights and child poverty

The well-being of children requires political action at the highest level. We make a solemn commitment to give priority to the rights of children.

This commitment was made by the former Prime Minister, Margaret Thatcher, at the World Summit on Children in New York in November 1989, when she first committed the UK to the 1989 UN Convention on the Rights of the Child. It is fair to assume that it is equally binding on the present Government which has since ratified the Convention.

As this study has demonstrated, the rights which have been particularly hit by the rising child poverty in the UK are as follows: the right to benefit from an adequate standard of living, including the right to a decent standard of housing with the duty of the State to help parents achieve this; the right to the highest level of health possible; and the right to education with equal opportunities. Here is an opportunity, therefore, for the Government to redeem the previous Prime Minister's pledge by examining comprehensively how its policies across the board affect children, and take appropriate action to further children's rights[6].

Mass unemployment, as we have seen (chapter 2), is the biggest threat to a child's right to an acceptable living standard, followed closely by an increasing incidence of low paid employment in peripheral, insecure jobs. Since many people alternate between bouts of unemployment and temporary low paid jobs (Daniel, 1990), the latter is not a way out of poverty: it tends to increase dependence on benefits when they are taken up, and hardship when they are not, as is frequently the case. Both these trends have been reinforced by the economic restructuring of society in the last 13 years, and children have had to bear the brunt of these changes. Is it fair that a disproportionate amount of the price should, thus, have to be paid by the most vulnerable sectors of society? And should the State be subsidising, in effect, low waged, low productivity jobs in the peripheral labour market? Or should it be encouraging a transition to a high wage, high productivity economy which offers secure employment to all, not just to a minority of the working population? And, finally, should not the Government, concerned about the welfare of low income families with children, seriously consider restoring full employment once again as the goal of economic policy, to be achieved in progressive stages so as not to lead to excessive inflation?

Child poverty also has implications for the policy on childcare, since many lone mothers are prevented from taking jobs because of the lack of affordable, good quality childcare. The issue here is as to how the childcare policy can be adapted to the changing needs of the economy in general, and the changing employment patterns in particular.

However, since significant reductions in unemployment can only be achieved in the medium-term, in the mean time there is a strong case in our view for examining the adequacy of various benefits, such as unemployment benefit, income support, family credit and housing benefit, and increasing these to provide at least a reasonable minimum standard of living, especially to low income families with children. Once agreed, such a national minimum standard needs to be uprated annually in line with average earnings. This is of course likely to significantly increase expenditure on social security in the short-term. However, if one were to look at tax and social security policies together, it should be possible to contain such increases by progressively reducing tax expenditures in areas such as occupational pensions, mortgage interest tax relief and so on, which tend to benefit for the most part the higher income groups in society. Likewise, there is a good case, in our view, for re-examining the argument between the provision of universal versus selective, means-tested benefits so as to restore the balance in favour of the universal principle. Once again, it is possible to claw back the additional expenditure from the higher income groups by making these benefits taxable.

Children's right to decent housing cannot be a reality for the increasing numbers of families with children in temporary, mostly bed and breakfast, accommodation, let alone for the young people sleeping rough on the streets. Likewise, the right of those families living in cold, damp and mouldy houses in run-down inner city estates is also being infringed. To restore their right to a decent home, it is necessary we feel to examine polices, such as the sale of council houses, which have had the effect of reducing the supply of low cost social housing; or others, which have over-emphasised owner-occupation at the expense of privately rented accommodation, and have tended to put even reasonable housing in the private sector out of reach of most low income families with children.

The right to the highest possible health for many deprived children is likely to remain an aspiration so long as there are strong social class inequalities in childhood mortality, morbidity and growth. At the time of the publication of the Government's Green Paper *The Health of the Nation* in 1991, William Waldegrave, the then Minister for Health, described the reduction of inequalities in health as a 'perfectly legitimate objective' but declined to commit the Government to its achievement because the divisions were so fundamental and long lasting and the issues so complex that they were not suitable for a Government target (*Health Visitor*, July 1991). It is not clear though for whom it is a legitimate target, if not for the Government.

By contrast the House of Commons Health Committee had this to say on the subject:

Without reductions in the persistent social and geographical inequalities in health, a proportion of the population will remain vulnerable during pregnancy...Further significant improvements in relation to pregnancy outcome depend on improving social

conditions such as alleviating poverty, poor housing and inadequate diet.
(1991, p.xxxi)

The Committee therefore stressed that the Government should tackle the link between poverty and poor health outlined in the Green Paper. A recent study by Quick and Wilkinson (1991) goes further in arguing that improvement in health depends less on economic growth than on reducing income inequalities. That is the way, they argue, not only to the reduction of health inequalities, but also to an overall improvement in the health of the population generally.

Given the importance of school meals for children in general and those from low income groups in particular, and given the well-documented deficiencies in the diets of British schoolchildren, especially those from lower income families, there seems to be a strong case for the Government ensuring that a school meal of adequate minimum quality and quantity is available to all those pupils who want it, and at an affordable price. This is best done, in our view, by the Government accepting the call of the Parliamentary Committee on Education, Science and Arts and a number of other bodies to reinstate nutritional standards for school meals, suitably updated, in the light of the recommendations for dietary changes made by the Government's own Committee on Medical Aspects of Food Polices (COMA) in 1991, and the earlier report of the National Advisory Committee on Nutrition Education (NACNE) (Health Education Authority, 1983).

The right to equality of opportunity in education is also seriously compromised, we believe, when there are strong structural inequalities due to social class, race and to a lesser extent gender in educational outcomes – a third of school pupils in deprived inner city schools are under-achieving – and in access to opportunities in further and higher education. In addition to the deprived socio-economic background of children, the other crucial variable explaining educational disadvantage was found to be resources: widening disparities both within and between local education authorities were exacerbated by overall insufficiency to cope with the burgeoning new needs arising from major recent changes in curriculum, assessment, examinations and educational reorganisation. If the Government is serious about promoting equality of opportunity in education and reducing disparities in educational achievement, a significant increase in resources focused specifically on impoverished schools would seem to be a necessary, if not a sufficient, condition.

An alternative political morality?

Over and above certain discrete measures in specific areas such as health and education outlined above, it is obvious that any substantial and lasting improvement in health and educational outcomes is unlikely to be achieved until there is a sustained, all-round attack on child poverty and poor housing and living conditions, given that deep-seated deprivation is the common thread linking poor housing, ill-health and educational disadvantage of children, even if the relationship is often complex. This is clearly not a cheap option – its realisation is critically dependent upon the adoption and vigorous pursuit of full employment as the primary goal of economic policy.

Some may ask if the country can afford it. The real question is **not** whether we can afford it, but rather can we afford not to. Unemployment is the biggest drain on the economy, as well as on society. Both historical precedent and recent experience in the UK and in Europe (the frequent eruption of riots in the UK in the 1980s, and the spreading of racial attacks here and in Europe in the wake of economic recession) suggests that social cohesion and political stability are liable to be strained if policies generating largescale unemployment over the medium to long-term lead to a widespread feeling of despair and frustration.

Finally, if the last 13 years can be summed up as reflecting too often a philosophy of 'me-tooism', it is fitting to conclude this study by positing an alternative philosophy. Our use of the concept of poverty ('relative poverty')

...poses questions about inequality, exclusion, discrimination, (and) injustice... If this is to have any practical cutting edge it calls for nothing less than a new morality. (Donnison, 1982, p.7)

This morality needs to be aligned with the society's interest in improving the quality of life of the **whole** community – poor, and not just the rich; children, and not just adults – since excessive private affluence and public squalor tend to diminish the quality of life of the better-off too.

Notes

1. A speech by the Rt. Hon. John Moore MP, Secretary of State for Social Security on 11.5.1989.
2. Rt. Hon. John Moore, MP, in a speech on 'The Future of the Welfare State', 26.9.1987.
3. Letter from the Prime Minister Rt. Hon. Margaret Thatcher, MP, to Rt. Hon. Neil Kinnock, MP, on 30.5.1989.
4. Letter from Rt. Hon. Nicholas Scott, MP, Minister of State for Social Security, to Peter Barclay, CBE, Chair of the Social Security Advisory Committee, 25.8.87.
5. The idea originated from Marx, but has had considerable airing in the media since it was captured by the 'New Right' in the sixties and seventies in the U.S and in the eighties in the UK. For two contrasting approaches to the subject, see Smith (1992) and Mann (1992).
6. For a recent study of the implications for the UK of the UN Convention on the Rights of the Child, see Newell (1991).

Appendix

Table I.1   Proportion of adults and children below half of contemporary average income in the UK

Year	Before Housing Costs		After Housing Costs	
	Adults%	Children%	Adults%	Children%
1979	8	9	9	10
1981	9	12	11	16
1987	16	20	19	24
1988/89	19	22	22	25
1990/91	21	26	24	31

Source: DSS *HBAI, 1992, 1993* (Tables F1 and F3).

Table I.2   Proportion of dependent children with incomes below various thresholds which change with average income (AHC)[1] in the UK 1979–1990/91

Income below given proportion of the average	1979		1988/89		1990/91	
	number (million)	%	number (million)	%	number (million)	%
0.5	1.4	10	3.1	25	3.9	31
0.6	2.8	20	4.4	35	5.0	40
0.7	4.7	34	5.7	46	6.3	50
0.8	6.6	48	7.0	56	7.6	60
1.0	9.7	71	9.1	73	9.4	75

Source: DSS *HBAI, 1992, 1993* (Table F3).
Notes: 1. AHC = After Housing Costs

Table I.3   Distribution of wealth in the UK 1979-89

	1979	1983	1987	1989[1]
Marketable wealth				
Percentage of wealth owned by[2]:				
Most wealthy 1%	20	20	18	18
Most wealthy 5%	37	37	37	38
Most wealthy 10%	50	50	51	53
Most wealthy 25%	72	73	74	75
Most wealthy 50%	92	91	91	94
Least wealthy 50%	8	9	9	6
[3]Gini Coefficient	65	65	66	67
Marketable wealth less value of dwellings				
Percentage of wealth owned by[2]:				
Most wealthy 1%		26[4]	25[5]	28
Most wealthy 5%		45	46	53
Most wealthy 10%		56	58	66
Most wealthy 25%		74	75	81
Most wealthy 50%		87	89	94
Least wealthy 50%		13	11	6
Marketable wealth plus occupational and state pension rights (historic valuation)				
Percentage of wealth owned by[2]:				
Most wealthy 1%	11	11	11	11
Most wealthy 5%	23	24	25	26
Most wealthy 10%	34	33	36	38
Most wealthy 25%	55	56	59	62
Most wealthy 50%	78	80	81	83
Least wealthy 50%	22	20	19	17
[3]Gini Coefficient	44	46	50	50
Marketable wealth plus occupational and state pension rights (latest valuation)				
Percentage of wealth owned by[2]:				
Most wealthy 1%	12	11	11	11
Most wealthy 5%	25	24	25	26
Most wealthy 10%	36	35	36	38
Most wealthy 25%	58	57	59	62
Most wealthy 50%	80	80	81	83
Least wealthy 50%	20	20	19	17
[3]Gini Coefficient	47	47	50	50

Source: Economic Trends, 1991; Social Trends, 1992.
Notes: 1. Provisional.
2. Percentages and total marketable wealth are of population aged 18 and over.
3. This is a measure of inequality: the higher the number, the greater the inequality.
4. Relates to year 1981.
5. Relates to year 1986.

Table I.4 Dependent children in the UK below various income thresholds of contemporary average income (AHC)[1] by economic status 1979–1990/91

Economic status	1979			1988/89			1990/91		
	Children below various proportions of income below average								
	0.5	0.6	0.7	0.5	0.6	0.7	0.5	0.6	0.7
Full-time workers[2]									
%	4	12	26	11	21	33	15	25	37
No. (1,000s)	476	1,379	2,942	1,089	2,044	3,165	1,431	2,315	3,435
Lone parents									
%	(28)	(57)	(76)	(64)	(82)	89	(74)	83	88
No. (1,000s)	280	570	760	896	1,148	1,246	1,258	1,411	1,496
Unemployed									
%	73	86	89	90	96	97	88	92	97
No. (1,000s)	352	413	425	740	787	795	734	773	808
All economic types									
%	(10)	(20)	34	25	35	46	31	40	50
No. (millions)	(1.4)	(2.8)	4.7	3.1	4.4	5.7	3.9	5.0	6.3

Source: DSS: *HBAI 1993* (Table F3); data on unemployed received from DSS in a personal communication dt. 15.7.93

Notes: 1. AHC = After Housing Costs
2. This includes self-employed: there may be one or more FT workers in a family.
3. Figures in brackets( ) are particularly uncertain.

Table I.5   Education and day care of children under five in the UK 1981-1990

	1981	1986[1]	1988	1989	1990
A. Children under 5 in schools[2]					
(Public sector schools) (thousands)					
Nursery schools:					
full-time	22	19	18	17	17
part-time	67	77	80	65	67
Primary schools:					
full-time	281	306	314	317	346
part-time	167	228	243	273	286
As a percentage of all children aged 3 or 4	*44.3*	*46.7*	*48.4*	*49.1*	*51.2*
B. Day care places[3] (thousands)					
Local authority day nurseries	32	33	34	34	33
Local authority playgroups	5	5	6	4	3
Registered day nurseries	23	29	40[6]	49[6]	64[6]
Registered playgroups	433	473	479	480	491
Registered child minders[4]	110[5]	157	189	216	238
Total	603[5]	698	747	783	830

Source: Social Trends 1992.

Notes: 1. Data for 1985 have been used for Scotland for children under 5 in schools.
2. Pupils aged under 5 at December/January of academic year.
3. Figures for 1966 and 1971 cover England and Wales at end-December 1966 and end-March 1972 respectively. From 1976 data are at end-March except for the Northern Ireland component which is at end-December of the preceding year up to 1988.
4. Includes child minders provided by local authorities.
5. Because of a different method of collection of data between 1978 and 1981, these figures are less reliable.
6. No figures are available for registered nurseries in Scotland. An estimate has been made for the purposes of obtaining a United Kingdom total.

Table I.6 Education and day care of children under five by age and region in the UK 1989[1]

Region	Under fives in maintained schools[2] As percentage of population in age group			Total (thousands)
	Aged 2	Aged 3	Aged 4[3]	
North	8.7	62.0	96.1	53.9
Yorkshire & Humberside	4.5	50.6	89.4	73.0
East Midlands	4.1	36.4	80.3	47.3
East Anglia	0.8	15.2	78.6	16.9
South East	2.5	24.9	58.8	148.3
South West	1.2	12.6	80.4	36.2
West Midlands	4.9	42.7	83.8	71.2
North West	8.1	46.5	94.3	100.8
England	4.1	34.0	76.8	547.6
Wales	0.4	46.4	92.9	50.4
Scotland	0.3	18.2	60.1	49.8
Northern Ireland	-	15.0	75.3	30.1

Source: *Social Trends* 1992.
Notes: 1. At January, except Scotland – at September 1988.
2. Ages at 31 August 1988 for England and 31 December 1988 for Scotland, Wales and Northern Ireland.
3. Excludes pupils aged 4 at 31 August 1988 who attained the age of 5 by 31 December 1988.

Bibliography

Abel-Smith, B and Townsend, P (1965) *The Poor and the Poorest*. Bell

Sir Donald Acheson (1992) Talk given to a conference, Unhealthy Housing: The Public Health Response at Warwick University, 18-20 December

Adams, M (1987) *The Distribution of Earnings: 1973 to 1986*. Research Paper 64, Department of Employment

Alcock, P (1991) The end of the line for social security: the Thatcherite, restructuring of welfare, *Critical Social Policy*, 30, 1990-91

Amin, K with Oppenheim, C (1992) *Poverty in Black and White: Deprivation and Ethnic Minorities*. Child Poverty Action Group

Arber, S (1987) Social class, non-employment and chronic illness; continuing the inequalities in health debate, *British Medical Journal*, 294, 1069-73

Ashton, P (1984) Poverty and its Beholder, *New Society*, 18.10.84

Association of County Councils and Metropolitan Authorities (1992) *School Leavers Destinations: An analysis of young people's career choices made by the heads of LEA careers services*. Roy Slade (ed.) for the ACC/AMA, ACC Publications Ref No 88259

Association of Metropolitan Authorities (1990) *Homelessness: report of local authority housing and racial equality working party.*

Atkinson, A.B (1990) *The Department of Social Security Report on Households Below Average Income 1981-87*, London School of Economics WSP/RN/22

Atkinson, A.B and Micklewright, J.C (1989) Turning the screw: benefits for the unemployed, 1979-88 *in* Atkinson (1989) *Poverty and social security*. Harvestor Wheatsheaf

Audit Commission (1989) *Housing the Homeless – The Local Authority Role*. HMSO

Audit Commission (1992) *Developing Local Authority Housing Strategies*. HMSO

Balarajan, R (1986) On the state of health in Inner London, *British Medical Journal*, 292, 911-14

Balarajan, R and Raleigh, V.S (1990) Variations in perinatal, neonatal, postneonatal and infant mortality in England and Wales by mother's country of birth, 1982-85 *in* Britton, M (ed.) *Mortality and Geography: A review in the mid-1980s.* HMSO: OPCS Decennial Supplement for England and Wales, Series DS no.9

Balarajan, R, Yuen, P and Machin, D (1992) Deprivation and general practitioner workload, *British Medical Journal*, 304, 529-34

Baldwin, S (1985) *The Costs of Caring.* Routledge and Kegan Paul

Barnes, J. H and Lucas, H (1975) Positive discrimination in education: individuals, groups and institutions *in* Barnes, J *(ed.) Educational Priority, Vol, 3; Curriculum Innovation in London's EPAs,* HMSO

Bartholomew, R, Hibbett, A and Sidaway, J (1992) Lone parents and the labour market: Evidence from the labour force survey, *Employment Gazette*, November

Bebbington, A.C (1991) The expectation of life without disability in England and Wales: 1976-88, *Population Trends*, 66, 26-29

Bennett, M and Kell, J (1989) *A Good Start: Four year olds in Infant schools.* Blackwell

Bentham, G (1990) Poverty, cold weather and the rise in infant mortality in England in 1986, School of Environmental Sciences, University of East Anglia, Paper presented at the annual conference of the Institute of British Geographers, Glasgow, 4 January

Bernstein, B (1971) *Class, Codes and Control.* Routledge

Berthoud, R (1986) *Selective Social Security.* London Policy Studies Institute

Berthoud, R and Brown, J.C (1981) *Poverty and the Development of Anti-Poverty Policy in the United Kingdom.* Heinemann

Berthoud, R and Kempson, E (1992) *Credit and debt in Britain: The PSI Report*

Beveridge, W (1942) *Social Insurance and Allied Services.* HMSO cmd. 6404

Bird, M (1987) *Non-Attendance: A case study of fifth-year pupils.* ILEA: RS 1141/87

Black, J (1985) Child Health in ethnic minorities, *British Medical Journal*, 290, 615, 23 February

Black, M.E and Colleagues (1991) Utilisation by homeless people of acute hospital services in London, *British Medical Journal* 303, 958-961, 19 October

Blackburn, C (1991) *Poverty and Health: Working with families.* OUP

Blackburn, C and Graham, H (1991) *Smoking Among Working Class Mothers.* Coventry: University of Warwick: Department of Applied Social Studies

Blackman, T and Colleagues (1989) Housing and health: a case study of two areas in West Belfast, *Journal of Social Policy*, 18,1,1-26

Blatchford, P and Colleague (1985) Educational achievement in the infant school: the influence of ethnic origin, gender and home on entry skills, *Educational Research* 27, 1, 52-60

Blaxter, M (1983) Health Services as a defence against the consequences of poverty in industrialised societies, *Social Science and Medicine*, 17, 1139-48

Blaxter, M (1990), *Health and Life styles*. Tavistock/Routledge

Bloor, M, Sampier, M and Prior, L (1987) Arte fact explanations of inequalities in health: an assessment of the evidence, *Sociology of Health and Illness*, 9, 231-64

Boardman, B (1991a) *Ten years cold-lessons from a decade of fuel poverty*. Neighbourhood Energy Action

Boardman, B (1991) *Fuel Poverty*.

Bone, M and Meltzer, H (1989) *The Prevalence of Disability Among Children*. HMSO: 1989

Booth, C (1988) Conditions and occupations of the people of East London and Hackney, *Journal of the Royal Statistical Society*, vol.50, No1

Borooah, V.K (1988) The growth of public expenditure in the United Kingdom, 1960-86 *in* Lybeck, J.A and Henrekson, M (*eds.*) (1988) *Explaining the Growth of Government*. North-Holland: Elsevier Science Publishers BV

Borooah, V.K, McGreggor, P.P.L and Mckee, P.M (1991) *Regional Income Inequality and Poverty in the United Kingdom*. Aldershot: Dartmouth

Bradshaw, J (1990) *Child Poverty and Deprivation in the UK*. National Children's Bureau

Bradshaw, J (1991) *Developments in Social Security Policy*, University of York

Bradshaw, J, Hicks, L and Parker, H (1992) *Summary Budget Standards for Six Households*. Working Paper No 12 (Revised) York University, Department of Social Policy and Social work: Family Budget Unit

Bradshaw, J, Mitchell, D and Morgan, J (1987) Evaluating adequacy: The potential of budget standards, *Journal of Social Policy*, 16,2

Bradshaw, J and Holmes, H (1989) *Living on the Edge: a study of the Living Standards of Families on Benefit in Tyne and Wear*. Tyneside Child Poverty Action Group

Bradshaw, J and Morgan, J, (1987) *Budgeting on Benefit: the consumption of families on social security*. Family Policy Studies Centre. 65pp (Occasional Paper No.5)

Bradshaw, J and Millar, J (1991) *Lone Parent Families in the UK*. Department of Social Security Research Report No.6 HMSO

Britton, M (1989) Mortality and Geography, *Population Trends*, 56, 16-23

Brown, C (1984) *Black and White Britain: The Third PSI Survey*. Gower

Brown, J.C (1990) The Focus on Single Mothers *in* Murray (1990) *The Emerging British underclass*. The Institute of Economic Affairs

Brown, M and Madge, N (1982) *Despite the Welfare State*. Heinemann: SSRC: DHSS studies in Deprivation and Disadvantage

Bruegel, I (1989) Sex and race in the labour market, *Feminist Review*, 32

Burghes, L (1980) *Living from Hand to Mouth: A study of 65 families living on supplementary benefit*. Child Poverty Action Group/Family Services Unit

Carmichael, C. L, Rugg-Gun, A.J and Farrell, R.S (1989) The relationship between floridation, social class and carers' experience in 5-year-old children in Newcastle and Northumberland in 1987, *British Dental Journal*, 167, 2, 57-61, July

Carr-Hill, R (1986) *Trends in Health*, mimeo (as quoted in Bradshaw 1990)

Carr-Hill, R.A. (1988) Time trends in inequalities in health, *Journal of Biosocial Science*, 20, 253-263

Carroll, T (1992) Season of birth and school attendance, *The British Journal of Educational Psychology*, 62,3, November

Carstairs, V (1981) Multiple deprivation and health state, *Community Medicine*, 3, 4-13

Cato, V and Whetton, C (1991) *An Inquiry into Local Education Authority Evidence on Standards of Reading of Seven-year-old children*. DES and NFER Report

Central Statistical Office, *Economic Trends*, 1991, 1992

Central Statistical Office, *Regional Trends*, 1991

Central Statistical Office, *Social Trends*, 1991, 1992

CHAR (1992) *Plans No Action – The Children Act and homeless young people* Chartered Institute of Public Finance, *School Meals Census* 1986-88

Chinn, S, Rona, R.J and Price, C.E (1989) The Secular Trend in the Height of Primary School Children in England and Scotland 1972 to 1979 and 1979 to 1986, *Annuals of Human Biology*, 16, 387-395

Clarke, L (1989) *Children's Changing Circumstances: Recent Trends and Future Prospects*. University of London: Centre for Population Studies

Clarke, M.M (1988) *Children Under Five: Educational research and evidence*. Gordon and Breach Science Publishes: Final Report to the Department of Education and Science

Coalition for Child Benefit (no date) *Child Benefit: Looking to the Future*

Coalition on Young People and Social Security (1992) *A Broken Promise: The Failure of Youth Training Policy*. Youthaid and The Children's Society

Cohen, B and Fraser, N (1991) *Childcare in a Modern Welfare System: Towards a New National Policy*. Institute for Public Policy Research

Cohen, R and Colleagues (1992) *Hardship Britain: Being poor in the 1990s*. Child Poverty Action Group

Cole-Hamilton, I, Dibb, S and O'Rourke, J (1991) *School Meals*. CPAG Fact Sheet

Cole-Hamilton, I and Lang, T (1986) *Tightening Belts: A report on the impact of poverty on food*. London Food Commission

Coleman, A (1985) *Utopia on Trial: Vision and reality in planned housing*. Hilary Shipman

Commission for Racial Equality (1992a) *CRE Submission to the National Commission on Education*. CRE

Commission for Racial Equality (1992b) *Set to Fail?: Setting and banding in secondary schools*. CRE

Committee on Medical Aspects of Food Policy (1991) *Dietary Reference Values*. Department of Health: HMSO

Conway, J (*ed.*) (1988) *Prescription for Poor Health: The Crisis for Homeless Families*. London Food Commission, Maternity Alliance, SHAC, Shelter

Cooper, J (1991) Births outside marriage: recent trends and associated demographic and social changes, *Population Trends*, 63, Spring

Coulter, F.A.E, Cowell, F.A and Jenkins, S.P (1991) Family Fortunes in the 1970s and 1980s *in* Blundell, R, Preston, I and Walker, I (forthcoming) *Measuring Household Welfare*. Cambridge University Press

Council of Mortgage Lenders (1992) *Mortgage Arrears and Possession Statistics*

The Court Report of the Committee on Child Health Services (1976) *Fit for the Future*. Department of Health and Social Security: HMSO: cmnd 6684

Cox, B and Others (1987) *Health and Life-style survey: Preliminary Report*. Health Promotion Research Trust

CPAG (1992) *Fuel Rights Handbook*

Craig, G (1992), *Replacing the Social Fund: A strategy for change*. York: University of York Social Policy Research Unit.

Cross, C (1978) *Ethnic Minorities in the Inner City: The ethnic dimension in urban deprivation in England*. Commission for Racial Equality

Crowe, J (1991) *Right to Fuel*, Secretary, National Right to Fuel Campaign

Curwen, M and Davis, T (1988) Winter mortality, temperature and influenza: has the relationship changed in recent years? *Population Trends*, 54, 17-20

Cuttance, P (1988) Intra-system variation in the effective of schooling, *Research Papers in Education*, 3, 3, 180

Dale, R.R and Griffiths, S (1965) *Down Stream*. Routledge

Daniel, W.W (1990) *The Unemployed Flow*. Policy Studies Institute

Davie, R, Butler, N and Goldstein, H (1972) *From Birth to Seven: A report of the National Child Development Study* (1958 Cohort), National Children's Bureau

Davies, J (Summarised by Mortimer, P and Dowson, J) *Attendance at Three Secondary Schools*. ILEA: RS 761/80

Davey Smith, G, Blane, D and Bartley, M (1992) Explanations for socio-economic differentials in mortality, *Social Science and Medicine*, as quoted in Whitehead, M (1992)

Department of Education and Science (1981) *Report by HMI on the Effects on the Education Service in England of Local Authority Expenditure Policies – Financial year 1980-81*

Department of Education and Science (1985a) White Paper, *Better Schools*. HMSO

Department of Education and Science (1985b) *Report by HMI on the Effects of Local Authority Expenditure Policies on Education Provision in England*, 1984

Department of Education and Science (1986) *Report by HMI on the Effects of Local Authority Expenditure Policies on Education provision in England 1985*

Department of Education and Science (1989) *Education Observed 13: Attendance at School*. DES: A Report by HMI

Department of Education and Science (1990a) *A Survey of the Education of Children Living in Temporary Accommodation: April-December 1989*, HMI Report: Reference 178/90/NS

Department of Education and Science (1990b) *The Teaching and Learning of Reading in Primary Schools* HMSO: A Report by HMI

Department of Education and Science (1990c) *Standards in Education 1988-89: The annual report of HM Senior Chief Inspector of Schools*

Department of Education and Science (1991a) *Standards in Education 1989-90: The annual report of HM Senior Chief Inspector of Schools*.

Department for Education (1991b) School Examination Survey 1989/90, *Statistical Bulletin*, 22/91, December

Department of Education and Science (1991c) Educational and Economic activity of young people aged 16 to 18 years in England from 1974/75 to 1989/90, *Statistical Bulletin*, 13/91

Department of Education and Science (1991d) *Higher Education: A New Framework*. HMSO cm 1541

Department of Education and Science (1991e) Education expenditure from 1979-80, *Statistical Bulletin*, 21/91

Department of Education and Science l (1992a) *Education in England 1990-91: The annual report of HM Senior Chief Inspector of school*

Department for Education (1992b) School Examination Survey 1990/91, *Statistical Bulletin*, 15/92, July

Department for Education (1992c) Participation in Education by 16-18 year olds in England: 1979-80 to 1991-92, *Statistical Bulletin*, 14/92

Department of Education and Science (1992d) Education statistics for the United Kingdom 1991 Edition, *Statistical Bulletin*, 3/92

Department of Education and Science (1992e) Student members in higher education – Great Britain 1980 to 1990, *Statistical Bulletin*, 8/92

Department of Education and Science (1992f) *Education Statistics 1991*

Department of Education (1992g) Pupil/teacher ratios for each Local Education authority in England – January 1991, *Statistical Bulletin* 2/92

Department for Education (1992h) Education expenditure from 1979-80, *Statistical Bulletin* 10/92

Department for Education (1992j) The Implementaion of Local Management of Schools: *A Report by HM Inspectorate 1989-92*, HMSO

Department for Education (1993) The Implementation of the Curriculum Requirements of the ERA: *An Overview by HM Inspectorate on the second year 1990-91*, HMSO

Department of Employment *New Earnings Survey*, 1991

Department of Employment *Labour Force Surveys* 1984-1991

Department of Employment *Employment Gazette* (Monthly) various issues

Department of Environment (1977) *Final Reports of the Inner Area Studies in Lambeth, Liverpool and Birmingham*

DoE (1988) *English House Conditions Survey 1986*, HMSO

Department of Environment (1991a) *Annual Report*, 1991 HMSO: CM 1508

Department of Environment (1991b) *Homelessness Statistics*

DoE (1991c) *English House Condition Survey 1986, Supplementary (Energy) Report* HMSO

Department of Health and Social Security (1967) *Circumstances of Families*, HMSO

Department of Health and Social Security (1978) *Eating for Health*

Department of Health and Social Security (1980) *The Black Report*

Department of Health and Social Security (1985) *The Reform of Social Security* HMSO:Cmnd 9517

Department of Health and Social Security (1987) *Impact of the Reformed Structure of Income-Related Benefits*, DHSS

Department of Health and Social Security (1988) *Low Income Statistics: Report of a Technical Review*

Department of Health and Social Security *Social Security Statistics 1979-1989*. HMSO

Department of Health (1989) *The Diets of British Schoolchildren*. HMSO

Department of Health (1990a) *An Epidemiological Review of Child Health*. (unpublished)

Department of Health (1990b) *The State of Public Health*, 1989. HMSO

Department of Health (1991a) *On the State of the Public Health for the year 1990* HMSO

Department of Health (1991b) *The Health of the Nation*. HMSO: Green Paper

Department of Social Security (1990a) *Households Below Average Income: A Statistical Analysis 1981-87*

Department of Social Security (1991a) *Households Below Average Income: Stocktaking*. Report of a Working Group

Department of Social Security (1991b) *Income Related Benefits: Estimates of Take-up 1987*. Technical Notes

Department of Social Security (1991c) *Annual Report by the Secretary of State for Social Security on the Social Fund*. HMSO: CM 1580

Department of Social Security (1992a) *Households Below Average Income: A Statistical Analysis 1979-1988/89*

Department of Social Security (1992b) *Report of Severe Hardship Claims Unit*

Department of Social Security (1993a) *Income Related Benefits - Estimates of Take-up 1989*

Department of Social Security (1993b) *Households Below Average Income: A statistical analysis 1979-1990/91*. HMSO

Department of Social Security *Social Security Statistics 1990-92*. HMSO

Ditch, I, Pickles, S and Whiteford, P (1992) *The New Structure of Child Benefit: A Review Report Prepared for the Coalition of the Child Benefit*

Donnison, D (1982) *The Politics of Poverty*. Martin Robertson

Douglas, J.W.B (1964) *The Home and the School*. MacGibbon and Kee

Drew, D, and Gray, J (1990) The Fifth Year examination achievements of Black, Young People in England and Wales, *Educational Research*, 32,3

Drew, D and Gray, J (1991), The Black-White gap in examination results: a statistical critique of a decade's research, *New Community*, 17, 2, 159-72

Duffy, K. B and Lincoln, I.C (1990) *Earnings and Ethnicity*. Leicester City Council

Dunnell, K (1990) Monitoring children's health, *Population Trends*, 60, 16-19, Summner

Durward, L (1984) *Poverty in Pregnancy*. Maternity Alliance.

Education, Science and Arts Committee (1988) *Educational Provision for the Under Fives*. House of Commons: First Report: Session 1988-89 HMSO

Education Science and Arts Committee (1982) *School Meals*. House of Commons: Seventh Report: 1981-82 HMSO

Education, Science and Arts Committee (1991) *Standards of Reading in primary schools*. House of Commons: Third Report: Vol 1: Session 1990-91: HMSO

Edwards, H with Stanyer, A (1987) Mrs Thatcher's diary: Policies affecting poor families – May 1979-April 1987 *in* Walker A and Walker, C (*eds.*) (1987) *The Growing Divide*, Child Poverty Action Group

Edwards, R (1991a) *Lone Parent Families Poverty and Employment*. National Children's Bureau: Highlight No. 102

Edwards R (1991b) *Homeless Families*. National Children's Bureau: Highlight No.99

Eggleston, J and others (1986) *Education for some: The Educational and Vocational Experiences of 15-18 year old Young People from Minority Ethnic Groups*. DES: Trentham Books

Employment Institute (1991) Public spending – a break with the past? *Economic Report*, 6,6, December

Employment Policy Institute (1992) Figuring Out Unemployment, *Economic Report*, 7,2, September

Enfield Health Authority: Director of Public Health (1990) *On the Health of Enfield People: Annual Health Report*

Equal Opportunities Commission (1990) *The Key to Real Choice: an Action plan for childcare*

Ermisch, J (1986) *The Economics of the Family: Applications to Divorce and Re-marriage*. CEPR: Discussion Paper No.40

Essen, J, Fogelman, K.R and Head, J (1978) Childhood housing experiences and school attainment, *Child: Care, health and Development*. 4, February

European Economic Community (1981) *Final Report on the First Programme of Pilot Schemes and Studies to Combat Poverty*. Brussells: Commission of the European Communities

Fagin, L and Little, M (1984) *The Forsaken Families: The Effects of Unemployment on Family Life*. Penguin

Family Policy Study Centre (1990) *One Parent Families*. Factsheet 3

Fanning, D.M (1967) Families in flats, *British Medical Journal*, IV, 382-6

Ferguson, D.M and O'Mahony, B (1991) *Young, Black and Homeless in Britain*. Barnardo's

Field, F (1990) Britains Underclass: *Countering the Growth* in Murray, C (1990) *The Emerging British Underclass*, The Institute of Economic Affairs

Fogelman, K (ed.) (1976) *Britain's Sixteen year olds*: National Children's Bureau

Fogelman, K and Goldstein, H (1976) Social Factors associated with changes in educational attainment, *Educational Studies 2*

Foster, S and Burrows, L (1991) *Urgent Need for Homes*. Shelter

Frayman, H (1991) *Breadline Britain 1990s: The Findings of the Television Series*. Domino Films/LWT

Furley, A (1989) *A Bad Start in Life: Children, Health and Housing*. Shelter

Galloway, D. M (1979) *A study of persistent absence from school in Sheffield: prevalence and assoicated educational psychological and social factors*, PhD. Thesis, City of Sheffield Polytechnic as cited in Grimshaw and Pratt, 1986

Galloway, D (1985) *Schools and Persistent Absentees*. Pergamon Press

Gans, H.J. (1970) Poverty and Culture: Some Basic Questions About Methods of Studying Life-Styles of the Poor *in* Townsend, P (*ed.*) (1970) *The Concept of Poverty*: Heinemann

Gardner Merchant (1991) *What Today's Children Are Eating – School meals survey*

Garner, C.L (1989) *Does Deprivation Damage?* Centre for Educational Sociology

Garrow, J.S. (1991) *Obseity and Overweight*. Health Education Authority

Gillborn, D and Drew, D (1992) 'Race', Class and School Effects, *New Community*, 18,4,551-65

Glennerster, H and Low, W (1991) Education and the Welfare State: does it add up? *in* Hills, J (*ed.*) (1991) *The State of Welfare: The Welfare State in Britain since 1974*. The Clarenden Press

Godfrey, C and Bradshaw, J (1983) Inflation and poor families, *New Society* 65, 1083

Godley, W (1992) Escape from the Infinite recession, *New Statesman and Society*, 20 March

Goldblatt, P (*ed.*) (1990) *Longitudinal study – 1971-81: Mortality and Social organisation*, HMSO: OPCS: Series LS No.6

Gorman, T and Fernandes, C (1992) *Reading in Recession*. NFER

Graham, H (1984) *Women, Health and the Family*. Wheatsheaf Books

Graham, H (1986) *Caring for the Family*. Health Education Council: Research Report, No.1

Graham, P (1989) Social class, social disadvantage and child health, *Children and Society*, 2, 9-19

Grant, J (1991) *The State of the World's children*. New York: OUP

Gray, J and Colleagues (1983) *Reconstruction of Secondary Education: Theory, Myth and practice since the war*. Routledge

Gray, J and Jesson, D (1990) *Truancy in secondary schools amongst fifth-year pupils*. Sheffield University: Educational Research Centre

Greve, J (1991) *Homelessness in Britain*. Joseph Rowntree Foundation

Grimshaw, R.H and Pratt, J.D (1986) Counting the absent scholars: some implications for managerial practice arising from a survey of absenteeism in a city's secondary schools, *School organisation*, 6, 1, 155-73

Hackett, A and others (1984) A two-year longitudinal nutritional survey of 405 Northumberland children intially aged 11.5 years, *British Journal of Nutrition*, 51, 67-75

Hakim, C (1982) The Social consequences of unemployment, *Journal of Social Policy* 11,4

Hall, S, (1986), Current epidemiology of childhood infections *in* Alberman, E.D and Peckham, C.S (*eds.*) *Childhood Epidemiology*, *British Medical Bulletin*, 42,2, 127-30

Halsey, A.H (1975) Sociology and the equality debate, *Oxford Review of Education*, 1,1

Halsey, A.H (1992) *Opening Wide the Doors of Higher Education*. National Commission on Education: Briefing No6

Hansard   22.12.83   Col 561
             24. 7.86   Col 450
             16.11.87   Col 442
             18.11.87   Col 1172
             13. 2.88   Col 737-742
             31.10.89   Col 200-208
              1. 5.90   Col 491
             18. 4.91   Col 238

Hansard   16. 5.91   Col 413
           20. 5.91   Col 361
           21. 5.91   Col 417-418
           10.12.91   Col 417
           17.12.91   Col 126-29
           23. 1.92   Col 518
            3. 2.92   Col 42-44
           21. 5.92   Col 247-250
           17. 6.92   Col 531-534
           24. 6.92   Col 249
           16.12.92   Col 325-326
           11. 1.93   Col 545-546

Haskey, J (1989a) One-parent families and their children in Great Britain: numbers and characteristics, *Population Trends*, 55, Spring

Haskey, J (1989b) Current prospects for the proportion of marriages ending in divorce, *Population Trends*, 55

Haskey, J (1990) Children in families broken by divorce, *Population Trends*, 61 Autumn

Haskey, J (1991) Estimated numbers and demographic characteristics of one parent families in Great Britain, *Population Trends* 65, Autumn

Haskey, J and Kelly, S (1991) Population estimates by cohabitation and legal marital status – a trial of new estimates, *Population Trends*, 66, Winter

Heady, P and Smyth, M (1989) *Living Standards During Unemployment: Volume I: The Results*. HMSO

Health Committee (1991) *Maternity Services: Preconception*. HMSO: House of Commons: Fourth Report: vol.1: Session 1990-91

Health Visitors Association and the British Medical Association (1989) *Homeless Families and their Health*. BMA

Hills, J (1991) *Unravelling Housing Finance*. OUP

Hills, J and Mullings, B (1991) Housing: A decent home for all at a price within their means *in* Hills, J (*ed*) (1991) *The State of Welfare: The Welfare State in Britain since 1974*. The Clarendon Press

Holt, R (1991) Food and drinks at four daily time intervals in a group of young children, *British Dental Journal*, 170, 137-43

Holtermann, S (1992) *Investing in Young Children: Costing an Education and Day Care Service*. National Children's Bureau

House of Commons Standing Committee E, 10.12.87, col.510

Howarth, V (1987) *A Survey of Families in Bed and Breakfast Hotels*. The Thomas Coram Foundation

Huby, M and Dix, G (1992) *Evaluating the Social Fund*. Department of Social Security Research Report No 9 HMSO

Hutchinson, S and Varlaam, A (1985) *Bangladeshi Mothers: Views of Schooling in Tower Hamlets*, ILEA:Research and Statistics Branch RS 1029/86

Huws, K, Hurstfield, J and Holtmatt, R (1989) *What Price Flexibility?* Low Pay Unit

Hyndman, S.J (1990) Housing dampness and health among British Bengalis in East London, *Social Science and Medicine*, 30, 131-41

Illsley, R, (1986) Occupational class, selection and the production of inequalities in health, *Quarterly Journal of Social Affairs*, 2,2, 151-65

Inner London Education Authority (1981) *School Examination Results in the ILEA 1979 and 1980*. ILEA RS787/81

The Institute for Fiscal Studies (1992) *Alternative Proposals on Tax and Social Security*. IFS commentary no 29

Jarman, B and colleagues (1988) Uptake of immunisation in district health authorities in England, *British Medical Journal*, 296, 1775-78

Jesson, D and Gray, J (1991) *Pupil Performance in Context*. Nottingham County Council: Education and University of Sheffield: Division of Education

Jesson, D (1992) *Personal Communication*

Johnson, P and Webb, S (1990) *Poverty in Official Statistics: Two Reports*. The Institute for Fiscal Studies: IFS Commentary No 24

Jones, I.G and Cameron, D (1984) Social class: an embarrassment to epidemiology? *Community Medicine*, 6, 37-46

Joseph, K and Sumption, J (1979) *Equality*. John Murray

Joseph Rowntree Foundation (1991) *Inquiry into British Housing*. Second Report

Judge, K and Benzeval, M (1993a) Health inequalities: new concerns about the children of single monthers, *British Medical Journal* 306, 6879, 13 March

Judge, K and Benzeval, M (1993b) Analysis of data from the *General Household Surveys 1985-1989* (made available in a personal communication).

Judge, K and Benzeval, M (1993c) Analysis of Public Health Common Data Set 1989 – (made available in a personal communication at 21.1.93)

Judge, K and Benzeval, M (1993d) Analysis of data from *The Survey of Londoners' Living Standards* by Townsend (1986) (made available in a personal communication).

Kiernan, K and Wicks, M (1990) *Family Change and Future Policy*. Family Policy Studies Centre and Joseph Rowntree Foundation

Knight, I (1984) *The Heights and Weights of Adults in Great Britain.* HMSO

Kurtz, Z (1992) *The Challenge to health services for children of school-age in Inner London,* (unpublished)

Kysel, F (1987) *Ethnic Background and Examination Results 1985 and 1986.* ILEA: RS1120/87

Lang, T and others (1984) *Jam Tommorrow?* Manchester Polytechnic: Food Policy Unit

Lawlor, J and Kennedy, C (1992), Measures of unemployment: the claimant count and the Labour Force Survey, *Employment Gazette,* July

Le Grand, J, Winter, D and Woolley, F (1991) The National Health Service: Safe in whose hands? *in* Hills, J (*ed.*) (1991) *The State of Welfare: The Welfare State in Britain since 1974.* Clarendon Press

Lister, R (1989) Social Security *in* McCarthy, M (*ed.*) (1989) *The New Politics of Welfare.* Macmillan

Lister, R (1991) Concepts of Poverty, *Local Government Policy-making,* May, p192

Littlewood, J and Tinker, A (1981) *Families in Flats.* HMSO

Lobstein, T (1988) Poor children and cheap calories, *Community Paediatric Group Newsletter,* Autumn

London Borough of Croydon (1992) *Reading Competence at Age 7,* LB Croydon: Education Department

London Research Centre (1991) *Length of stay in temporary accommodation: A study of homeless households in London*

London University: Kings College School of Medicine and Dentistry (1986) *Trends in Health.* Mimeo

Lonsdale, S (1985) *Work and Inequality.* Longman

Low Pay Unit (1992) *Poor Britain: Poverty Inequality and Low Pay in the Nineties.* LPU

Lowry, S (1991) *Housing and Health,* British Medical Journal

Lynes, T (1992) *The wrong side of the Tracks: factsheet on unemployment and benefits.* Child Poverty Action Group

Mack, J and Lansley, S (1985) *Poor Britain.* Unwin

Madge, N (1983) Unemployment and its effects on children, *Journal of Child Psychology and Psychiatry,* 24,2,311-319

Martin, C and Hunt, S (1989) Disadvantage and Disease *in* Research Unit *in* Health and Behaviour Change (1989) *Changing the Public Health,* John Wiley

Martin, J and White, A (1988) *The Financial circumstances of disabled adults living in private households,* HMSO: OPCS Disability Survey Report 2

Mann, K, (1992) *The Making of an English 'underclass'?: The social divisions of welfare and labour*. Open University Press

Maughan, B and Rutter, M (1986) Black Pupils' progress in secondary schools II: examination achievements, *British Journal of Developmental Psychology*, 419-29

Middleton, B (1983) *Factors affecting the performance of West Indian Boys in a secondary school*. York: University of York: unpublished MA dissertation as cited in Tomlinson (1987)

Millar, J (1989) *Poverty and the Lone Parent: The challenge of social policy*. Avebury

Millar, J (1991) Bearing the cost *in* Becker, S (*ed.*) (1991) *Windows of opportunity: public policy and the poor*. Child Poverty Action Group

Moore, R (1991) Cold, damp and mouldy housing in England (A paper delivered at *Unhealthy Housing: The Public Health Response* 18-20 December, 1984)

Morris, J and Winn, M (1990) *Housing and Social Inequality*. Hilary Shipman

Mortimore, J and Blackstone, T (1982) *Disadvantage and Education*. SSRC – DHSS Studies in Deprivation and Disadvantage 4: Heinemann

Mortimore, P (1983) *Achievement in Schools*. Research Statistics Branch, ILEA (RS 829/82)

Mortimore, P, and colleagues (1988) *School Matters: The junior years*. Open Books

Mortimore, P and Coulter, A (1982) *Non Attendance at School: Some research findings*. ILEA: RS860/82

Moser, K.A, Fox, A.J and Jones, D.R (1984) Unemployment and mortality in the OPCS Longitudinal Study, *The Lancet*, 1324-28, 8 December

Moss, P (1989) The indirect costs of parenthood: a neglected issue in social policy, *Critical Social Policy*, 24, pp 20-37

Muelbauer (1991) *The Independent*, 22 December

Murie, A (1983) *Housing Inequality and Deprivation*. Heinemann: SSRC/ DHSS: Studies in Deprivation and disadvantage

Murray, C (1990) *The Emerging British Underclass*, The Institute of Economic Affairs

McCormick, A, Fleming, D, and Rosenbaum, M (1990) Socio-economic characteristics of people who consult their general practitioner, *Population Trends*, 59, 8-10, spring

McNeil, G and others (1991) Nutrient intakes in school children: some practical considerations, *Proceedings of the Nutrition Society*, 50, 29-35

Maclure, A and Stewart, G (1984) Admission of children to hospitals in Glasgow: relation to unemployment and other deprivation variables, *Lancet*, 682-5, 22 September

National Advisory Committee on Nutrition Education (1983) *A Discussion Paper on Proposals for Nutritional Guidelines for Health in Britain.* Health Education Authority

National Association of Citizens Advice Bureaux (1992) *Severe Hardship: CAB Evidence on Young People and Benefits.* E/3/92 NACAB

National Audit Office (1990) *Homelessness: A report by the Comptroller and Auditor General.* HMSO

National Audit Office (1990) *Report on Maternity Services.* HMSO: HC 297

National Audit Office (1991) *Repair and Maintenance of School Buildings.* HMSO

National Children's Bureau (1987) *Investing in the Future: Child health ten years after the Court Report*

National Children's Homes (1989) *Housing: Vulnerable young single homeless people*

National Children's Homes (1992a) *The NCH Factfile: Children in Britain*

National Children's Home (1992b) *Runaways: exploding the myths*

National Dairy Council (1982) *What are the Children Eating these days?*

National Economic Development Council (1977) *International price competitiveness, non-price factors and export performance.* NEDO

National Federation of Housing Associations (1989) *Single Homeless in London*: Research Note No.4

Nelson, M (1991), Nutrition and the school-child, food, vitamins and IQ, *Proceedings in the Nutrition Society*, 50, 29-35

Nelson, M and Naismith, D (1979) The nutritional status of poor children in London, *Journal of Human Nutrition*, 33, 1, 33-46

Nelson, M, and others (1990) Nutrient intakes, vitamin-mineral supplementation and intelligence in British schoolchildren, *British Journal of Nutrition*, 64, 13-22

Nelson, M, and Paul, A (1983), The nutritional contribution of school dinners and other mid-day meals to the diets of school-children, *Human Nutrition: Applied Nutrition*, 37A(2), 128-35

Newell, P (1991) *The UN Convention and Children's Rights in the UK.* National Children's Bureau

Nuttal, D.L (1990) *Differences in Examination Performance*, ILEA: RS 1277/90

Nuttal, D and Goldstein, H (1989) Differential School Effectiveness, *International Journal of Educational Research*, 13, 769-76

Nuttal, D.L, Thomas, S and Goldstein, H (1992) *Report on Analysis of 1990 Examination Results*. AMA

Union de Foyers de Jeunes Travailleurs (1989) Le Rapport sur le Logement des Jeunes en Europe pour la Grande-Bretagne, *Oeil*

OPCS (1978) *Occupational Mortality*: Decennial Supplement, 1970-72 HMSO: DS No1

OPCS (1988) *Childhood Occupational Mortality 1979, 1980, 1982 and 1983: Decennial Supplement*. HMSO

OPCS (1991a) *Private Renters Survey: Preliminary results*

OPCS (1991b) *Supplementary Monitor on People Sleeping Rough*

OPCS (1992) *General Household Survey* 1989, 1990, 1991. HMSO

OPCS (1992), *Mortality Statistics 1990 – Perinatal and infant: social and biological factors*. HMSO: Series DH3 no24

OPCS (1992) *Population Trends*, 69, Autumn

OPCS (1993) *Population Trends*, 71, March

Oppenheim, C (1988) *The Social Security Act: A Brief Guide*. Child Poverty Action Group

Oppenheim, C (1990) *Poverty: The Facts Child Poverty Action Group*

Orshansky, M (1969) How Poverty is measured, *Monthly Labour Review*, February

Osborn, A.F and Butler, N.R (1985) *Ethnic Minority Children: A comparative study from birth to five years*. University of Bristol: Department of Child Health and Education Study; and Commission for Racial Equality

Pamuk, E.R (1988) Social class inequality in infant mortality in England and Wales from 1921-1980, *European Journal of Population Studies*, 4, 1-21

Parekh, B (1983) Educational opportunity in multi-ethnic Britain *in* Glaza, N and Young, K (*eds.*) *Ethnic Pluralism and Public Policy*. Heinemann

Pearce, B and Wilcox, S (1991) *Home Ownership, Taxation and the Economy*. Joseph Rowntree Foundation

Pearson, D, Burns, S and Cunningham, K (1977) Dietary surveys of immigrant school girls in Leicester, *Journal of Human Nutrition*, 31, 362

Peckham, C, and others (1989) *National Immunisation Study: Factors influencing immunisation uptake in childhood*. Action Research for the Crippled Child

Peckam, C and others (1983) Prevalence of obesity in British children born in 1946 and 1958, *British Medical Journal*, 286, 1237-42

Pharoah, P.O.D (1986) Perspective and Patterns *in* Alberman, E.D, Peckam, C.S *(eds)* Childhood Epidermiology, *British Medical Bulletin*, 42,2,119-26

Phillimore, P (1989) Mortality variations within two poor areas in North East England, University of Newcastle: Department of Community Health, as quoted in Townsend (1990a)

Piachaud, D, (1987) Problems in the Definition and Measurement of Poverty, *Journal of Social Policy*, 16,2, pp147-64

Piachaud, D (1981) Peter Townsend and the Holy Grail, *New Society*, 10 September

Piachaud, D *Poverty and Social Security*, Paper for Social Services Committee, no date

Pickin, C.A, and Ramsell, P.J (1991) *A profile of single homeless people in Manchester: their health status and access to health care*, (A paper delivered at a conference *Unhealthy housing: the public health response*, held at Warwick University, Coventry, 18-20 December 1991)

Pilling, D, (1990) *Escape from disadvantage*. The Falmer Press

Platt, S.D and colleagues (1989), Damp housing mould growth and symptomatic health state, *British Medical Journal*, 298, 1673-78, 24 June

Platt, S.D, Martin, C and Hunt, S (1991), Womens' mental health in deprived areas *in* Goldberg, D *(eds.)* *The Public Health Impact on Mental Disorder* New York: Hogrefe and Huber

Plowden Report (1967) *Children and their Primary Schools*. Central Advisory Council for Education: HMSO

Pollitt, N with Booth, A and Kay, H (1989) *Hard Times: Young and Homeless*. Shelter

Polytechnics Central Admission System (1991) *Statistical Supplement to the Annual Report*

Power, C, Manor, O and Fox, J (1991) *Health and Class: The Early Years*. Chapman and Hall

Public Accounts Committee (1990) *Maternity Services*. HMSO: House of Commons Session 1989-90, 35th Report

Public Accounts Committee (1991) *Homelessness*. HMSO: House of Commons: Twentysecond Report

Quick, A and Wilkinson, RG (1991) *Income and Health: Towards equality in health*. Socialist Health Association

Rein, M (1970) Problems in the definition and measurement of poverty, *in* Townsend, P *(ed)* *The Concept of Poverty*. Heinemann

Report by Her Majesty's Inspectors on the Effects of Local Authority Expenditure Policies on Education Provision in England – 1984. Department of Education and Science, May 1985

Report by Her Majesty's Inspectors on the Effects of Local Authority Expenditure Policies on Education Provision in England – 1985. Department of Education and Science, May 1986

Report of a Research Working Group (the Black Report) (1980) *Inequalities in Health*. Department of Health and Social Security

Research Unit in Health and Behavioural Change (1989) *Changing the Public Health*. John Wiley

Reynolds, D and others (1980) School factors and truancy *in* Hersov, L and Berg, I *Out of School*. John Wiley

Ringen, S (1988) Direct and Indirect Measures of Poverty, *Journal of Social Policy*, 17,3

Ritchie, J, Jacoby, A and Bone, M (1981) *Access to Primary Health Care*. HMSO: OPCS

Robinson, P (1990) *Racial Disadvantage and the Economic Cycle*. Campaign for Work: Research Report 2, 5, July

Rodrigues, L and Botting, B (1989) Recent trends in postneonatal mortality in England, *Population Trends*, 56, 7-9

Roll, J (1990) *Young People: growing up in the Welfare State*. Family Policy Studies Centre

Roll, J (1992) *Understanding Poverty*. Family Policy Studies Centre

Rona, R.J and Chinn, S (1982) *National Study of health and growth: social and family factors and obesity in primary school children*, Annals of Human Biology, 9, 147-156

Rona, R.J and Chinn, S (1984) Parents' attitudes towards school meals for primary school children in 1981, *Human Nutrition:* Applied Nutrition, 38A, 187-98

Rose, G (1990) Reflections on the changing times, *British Medical Journal*, 301, 683-87

Rosenberg, K (1984) Poverty and the health of children, Letter in *Lancet*, 814, 6 October

Rowntree, B. Seebohm (1901) *Poverty: A Study of Town Life*. Macmillan

Royal College of Physicians (1983) Obesity, *Journal Royal College of Physicians*, 17, 1

Royal College of Physicians: Faculty of Public Health Medicine: Working Group on Housing and Health (1991); *Housing or Homelessness – A public health perspective*. BMA

Royal Commission on the Distribution of Income and Health (1979) Report No 7: *Fourth Report on the Standing References*, Cmnd 7595: HMSO

Runciman, W.G (1966) *Relative Deprivation and Social Justice*. Routledge and Keegan Paul

Rush, D and Cassano, P (1983) Relationship of cigarette smoking and social class to birth weights and perinatal mortality among all births in Britain, 5-11 April 1970, *Journal of Epidemiology and Community Health*, 37, 249-55

Rutter, M and Madge, N (1976) *Cycles of Disadvantage: A review of research*. Heinemann

Rutter, M and others (1979) *Fifteen Thousand Hours: Secondary schools and their effects on children*. Open Books

Sammons, P and Newbury, K (1989) *Ethnic Monitoring in Further and Higher Education: An account of the ILEA's initiative*. Further Education Unit.

Scarr, S and colleagues (1983) Development status and school achievements of minority and non-minority children from birth to 18 years in a British Midlands town, *British Journal of Development Psychology*, 1, 31-48

Scheuer M.A and colleagues (1991) *Homelessness and the Utilisation of Acute Hospital Services in London*. King's Fund Institute

Schorr, A. L (1964) Housing policy and poverty *in* Townsend P *(ed.)* (1970) *The Concept of Poverty*. Heinemann

Sen A. K (1978) *Three Notes on the concept of poverty*. Geneva: International Labour Organisation

Shiner, P and Leddington, S (1991) Sometimes it makes you frightened to go to hospital ...they treat you like dirt, *Health Service Journal*, 7 November

Sinfield, A (1993) Social Security through taxation *in* Pieters D *(ed.) Social Security, Taxation and Europe*, Antwerp: Maklu

Single and Homeless in London Working Party (1989) *Report on Homelessness*

Smith, A (1812) *The Wealth of Nations*. Ward, Lock (first published 1776)

Smith, D. J *(ed.)* 1992 *Understanding the Underclass*. Policy Studies Institute

Smith, D. J and Tomlinson, S (1989) *The School Effect: A study of multi-racial comprehensives*. PSI

Smith, S. J (1991) *Race and Housing in Britain*. Joseph Rowntree Foundation

Smith, S. J (1989) *The Politics of 'Race' and Residence*. Polity Press

Social Security Advisory Committee (1981) *First Report of the SSAC*

Social Security Advisory Committee (1992) Eighth Report of the SSAC

Social Security Committee (1990) *Households and Families Below Average Income*: A regional analysis 1980-85, HMSO (Prepared by the Institute for Fiscal Studies on behalf of House of Commons SSC, Session 1989-90 378-I)

Social Security Committee (1991) *Low Income Statistics: Households Below Average Income Tables 1988*. HMSO: First Report (Prepared by the Institute for Fiscal Studies)

Social Services Committee (1989) *Social Security: Changes implemented in April 1988*. Ninth Report HC 437 HMSO

Social Services Committee (1993) *Low Income Statistics: Low Income Families 1979-89*. House of Commons: The Second Report: HC 359, Session 1992-93

Sparrow, M and Ryan, M (1983) Children living off the ground, *Concern*

Spencer N.J (1991b) Child poverty and deprivation in the UK, *Archives of Disease in childhood*, 66, 1255-57

Spencer N.J and Lewis, M.A (1991a) Multiple admission under two years of age, *Archives of Disease in Childhood*, 66, 938-40

Spencer, N.J, Lewis, M. A and Logan, S (1993) Multiple admission and deprivation, *Archives of Disease in childhood*, 68, 6 June

Stark, O, Peckham, C. S and Ades, A (1986) Weights of British and French children, letter, *Lancet*, 1,8485, 12 April 862

Stewart, I (1991) Estimates of the Distribution of Personal Wealth II: Marketable Wealth and Pension Rights of Individuals 1976 to 1989, *Economic Trends*, 457 November

Stoll, P and O'Keeffe, D (1989) *Officially present: An investigation into post-registration truancy in nine maintained seconday schools*. IEA Education Unit

Storie, J (1990) *Bed, Breakfast and Social Work*. University of East Anglia: Social Work Monographs 86

Strachan, D. P and Elton, R. A (1986) Relationship between respiratory morbidity in children and the home environment, *Family Practice*, 3 137-42

Strathdee, R (1989) *Nobody wants to know*. Gingerbread

Svenson, M and MacPherson, S (1988) Real Losses and unreal figures: the impact of the 1986 Social Security Act *in* Becker, S and MacPherson, S *(eds.)* (1988) *Public Issues Private Pain*. Insight

Swann Report (1985) *Education For all*. DES: HMSO

Sylva, K and Moss, P (1992) *Learning Before School*. National Commission on Education: Briefing No. 8

Taylor, D (1989) The vacancies argument, *Unemployment Bulletin*, 29 Spring

Taylor, G and James, S (1990) *A Crying Shame: The child victims of homelessness*. London Boroughs Association

Taylor, P (1992) *Ethnic Group Data for University Entry – Project Report for CVCP Working Group on Ethnic Data*. University of Warwick: ESRC Centre for Research in Ethnic relations

Thomas, A and Niner, P (1989) *Living in temporary accommodation: a survey of homeless people.* HMSO, DoE

Thorton, R (1989) *The New Homeless.* SHAC

Tibbenham, A (1977) Housing Truancy, *New Society,* 39 501-2

Titmuss, R (1958) *Essays on the Welfare State*

Tizard, B and colleagues (1988) *Young Children at School in the Inner City.* Lawrence Erlbaum

Todd, J and Dodd, T (1985) *Children's Dental Health in the UK 1983.* HMSO OPCS Monitor SS83/2

Tomlinson, S, Curriculum option choices in multi-ethnic schools *in* Troyna B *(ed.)* (1987) *Racial Inequalities in Education.* Tavistock and Routledge

Tomlinson, S and Hutchinson, S (1991) *Bangladeshi Parents and Education in Tower Hamlets.* Advisory Centre for Education and the University of Lancaster Department of Educational Research

Townsend, P *(ed)* (1970) *The Concept of Poverty.* Heinemann

Townsend, P (1979) *Poverty in the United Kingdom: A survey of household resources and standards of living.* Penguin

Townsend, P (1981) Peter Townsend Replies, *New Society,* 17 September 1981

Townsend, P (1990a) Deprivation, *Journal of Social Policy,* 16,2,pp 125-46

Townsend, P (1990b) The Relationship between Deprivation and Ill-Health: New evidence (A paper prepared for a seminar on Deprivation and Health Manchester University 21 February 1990)

Townsend, P (1991) *The Poor are Poorer: A statistical report on changes in the living standards of rich and poor in the UK 1979-89.* Statistical Monitoring unit Department of Social Policy and Social Planning University of Bristol.

Townsend, P and Davidson, N (1982) *Inequalities in Health: The Black Report.* Penguin

Townsend, P and Davidson, N *(eds.)* (1992) *Inequalities in Health: The Black Report.* Penguin, New edition

Townsend P, Phillimore, P and Beattie, A (1987) *Health and Deprivation: Inequality and the North.* Croom Helm

H.M Treasury (1992) *Public expenditure analysis to 1994-95: Statistical supplement to the 1991 Autumn Statement.* January cm 1920

Troyna, B *(ed)* (1987) *Racial Inequality in Education.* Tavistock

Turner, M (1990) *Sponsored Reading Failure.* Institute of Economic Affairs: Education Unit

Unemployment Unit and Youth Aid, *Working Brief.* (Various issues)

The Universities Central Council on Admissions, *Statistical Supplement to the Annual Reports 1980, 1990 and 1991*

Veit-Wilson, J (1987) Consensual approaches to poverty lines and social security, *Journal of Social Policy*, 16, 2

Wadsworth, M (1986) Serious illness in chillhood and its association with later-life achievement *in* Wilkinson, R *(ed.)* (1986a).

Wagstaff, A and others (1991) On the measurement of inequalities in Health, *Social Science and Medicine*, 33, 545-57

Walker, A (1990) Blaming the victims *in* Murray, C (1990) *The Emerging British Underclass*, The Institute of Economic Affairs.

Walker, M, Shaper A.G and Wannamethee, G (1988) Height and social class in middle aged British men, *Journal of Epidemiology of Community Health*, 42, 299-303

Walker, R (1987) Consensual Approaches to the Definition of Poverty: Towards an alternative methodology, *Journal of Social Policy*, 16,2,213-26

Weatherall, R and Shaper, A. G (1988) Overweight and obesity in middle-aged British men, *European Journal of Clinical Nutrition*, 42, 221-31

Wedderburn, D *(ed)* (1974) *Poverty Inequality and Class Structure*. Cambridge University Press

Wedge, P and Prosser, H (1973) *Born to Fail?* Arrow Books in association with National Children's Bureau

West,P and others (1990) Social class and health in youth: Findings from the West of Scotland Twenty-07 study, *Social Science Medicine*, 30,6,665-73

White, J, Cole-Hamilton, I and Dibb, S (1992) *The Nutritional Case for School Meals*. School Meals Campaign, June

White, M (1985) Life stress in long-term unemployment, *Policy Studies*, 5,4

Whitehead, M (1987) *The Health Divide: Inequalities in health in the 1980s*. Health Education Council

Whitehead, M (1992) *The Health Divide*. Penguin: New edition-revised and updated

Whitehead and others (1992) *Housing the Nation: Choice, access and priorities*. University of Cambridge, Department of land Economy

Whiteside, N (1988) Unemployment and health: an historical perspective, *Journal of Social Policy*, 17, 2, 177-94

Wilkinson, R. G (1986a) Socio-economic Differences in Mortality: Interpreting the data on their size and trends *in* Wilkinson *(ed.) Class and Health: Research and longitudinal date*. Tavistock

Wilkinson, R. G (1986b) Occupational class, selection and inequalities in health: a reply to Raymond Illsley, *Quarterly Journal of Social Affairs*, 2,4,415-22

Williams, M (1991) *Housing, health and the longitudinal study* - a paper presented at a conference. *Unhealthy housing: The Public Health Response* held at Warwick University Coventry 18-20 December

Willmott, P and Hutchinson, R (1992) *Urban Trends 1: A report on Britain's Deprived Urban Areas.* Policy Studies Institute

Winter, D (1991) *A Cohort Analysis of Chronic Morbity and Unemployment in the General Household Survey.* London School of Economics: Discussion Paper WSP/59 April

Wood, D and Smith, P (no date) *Employers Labour Use Strategies: First Report on the 1987 Survey.* Department of Employment: Research Paper No 63

Woods, J (summarised by Varlaam A) *Absenteeism in Secondary Schools.* ILEA RS 762/80

Wright, C (1987) Black students – white teachers *in* Troyna, B *(ed.) Racial Inequality in Education.* Tavistock and Routledge

Youthaid and the Children's Society (1992) *A Broken Promise – the failure of Youth Training Policy.* Youthaid

Index of names

A

Abel-Smith, B., and Townsend, P. 27
Acheson, *Sir* Donald 134
Alcock, P. 25
Amin, K., and Oppenheim, C. 56, 57, 145
Arber, S. 124

B

Balarajan, R. 96, 117
and Raleigh, V.S. 100
Baldwin, S. 110
Ballard, Barbara xv
Barnes, J.H., and Lucas, H. 150-51
Bartholomew, R. 62
Bebbington, A.C. 107
Bennett, Fran xv
Bennett, M., and Kell, J. 79
Benzeval, Michaela xv, 140
and Judge, Ken 103, 104-6, 139-41
Bernstein, B. 145-6
Berridge, David xv
Berthoud, R.
and Brown, J.C. 53, 56, 60-61, 85, 130, 133
and Kempson 26
Beveridge, William, 26-7, *see also*
Beveridge Report [Subject Index]
Bird, M. 170
Black, M.E. 135, 136
Blackburn, C. 123
and Graham, H. 120
Blackman, T. 137-8
Blackstone, T. *see* Mortimore, P., and
Blackstone, T.
Blair, Bernadette xv
Blakemore, Fiona xv
Blatchford, P. 145, 152
Blaxter, M. 110, 120
Bloor, M. 119
Boardman, B. 132-3
Bone, M., and Meltzer, H. 110
Booth, Charles 2
Borooah, V.K. 87
McGreggor, P.P.L. and
McKee, P.M. 18, 19

Botting, Beverley xv
and Rodriguez, L. 104
Bradshaw, J. xv, xvii-xviii, 4, 26, 39, 70, 96
and Godfrey, C. 27
and Hicks, L. and Parker, H. 27, 123
and Holmes, H. 28, 123, 195
and Millar, J. 67-9
and Morgan, J. 27, 123
Brown, C. 56
Brown, J.C. 194
see also Berthoud, R., and
Brown, J.C.
Brown, M., and Madge, N. 160, 196
Bruegel, I. 56
Burghes, L. 123

C

Cameron, D., and Jones, I.G. 93
Carmichael, C.L 112
Carr-Hill, R. 112, 113
Carroll, T. 168
Carstairs, V. 110
Cassano, P., and Rush, D. 120
Cato, V., and Whetton, C. 149
Chinn, S.
and Rona, R.J. 113, 114
Rona, R.J., and Price, C.E. 112
Clarke, L. 6
Clarke, M.M. 79-80, 82
Cohen, B., and Fraser, N. 67, 82
Cohen, R. 26
Cole-Hamilton, I. 82-3
and Lang, T. 123
Coleman, A. 137
Conway, J. 117, 135
Coulter, A., and Mortimore, P. 161
Coulter, F.A.E., Cowell, F.A., and
Jenkins, S.P. 34
Cox, B. 95
Craig,G. 26
Cross, C. 57
Crowe, J. 133
Currie, Mark xv
Curwen, M., and Davies, T. 137

Cuttance, P. 158

D
Dale, R.R., and Griffiths, S. 147
Daniel, W. 39, 197
Davey Smith, G. 93
Davidson, M., and Townsend, P. 100
Davie, R. 138, 147
Davies, J. 169, 170
Davis, T., and Curwen, M. 137
Ditch, I., Pickles, S., and
  Whiteford, P. 25
Dix, G., and Huby, M. 26
Donnison, David 3, 7, 200
Douglas, J.W.B. 152
Drew, D.
  and Gillborn, D. 164
  and Gray, J. 161-4
Duffy, K.B., and Lincoln, I.C. 56
Durward, L. 123

E
Edwards, R. 67, 135-6
Eggleston, J. 180
Elton, R.A. and Strachan, D.P. 137
Ermisch, J. 194
Eshun, Ebah xv
Essen, J., Fogelman, K.R., and
  Head, J. 147

E
Fagin, L., and Little 124-5
Fanning, D.M. 137
Ferguson, D.M., and O'Mahoney, B.
  128, 130
Fernandes, C. and Gorman, T. 149
Field, F. 194
Fogelman, K. 169
  and Essen, J. 147
  and Goldstein, H. 150-51
Fowler, Norman 24
Fraser, N., and Cohen, B. 67, 82
Frayman, H. 15, 193
Furley, A. 134

G
Galloway, D. 168-70
Gans, H.J. 193, 195
Garner, C.L. 158
Garrow, J.S. 113
Gillborn, D., and Drew, D. 164

Glennerster, H., and Low, W. 78, 148,
  156, 173, 182
Godfrey, C., and Bradshaw 27
Godley, W. 39
Goldblatt, P. 119
Goldstein, H.
  and Fogelman, K. 150-51
  and Nuttal, D.L. 163-4
Gorman, T., and Fernandes, C. 149
Graham, H. 123, 136
  and Blackburn, C. 120
Grant, J. 119
Gray, J. 168, 168-71
  and Drew, D. 161-4
  and Jesson, D. 158, 161, 167-71
Greve, J. 84, 86, 126-30
Griffiths, S., and Dale, R.R. 147
Grimshaw, Roger xv
  and Pratt, J.D. 158, 168-9

H
Hackett, A. 114
Hall, S. 110
Halsey, A.H. 183
Haskey, J. 62, 63, 64, 67-9
  and Kelly, S. 64
Head, J., and Essen, J. 147
Heady, P., and Smyth, M. 44, 125
Herbison, Margaret 192
Hicks, L., and Bradshaw, J. 27, 123
Hilliard, Nicola xv
Hills, J. 84
  and Mullings, B. 84-5, 130-31
Holmes, H., and Bradshaw, J. 28, 123,
  195
Holt, R. 114
Holtermann, S. 67, 82
Holtmatt, R., and Huws, K. 57
Howarth, V. 127
Huby, M., and Dix, G. 26
Hunt, S. see Martin, C., and Hunt, S.
Hurstfield, J., and Huws, K. 57
Hutchinson, R., and Willmott, P.
  156-60
Hutchinson, S.
  and Tomlinson, S. 146
  and Varlaam, A. 146
Huws, K., Hurstfield, J., and
  Holtmatt, R. 57
Hyndman, S.J. 137

I

Illsley, R. 93, 119

J

James, S., and Taylor, G. 126, 130, 135
Jarman, B. 116
Jesson, D. 180
and Gray, J. 158, 161
Jones, I.G., and Cameron, D. 93
Joseph, *Sir* Keith 193, 195
Judge, Ken xv
and Benzeval, M. 103, 104-6, 139-41

K

Kell, J., and Bennett, M. 79
Kelly, S., and Haskey, J. 64
Kempson, E., and Berthoud, R. 26
Kiernan, K., and Wicks, M. 45
Knight, I. 113, 119
Kumar, Indira xv
Kurtz, Zarrina xv, 110
Kysel, F. 161-5

L

Lamont, Norman 40
Lang, T. 123
and Cole-Hamilton, I. 123
Lansley, S, and Mack, N. 2-3, 15, 145, 193
LeGrand, J., Winter, D., and Woolley, F. 71-4
Lewis, M.A., and Spencer, N.J. 118
Lincoln, I.C., and Duffy, K.B. 56
Lister, Ruth 25
Littlewood, J., and Tinker, A. 131
Lobstein, T. 123
Low, W. *see* Glennerster, H., and Low, W.
Lowry, S. 131, 137
Lucas, H., and Barnes, J.H. 150-51
Lynes, T. 41

M

McCormick, A. 117
McGreggor, P.P.L., and Borooah, V.K. 18, 19
Mack, J., and Lansley, S. 2-3, 15, 145, 193
McKee, P.M., and Borooah, V.K. 18, 19

Mcloughlin, Patrick 50
Maclure, A., and Stewart, G. 118, 124
McNeil, G. 115
MacPherson, S., and Svenson, M. 26
Madge, Nicola xv, 125
and Brown, M. 160, 196
and Rutter, M. 136, 147, 195-6
Major, John 40, 197
see also economic policy; social policy [Subject Index]
Mann, K. 200
Martin, C., and Hunt, S. 125, 131, 136, 138, 139
Martin, J., and White, A. 110
Maughan, B., and Rutter, M. 161
Meltzer, H., and Bone, M. 110
Middleton, B. 165
Millar, J. 24-5, 53, 58, 59, 61
and Bradshaw, J. 67-9
Moore, R. 132
Moore, John 193
Morgan, J., and Bradshaw, J. 27, 123
Morris, J., and Winn, M. 134
Mortimore, P. 92, 152, 167, 168-9
and Blackstone, T. 93, 146, 147, 148, 151, 165, 182
and Coulter, A. 161
Moser, K.A. 124
Moss, P. 67
and Sylva, K. 80, 82
Muelbauer, 84
Mullings, B., and Hills, J. 84-5, 130-31
Murie, A. 134
Murray, Charles 194-5
Murray, Iain xv

N

Naismith, D., and Nelson, M. 123
Nelson, M. 115
and Naismith, D. 123
and Paul, A. 114, 115
Newbury, K., and Sammons, P. 180
Newell, P. 200
Niner, P., and Thomas, A. 128
Nuttal, D.L. 161, 163, 164
and Goldstein, H. 163-4

O

Oeil 129
O'Keefe, D., and Stoll, P. 167, 170

O'Mahoney, B., and Ferguson, D.M. 128, 130
Oppenheim, C. 26, 59
and Amin,, K. 56, 57, 145
Orshansky, M. 3

P
Pamuk, E.R. 104
Parekh, B. 161
Parker, H., and Bradshaw, J. 27, 123
Paul, A., and Nelson, M. 114, 115
Payne, Lisa xv
Pearce, B., and Wilcox, S. 86
Pearson, D. 114
Pharoah, P.O.D. 96, 107
Phillimore, P. 138
Piachaud, D. 3, 194
Pickin, C.A. 135
Pickles, S., and Ditch, I. 25
Pilling, D. 160
Platt, S.D. 122, 137
Pollitt, N. 128-9
Power, C. 100, 119
Pratt, J.D., and Grimshaw, R. 158, 168-9
Price, C.E., and Chinn, S. 112
Prosser, H., and Wedge, P. 138, 146-7, 152-3

Q
Quick, A., and Wilkinson, R.G. 199

R
Raleigh, V.S., and Balarajan, R. 100
Randall, Simon 126
Rein, M. 27
Reynolds, D. 169
Ringen, S. 3
Ritchie, J. 117
Robinson, P. 57
Rodrigues, L., and Botting, B. 104
Rona, R.J., and Chinn, S. 112, 113, 114
Rose, G. 119
Rosenberg, K. 117-8
Rowntree, Joseph 2, 7
see also Joseph Rowntree Foundation [Subject Index]
Runciman, W. S. 3
Rush, D., and Cassano, P. 120

Rutter, M. 160, 163, 169
and Madge, N. 136, 147, 195-6
and Maughan, B. 161
Ryan, M., and Sparrow, M. 131

S
Sammons, P., and Newbury, K. 180
Scarr, S. 152
Scheuer, M.A. 135
Schorr, A.L. 136
Scott, Nicholas 193
Sen, A.K. 2-3
Sharper, A.G., and Weatherall, R. 113
Sinfield, A. 32
Smith, Adam 2
Smith, D.J. 200
and Tomlinson, S. 163
Smith, S.J. 127
Smyth, M., and Heady, P. 44, 125
Sparrow, M., and Ryan, M. 131
Spencer, N.J. 118, 120
and Lewis, M.A. 118
Stark, O. 113
Stewart, G., and Maclure, A. 118, 124
Stoll, P., and O'Keefe, D. 167, 170
Storie, J. 134
Strachan, D.P., and Elton, R.A. 137
Strathdee, R. 127
Svenson, M., and MacPherson, S. 26
Sylva, K., and Moss, P. 80, 82

T
Tawney, R.H. 193
Taylor, D. 44
Taylor, G, and James, S. 126, 130, 135
Taylor, P. 183
Thatcher, Margaret xvii, 40, 70, 79, 192, 193, 197
see also economic policy; social policy [Subject Index]
Thomas, A., and Niner, P. 128
Thornton, R. 129
Tibbenham, A. 147
Tinker, A., and Littlewood, J. 131
Titmuss, R. 193
Tizard, B. 152
Tomlinson, S. 165-6
and Hutchinson, S. 146
and Smith, D.J. 163
Townsend, P. xv, 2-3, 95, 122-3, 137-40

and Abel-Smith, B. 27
and Davidson, M. 100
Turner, M. 149

V
Varlaam, A., and Hutchinson, S. 146
Veit-Wilson, J. 3

W
Wadsworth, M. 119
Wagstaff, A. 93
Waldegrave, William 198
Walker, A. 193
Walker, M. 113
Weatherall, R., and Sharper, A.G. 113
Wedderburn, D. 1
Wedge, P., and Prosser, H. 138,
146-7, 152-3
West, P. 106
Whetton, C., and Catto, V. 149

White, A., and Martin, J. 110
White, J. 114, 115
White, M. 125
Whiteford, P., and Ditch, I. 25
Whitehead, M. 86-7, 92, 94-5, 110,
113, 123-4, 125
Whiteside, N. 123, 124, 125
Wicks, M., and Kiernan, K. 45
Wilcox, S., and Pearce, B. 86
Wilkinson, R.G. 93, 119
and Quick, A. 199
Williams, M. 130-31
Willmott, P., and Hutchinson, R.
156-60
Winn, M., and Morris, J. 134
Winter, D. 124
and LeGrand, J. 71-4
Woods, J. 169, 170
Woolley, F., and LeGrand, J. 71-4
Wright, C. 166

Index of subjects

A

A levels *see* examinations
accidents 120, 136
adolescents *see* young people
African origin, people of
  education and homelessness 147
  infant mortality 98-100
  lone parents 62
  see also minority ethnic groups
amenities, shared in rented housing
  129-30, 136
Asian people *see* minority ethnic
  groups; Bangladeshi; Indian;
  Pakistani
Association of County Councils 50
Association of Metropolitan
  Authorities 50, 127
attainment, educational *see* education
Audit Commission 84, 86-7, 126, 128
Audit Office, National 127-8, 130, 138,
  173
Australasian mothers, infant mortality
  98

B

Bangladeshi origin, people of
  education 146, 161-6, 183
  education and homelessness 147
  health 137
  infant mortality 98-101
  lone parents 62
  low pay 57
  unemployment 50-51
  see also minority ethnic groups
bed and breakfast accommodation 85,
  126-8, 134-5, 198
  see also homelessness
Belfast 137-8
  see also Northern Ireland
benefits
  adequacy 26-8, 192-3, 198
  changes in cf. earnings 29, 58-9
  expenditure 1979-1992 70-74
  lone parent families 62
  poor people's dependence on 8-9,
    20-29, 91-2

  see also Child Benefit; Family Credit;
    Housing Benefit; Income Support;
    social policy; Supplementary
    Benefit; taxation
Beveridge Report 7
  see also Beveridge, William [Names
    Index]
Birmingham
  education 156-60, 179
  health 116
Black people *see* minority ethnic
  groups
Black Report 92, 110, 119-21, 120, 146
Blackpool 147
books
  spending on in schools 76-8, 173-4
  see also reading
borstal leavers, homeless 128
boys' educational attainment 154
Bradford, education 156-60, 179
Brent
  education 156-60, 179
  see also London
British Association for the Study of
  Dentistry 112
British Medical Association 134-5
British Regional Heart Study 113

C

Canada, further education 180-82
Canadian mothers, infant mortality 98
Care, local authority, leavers homeless
  128
Careers Services 50
Caribbean *see* West Indian
central heating 132
CHAR 129
charities
  concerned about demand 38
  dependence on 26
child, definition 4
Child Benefit, *see also* benefits
Child Benefit xviii, 25
childcare 67, 81-2, 197-8
  see also under fives
child mortality 96-106, 110-111, 138-40

child poverty *see* poverty
Children Act 1989 129
children under five *see* under fives
children's rights 197-9
Children's Society 50
Citizens Advice Bureaux 28
class 92-3, 202
  childhood morbidity 106-111
  children's growth 113
  dental health 112
  educational attainment 150-52,
    160-63
  higher education 180-83
  infant and child mortality 100-06,
    111
  poor health 118-21, 190-91
  'underclass' 194-5, 200
  see also deprivation; inequality;
    poverty
clothing, as proportion of family
  expenditure 27
Coalition for Child Benefit 25
cohabitation 63-4
  see also lone parents
cold 131-3, 136-7
Commission for Racial Equality 165
Committee on Medical Aspects of
  Food Policies 199
Community Charge 25, 29
Council of Europe, definition of
  poverty 2
Council housing *see* housing; local
  authority housing
Council Tax 37
Court Report 1, 138, 146
Coventry, education 156-60, 179
Croydon 150
  see also London
CSEs *see* examinations
cycles of disadvantage 195-6

D
damp 131-3, 134, 136-7
day care of children under five 67,
  79-84, 204-5
deaths *see* mortality
debt 26, 86, 125-6s, inn 132-3
demographic change xvii
  declining school rolls 78-9
  underlying child poverty 61-69

dental health 111-12
  see also health
Department of Social Security *see* DSS
dependency culture 193-5
deprivation
  and class 122-3
  cost to nation 199-200
  cycles of 195-6
  definition 2-3
  and education 144-8, 150-51, 153,
    156-71
  and health 94, 100-106, 110-121,
    122-141, 143
  of recreation 27-8
  see also class; inequality; poverty
deregulation of labour market 58-61
  see also employment
diet 113-16, 199
  of homeless people 134-5
  income and health 123
disabled children 107, 110, 146
disabled people, lack of data on
  poverty 4
disadvantage, definition 2-3
discrimination, racial *see* minority
  ethnic groups
disease *see* health; morbidity
distribution of wealth *see* inequality
divorce 63-4
  see also lone parents; marriage
doctors, consultation of 116-17, 135,
  136
Dublin 124

E
early years *see* under fives
earnings *see* income; low pay
economic activity *see* employment;
  unemployment
economic policy
  inflation 40, 51-2, 61, 88-9
  underlying child poverty 39-51,
    197-8
  see also benefits; social policy;
    taxation; unemployment
economic trends 1979-1992 51-3, 88-9
Edinburgh 137
  see also Scotland
education
  expenditure 1979-1992 72-9, 83,
    171-6, 178, 199

education *continued*
  further and higher, and deprivation
    176-184, 199
  parental deprivation and 144-8,
    191-2
  primary, and deprivation 148-154
  secondary, and deprivation 154-67,
    199
  truancy, and deprivation 167-71
  under fives 79-82, 204-5
Education, Science and Arts
  Committee 82, 115, 150, 199
Eire 101
employment
  policies 58-61, 197-8
  and poverty 53-61, 203, *see also* low
    pay
  precarious 57-8, 60-61
  see also economic policy;
    unemployment
English House Conditions Survey
  129-32
environment of housing 131, 137-8
ethnic minority *see* minority ethnic
  groups
ethnicity, definition 4
European Community
  definition of poverty in 18
  subsidy on high-fat school meals 114
European countries
  infant mortality rates 96, 98, 123
  participation in further education
    180-83
ex-prisoners, homeless 128
examinations 145, 154-60
expenditure, public *see* benefits;
  economic policy; education; health;
  social policy

F
familial cycles of disadvantage 195-6
families, contributing to school
  funding 174-5
families headed by a lone parent *see*
  lone parents
families in poverty *see* deprivation;
  Households Below Average Income;
  Low Income Families; poverty
families in poverty *see* unemployment
Family Credit xviii, 7-9
  ceases to cover school meals 83

compared with Family Income
  Supplement 25
low take-up 24
see also benefits
Family Expenditure Survey 9, 12
Family Income Supplement 7-8
  children of families receiving 8-9
  compared with Family Credit 25
fathers, lone 67-9
  see also lone parents
fiscal policy *see* taxation
flats 131, 137
  see also housing
flexible employment 57-8
food *see* diet
food costs, as proportion of family
  expenditure 27, 123, 135
fuel 131-3
further education 176-84, 199
  see also education

G
Gardner Merchant 114, 115
GCSE *see* examinations
General Practitioner consultation
  116-17, 135, 136
Germany 137
girls
  educational attainment 154, 165-6
  illness 107-109
  truancy 168
  see also women
Glasgow 118, 124, 137
  see also Scotland
Government policy *see* economic
  policy; social policy; taxation
GP consultation 116-17, 135, 136
growth 112-3
  see also health; nutrition
Guyanese origin, people of
  low pay 57
  unemployment 50-51
  see also minority ethnic groups

H
handicapped *see* disabled people
Haringey
  education 156-60, 179
  see also London
HBAI *see* Households Below Average
  Income

health
    access to services 116-18
    child morbidity 106-110
    definition 94-5
    dental 111-12
    diet and nutrition 112-15, 123
    disability 110
    and education 146
    expenditure 1979-1992 71-4
    and housing 125-38
    and income 123
    inequalities 118-121, 198-9
    infant and child mortality 96-106
    measurement 95-6
    and multiple deprivation 138-43,
        189-91
    and unemployment 123-5
Health Visitors Association 134-5
hearing impairment 146
    see also disabled children
heat 131-3
Her Majesty's Inspectorate reports
    147, 150-51, 153, 171-6
higher education 176-84, 199
    see also education
HMI see Her Majesty's Inspectorate
homelessness xviii, 85-7, 198
    and education 147-8
    hidden 130
    poverty and health 125-138, 142-3,
        189
    see also housing
hospital attendance 117-18, 135-6
hospital leavers, homeless 128
hostel accommodation 126-8
House of Commons see Public
    Accounts Committee; Select
        Committee...; Social Services
        Committee
Households Below Average Income xv,
    xvii, 11-15, 53
    inclusion of lately published data in
        this study 5, 188
    statistical method 11-12, 15
    see also income; Low Income
        Families; poverty
households paying tax 32-3
housing
    costs 12-13, 85-6, 134
    expenditure 1979-1992 72-3, 83-7,
    198

health and poverty 125-138, 142-3,
    189-90
public sector see local authority
    housing
see also homelessness
Housing Associations 84, 128, 129
    see also local authority housing
Housing Benefit 13, 24-5, 84, 133
    see also benefits

I
IFS 8, 9, 17, 30, 32
ILEA see London, education
illegitimacy 64, 194
illness see health; morbidity
ILO 47
immunisation 116, 134-5
income
    and health 123
    low see Households Below Average
        Income; Low Income Families;
        low pay; poverty
    of poor people 20-38
Income Support xviii
    abolished for young people 4, 28, 47,
        129
    children of families receiving 8-9,
        10-11
    limitations 25, 29, 83
    as a measure of poverty 7-9, 192
    take-up 24
    trends in 1988-1992 22-3
    see also benefits; Supplementary
        Benefit
Indian origin, people of
    education 162-6
    infant mortality 98-101
    lone parents 62
    low pay 56
    unemployment 50-51
    see also minority ethnic groups
industrial tribunals 59
inequality
    definition cf. poverty 1-3
    increasing 1979-1991 xvii, 29-37
    narrowed 1971-76 34
    see also class; deprivation; poverty
infant mortality 96-104, 110-11, 137,
    138-40
infectious diseases 134, 136
    see also health; morbidity

infestation 134
inflation 40, 51-2, 61, 88-9
see also economic policy
Inner London Education Authority *see*
London, education
inner-city areas
health 116
minority ethnic groups 57
schools 142-3, 151, 153, 156-60,
168-70, 184-5, 191; 147
see also names of cities, e.g. London,
Dublin
Institute for Fiscal Studies 8, 9, 17, 30,
32
international economic trends xvii
International Labour Organisation 47
Ireland
mothers born in, infant mortality 98
see also Dublin; Northern Ireland

J
Japan, further education 180-82
Joseph Rowntree Foundation xv-xvi,
84, 86

K
King's Fund xv
Knowsley, education 156-60, 179
Kurdish children 147
see also minority ethnic groups

L
Labour Force Survey 44, 47, 50-51, 55
labour market *see* employment;
unemployment
language spoken, and educational
attainment 148, 152, 165
see also reading
LEAs *see* education
Leicester 114
life expectancy *see* mortality
literacy 148-9, 150-51
Liverpool, education 156-60, 179
local authority care leavers, homeless
128
local authority housing 84, 86-7, 126-7,
129, 131-3
see also housing; Housing
Associations
local authority spending
education 76-83, 171-6, 178
see also education

local authority taxes 25, 29, 37
local education authorities *see*
education
Local Government Act 1966 151
local management of schools 175
London
bed and breakfast accommodation
85, 126
demographic trends 62
education 147, 150-51, 152, 156-60,
161-5, 178-80
health 123, 137, 140-41
homelessness 126-7, 128, 135, 147
housing costs 86
immunisation 116
poverty 17-20, 159
unemployment 45-7
London Research Centre 127
lone parents 8, 11-15, 61-69, 187-8,
194-5, 203
benefit rates 24-5, 62, 133
debt 26, *see also* debt
homelessness 127, *see also*
homelessness
housing conditions 130-31
infant mortality 106
taxation 32
Low Income Families
statistics on 9, 12
see also Households Below Average
Income; income; poverty
low pay 53-61, 69, 89, 187
see also employment; income
Low Pay Unit 53-61

M
Manchester
education 156-60, 179
homelessness 135, 147
marriage 63-4, 136, 194
see also families; lone parents
mathematics, standards in 149-50, 152,
154
means-testing, increased use of 23-4,
198
mental health 124-5, 134-5, 136, 137-8
see also health
methodology of this study 4-5
Middlesborough 138
minority ethnic groups
concentration in inner cities 57

diet 114
discrimination in housing 57, 128, 131
education 146-7, 152, 160-63, 180-83, 191
growth 113
health 136
homelessness 127-8, 147
infant mortality 99-100
lack of data on poverty 4, 57, 188
lone parents 62
low pay 55-7, 61, 188
overcrowded housing 130
school meals 83
unemployment 50-51, 61, 188
moral issues 199-200
morbidity 106-111, 134, 136, s, he 140-41
morbidity, see also health
mortality, infant and child 96-106, 110-11, 137, 138-40
mortgages see housing; taxation
mothers see lone parents; women

N
National Advisory Committee on Nutrition Education 199
National Association of Citizens Advice Bureaux 28
National Association of Schoolmasters/ Union of Women Teachers 174
National Audit Office 127-8, 130, 138, 173
National Child Development Study 147, 150-51
National Children's Bureau xvi, 4, 113, 131
National Children's Home 128
National Commission on Education 82
national curriculum 145, 174-5
National Dairy Council 115
National Federation of Housing Associations 128
National Foundation for Educational Research 149, 150, 151
National Health Service see health
National Insurance Contributions 32
National Study of Health and Growth 112

Newham
education 156-60, 179
see also London
North of UK see regional trends
Northern Ireland
health and housing 137-8
infant mortality 98, 101
poverty 17-20
under fives provision 80-81, 205
unemployment 44, 45-7
see also Ireland
Northumberland 115
Nottingham 135
Nottinghamshire 158
nursery schools see education; under fives
nutrition see diet

O
O Levels see examinations
obesity 113
OECD 47
Office of Population Censuses and Surveys xv, 44, 124, 126
surveys of children's health 106, 110, 111, 114, 119
one-parent families see lone parents
OPCS see Office of Population Censuses and Surveys
Organisation for Economic Cooperation and Development 47
overcrowded housing 130, 136

P
Pakistani origin, people of
education 162-6, 183
infant mortality 98-101
lone parents 62
low pay 57
overcrowded housing 130
unemployment 50-51
see also minority ethnic groups
parental deprivation and education 144-8, 191-2
parents see families; households; lone parents
part-time work see employment
pay, low see low pay
pensions 34-7
personal social services see social services

play 131
Plowden Committee 147
policy *see* benefits; economic policy;
    education; social policy; taxation
Policy Studies Institute 39
poverty
    definitions 1-3, 15-17, 192-3
    income levels 20-29, 201, 203
    lone parent families 61-69
    national trends 1979-1991 xvii, 7-17,
    19, 91-3, 187, 201-3
    regional trends 1979-1991 17-20
    relationship with education 144-8,
    150-51, 153, 156-61
    relationship with health 122-143
    underlying factors 39-90, 187-8
    and wealth 29-37, 202
    see also class; deprivation;
    Households Below Average Income;
    inequality; low pay; unemployment
precarious employment 57-8, 60-61
pregnancy *see* women, pregnant
primary schools *see* schools, primary
prison leavers, homeless 128
Public Accounts Committee 127, 138
public expenditure *see* economic
    policy; social policy
pupil-teacher ratios 78-9

Q
quality of life 27-8, 196, 200

R
race *see* minority ethnic groups
racism, definition 4
reading 148-9, 150-51, 153, 172
    see also books; language
recreation, deprivation of 27-8
regional trends
    children's diet 114
    demographic 62
    dental health 112
    diet 114
    education 156-60, 178-80
    health 74, 138
    housing 86, 132
    immunisation 116
infant mortality 96-99
    poverty 1979-1991 17-20
    truancy 169

under fives provision 80-81, 204-5
    unemployment 44, 45-7
rent *see* housing
Research Unit in Health and
    Behavioural Change 120
rights of children 197-9
Rochdale, education 156-60, 179
Rowntree, Joseph *see* Joseph Rowntree
    Foundation
Royal College of Physicians 113, 135
Royal National Institute for Deaf
    People xvi

S
Salford, education 156-60, 179
Sandwell, education 156-60, 179
school meals 82-3, 114, 158, 199
schools *see* education
scope of this study 4-5
Scotland
    children's diet 114
    education 158
    health 112, 117-8, 124, 137
    heating costs 132
    immunisation 116
    infant mortality 98
    poverty 17-20
    under fives provision 80-81, 204-5
    unemployment 45-7
secondary schools *see* schools,
    secondary
Select Committee on Education,
    Science and Arts 82, 115, 150, 199
self-employment *see* employment
Sheffield 168-9, 180
Sheffield University 167
Shelter 84, 126, 128-30
Simon Community 136
Single Homeless in London Working
    Party 128
single mothers *see* lone parents
smoking 120
social class *see* class
Social Fund 26, 29
    see also benefits
social housing *see* housing associations;
    local authority housing
social policy 69-90, 196-200
    social services expenditure
    1979-1992 71-4

social policy *continued*
    see also benefits; economic policy;
        education; taxation
Social Policy Research Unit 26
Social Security Act 1980 22
Social Security Act 1986 24, 26, 83,
    133
Social Security Advisory Committee 8,
    9, 50
social security benefits *see* benefits
Social Services Committee, House of
    Commons 17-18
Somali children 147
    see also African origin, people of
South of UK *see* regional trends
statistical data, limitations of 188-9
statistics *see* subject, e.g. Low Income
    Families
stillbirths *see* infant mortality
suicide 125
Sunderland 138
Supplementary Benefit 7
    children of families receiving 8-11,
        22-3, 24, 192
    see also benefits; Income Support
Swann Report 160-61, 165

T
targeting of public expenditure xvii,
    24, 70
taxation xvii, 30-34, 198
    mortgage relief 84-5
    see also benefits; economic policy
teachers
    pupil ratios 78-9
    salaries 76-8, 87, 175
    stereotypes of pupils' ability 161-3,
        164-6
    see also education
teenagers *see* young people
teeth 111-2
Thomas Coram Foundation 127, 152
trade unions 58-9
training schemes 28, 50, 129
    see also further education
truancy 147, 167-71
    see also education

U
UCCA 183-4
UN Convention on the Rights of the
    Child 197
under fives
    dental health 111-2, 115
    homelessness 126-7, *see also*
        homelessness
    provision for 79-82, 204-5
    use of GPs and hospitals 116-18
under-achievement, educational *see*
    education
underclass 194-5, 200
underlying factors in child poverty
    39-90
unemployment
    benefits 1979-1991 23
    and debt 26
    and education 146
    and health 123-5, 141-2, 190
    minority ethnic groups 50-51, 61,
        188
    national trends 1979-1991 8, 41-5,
        51-3, 88-9, 187, 203
    policy 1979-1991 xvii, 39-51, 58-61,
        197-200
    regional trends 1979-1991 44, 45-7
    and taxation 32
    of young people 28, 47-50, 61, 125
    see also economic policy;
        employment
Unemployment Unit 28, 42, 47
UNICEF 4
United Nations 4, 197
United States, further education in
    180-82
Universities Central Council on
    Admissions 183-4

V
vaccination 116
verbal reasoning tests 161-3
vermin 134
visual impairment 146
    see also disabled children

W
wages
    deregulation of 58-9
    see also low pay

Wales
  dental health 112
  diet 115
  housing costs 86
  immunisation 116
  infant mortality 98
  poverty 17-20
  truancy 168, 169
  under fives provision 80-81, 205
  unemployment 45-7
warmth 131-3, 136-7
wealth, distribution of 29-37, 202
welfare state *see* social policy
West Indian/Guyanese origin, people of
  education 150, 152, 160-66, 183
  infant mortality 98-101
  lone parents 62
  low pay 56
  truancy 169
  unemployment 50-51
  see also minority ethnic groups
Wolverhampton, education 156-60, 179
women
  economic activity 64-9
  employment 57-8
  in higher education 182, 183
  housing deprivation 120, 126-8
  lack of data on poverty 4

lone parents 62, 64-9, 194-5, *see also* lone parents
low pay 54, 55-6, 57-8, 59, 69
precarious employment 57-8, 59-61
pregnant, homeless 126, 135
smoking 120
unemployment 42-4, 45
see also girls
World health Organisation 94, 134

Y
Yarmouth 147
York University Family Budget Unit 27
York University Social Policy Research Unit 26
young people
  definition of children 4
  further and higher education 176-84, 199
  homeless 128-9, 135-6
  truancy from school *see* truancy
  unemployment 28, 47-50, 61, 125
  withdrawal of benefit 4, 28, 129
Youth Cohort Study of England and Wales 167
Youth Training 28, 50, 129
Youthaid 42, 47, 50